PROGRAMMING
USING THE
C LANGUAGE

McGraw-Hill Computer Science Series

PROGRAMMING USING THE C LANGUAGE

ROBERT C. HUTCHISON

STEVEN B. JUST

Formal Systems, Inc.

McGraw-Hill Book Company

New York   St. Louis   San Francisco   Auckland   Bogotá   Caracas
Colorado Springs   Hamburg   Lisbon   London   Madrid   Mexico
Milan   Montreal   New Delhi   Oklahoma City   Panama   Paris
San Juan   São Paulo   Singapore   Sydney   Tokyo   Toronto

PROGRAMMING
USING THE
C LANGUAGE

34567890 DOCDOC 892109

ISBN 0-07-031541-8

This book was set in Times Roman by Bi-Comp, Inc.
The editor was David Shapiro;
the designer was Nicholas Krenitsky;
the production supervisor was Friederich W. Schulte.
Project supervision was done by The Total Book.
R. R. Donnelley & Sons Company was printer and binder.

Library of Congress Cataloging-in-Publication Data

Hutchison, Robert C.
  Programming using the C language.

  (McGraw-Hill computer science series)
  Includes index.
  1. C (Computer program language)   I. Just,
Steven B. II. Title. III. Series.
QA76.73.C25H88 1988   005.13'3   87-17038
ISBN 0-07-031541-8

CONTENTS

PREFACE

This book is intended to be a complete introduction to the C programming language that should be useful at several levels of reader expertise. We have endeavored to provide a thorough description of the C language and to show how C may be used to implement key computer science concepts, such as sorting algorithms, recursion, linked lists, queues, stacks, binary trees, hashing algorithms, and bitmaps.

It is our experience that currently most programmers do not learn C as a first programming language. However, as C becomes more popular, this situation will inevitably change. For first-time programmers we cover the details of the C language in considerable detail, provide useful hints about program organization and readability, and illustrate key concepts with many *complete* programs. We have also divided the discussions of both pointers and functions into introductory and advanced chapters.

Most programmers currently learn C as a second or third language. These readers should be able to pass quickly through the introductory chapters, familiarizing themselves with the C language implementation of basic concepts. Later chapters on pointers, functions, structures, unions, arrays and complex data types and access methods (linked lists, stacks, queues, binary trees) will provide new and challenging material at the appropriate level.

Finally, experienced C language programmers will be interested in the four case studies in which we implement complete systems with line-by-line program commentary.

For all readers we provide appendices on ANSI standard C, running C under UNIX and running C under MS-DOS.

ORGANIZATION

This book is divided into eight sections: six parts describing the C programming language and its applications, a section of case studies in which we implement reasonably large C programs with line-by-line commentary, and appendices. Below is a brief description of each of these sections:

Part 1 (Introduction)

New C language programmers will find this section useful. We relate the history of the development of the C programming language and describe the format of a typical C language program. In addition to being an interesting story, understanding the development of C will give the programmer an appreciation for certain C language attributes.

Part 2 (Data Types)

We introduce the basic C language variable types—integers, characters and floating point numbers.

Part 3 (Control Flow)

In this part we cover the basic C language control constructs including if, switch-case, while, do-while and for statements. We also introduce the reader to C language functions, return values and the concept of call by value.

The experienced programmer should be able to pass quickly through the first three parts.

Part 4 (Derived Variable Types)

This part introduces some of the key concepts of the C language including pointers, array names as expressions, structures and unions. Illustrative examples include sorting algorithms, regular expressions and the use of bit fields.

The beginning programmer, learning C as a first language, may want to treat the remaining sections as optional material.

Part 5 (More on I/O, Pointers, Functions and Variables)

More important C language concepts are covered including file I/O, pointers to arrays, arithmetic on pointer variables, the arrow operator, passing arguments to C programs, passing pointers, structures and arrays to functions, recursion, and variable storage classes.

Part 6 (Complex Data Types)

In this section we use the tools we have introduced in the previous five parts to implement programs that utilize linked lists, stacks, queues and binary trees. These data structures and access methods are developed within the context of complete programs and we provide explanations of underlying concepts.

Case Studies

The four case studies provide examples of relatively large software development in C. They will serve as good examples for more experienced C language programmers of the use of function hierarchies and isolation of machine dependent and independent procedures. In the first three case studies we implement a source file indentation program using a stack, a line printer spooling program using a prioritized queue and a dictionary program using hashing. In the fourth case study we discuss the concept of resource allocation and implement a free list, a bitmap and a map. Most important, all of the programs are accompanied by line-by-line commentary so that even less experienced programmers can follow the code. By their nature we have had to rely on some UNIX-specific functions in these examples, but they could be ported to other operating systems without significant effort.

Appendices

The first appendix is simply a reference chart of ASCII values that should be helpful in doing some of the exercises. The second appendix describes the major recommendations of the ANSI C standards committee. The third appendix discusses some important issues in running C under UNIX and the fourth appendix describes C under MS-DOS.

ACKNOWLEDGMENTS

Many people have helped us by reviewing the manuscript in various stages of its development, testing programs and suggesting revisions. In particular we would like to thank David Bern; Charles de la Motte; Bruce Leary; Tom Vaden; Dennis O'Brien; Lawrence A. Coon, Rochester Institute of Technology; Leonard J. Garrett, Temple University; Wayne B. Hewitt, Johnson County Community College; Arthur E. Oldehoeft, Iowa State University; and M. Satyanarayanan, Carnegie-Mellon University.

Robert C. Hutchison

Steven B. Just

PROGRAMMING USING THE C LANGUAGE

PART

1

INTRODUCTION

CHAPTER 1

INTRODUCTION

OVERVIEW

Throughout its history, the C programming language has been closely linked to the UNIX® operating system. Except for the very first versions of the UNIX operating system, which were written in assembly language, all implementations have been written largely in C. But C also has a life of its own, independent of the UNIX operating system, and C compilers now exist for nearly all operating systems across the spectrum of machine size. From the smallest personal computers to the largest mainframes, a significant percentage of software is being programmed in C, and many older systems originally coded in other languages are being rewritten in C.

This raises the obvious questions: Why is C so popular and why is it the language of choice for so many professional software developers? Understanding C's current popularity requires a brief review of its history.

A BRIEF HISTORY OF THE C PROGRAMMING LANGUAGE

The story of the development of UNIX and C has been retold many times. It is now a standard tale within the folklore of computer science. We do not intend to recapitulate the entire story here. (For readers interested in all the details, we suggest any of the articles written by the original system developers, Dennis Ritchie and Ken Thompson of AT&T Bell Laboratories. For example, Dennis Ritchie, "The Evolution of the C Programming Language," *Bell Laboratories Technical Journal,* vol. 63, no. 8, October 1984, pp. 1577–1593.) Rather, we intend to illuminate the developmental influences on C's structure. Understanding this developmental process offers insights into those features of C that account for its current popularity.

UNIX was originally developed in 1969 on a rather small machine (a DEC PDP–7) at Bell Laboratories in Murray Hill, New Jersey. It was written entirely in PDP–7 assembly language. The intent was to create an operating system that was "programmer-friendly," providing useful development tools, parsimonious commands, and a relatively open environment. After UNIX was up and running, Ken Thompson implemented a compiler for a new language called B. B in turn was heavily influenced by BCPL, a language developed for writing systems software. Within a year, a newer machine, a DEC PDP–11, was acquired. UNIX and the B compiler were transferred to the new machine. The PDP–11, though larger than the PDP–7, was still quite small by today's standards. It had 24K bytes of memory, of which the system used 16K, and one 512K fixed disk. Some consideration was given to rewriting UNIX in B, but B was interpretive and therefore slow; more importantly it was word oriented while the PDP–11 was byte oriented. For these reasons work was begun in 1971 on a successor to B, appropriately named C, that could be used for rewriting the UNIX operating system. By 1973, the operating system had been rewritten in C; current versions of UNIX are almost totally implemented in the C language.

Thus, C was originally developed on a small machine for the purpose of implementing the UNIX operating system. Although C is now used for a wide range of applications, those two developmental influences still strongly define the language structure.

THE CHARACTERISTICS OF C

All languages, including natural languages, have a characteristic "look." Many programmers encountering C for the first time will find its syntax cryptic and perhaps intimidating. There are few of the friendly English-like syntax structures found in other programming languages. C contains a variety of unusual looking operators and the typical C program uses pointers extensively. The new C programmer will discover a variety of language characteristics that are largely a consequence of the original constricted development environment and its original application—implementation of an operating system.

To set the stage for the information to be presented in subsequent chapters of this book we have highlighted below some of the more significant characteristics of the language.

Size of Language

C, as you would expect, is an extremely small language. Many of the functions commonly defined as part of other programming languages are not included in C. For example, C does not have any built-in input/output capabilities, it contains no string-handling functions (e.g., string copy, string compare), and arithmetic operations beyond those such as basic addition or subtraction are not defined. Clearly a language without these capabilities is not much use, so C provides this functionality through a rich set of function libraries. As a result, most C implementations include standard libraries of functions for input/output, string manipulation, and arithmetic operations. In fact, these features are so standardized across numerous implementations that, for all practical purposes, they can be considered part of the language. C also enables the programmer to develop his or her own function libraries; one of the characteristics of C programs is an extensive use of function calls.

Loose Typing

C treats data types somewhat more loosely than strongly typed languages. This is a carry-over from B which was an untyped language; it provides the programmer with some additional freedom but also requires caution.

Modern Control Constructs

For a language developed in 1971, before structured programming became *de rigeur,* C, surprisingly, contains all the control structures you would expect in a modern language. For loops, if-else constructs, case (switch) statements, and while loops are all part of the language.

Bitwise Control

To perform systems programming, the task for which C was first developed, it is frequently necessary to manipulate objects at the bit level. C provides a variety of operators for bitwise manipulation of data.

Pointer Implementation

The ability to address specific areas of memory directly is another systems programming requirement. C language accomplishes this by using pointers. Although other languages implement pointers, C is noted for its ability to perform pointer arithmetic. So, for instance, if the variable n points to the first element of an array x, then n+1 will be the address of the second element of x.

In Chapter 13 you will see how this facility is used extensively to manipulate arrays and strings.

C can be characterized as a small language with a rich array of optional library functions. It permits very low-level access to the hardware for systems software and provides high-level control constructs for applications programming. The language lends itself to software modularization; the typical C program will use function calls extensively.

CURRENT USES OF C

C's intimate ties to the UNIX system and its initial application as a systems programming language have been long since left behind. To be sure, C is still used for systems applications and it is still the language of choice for most UNIX users, but C is now also used for a variety of applications running under nearly all operating systems. Most of the major personal computer software houses use the C language almost exclusively for developing database systems, graphics packages, spread sheets, CAD/CAM applications, word processors, office automation, and scientific and engineering applications. C compilers are also now available on many mainframe systems.

C language was not designed by a committee; it was not mandated for use by the government; it is the product of a small number of talented people whose initial goal was not much more than to develop a tool for their own use. Because of its power, elegance, and portability, C will probably continue to flourish as a preferred software development tool.

CHAPTER

2

FORMAT
OF A
C PROGRAM

OVERVIEW

In this chapter we provide the information you will need to build a simple C language program. On a general level we discuss the essential parts of a C program, including the special comment character sequences / * and * /, variable declarations, expressions, the two types of C statements (simple and compound, or block), C language punctuation rules, and library and user-defined functions.

C PROGRAM COMPONENTS

A program written in the C language must have a few basic components.

1. a main() function: This is the function with which the operating system will start executing. Each and every C program must have one and only one main() function, defined as follows:

```
main()
{
        variable declarations;

        program statements;
}
```

2. variable declarations: All variables used in C language programs must be declared. As in other programming languages, C variable declarations include the name of the variable and its type. Examples of variable types are int, char, float, or one of several derived types. A derived type is made from a combination of other already known types. In the C language, these can be pointer variables, arrays, structures, or unions. These will be described in Chapter 9 through 11.

3. executable statements: Executable statements must follow the variable declarations. An executable statement is an expression followed by a semicolon, or a control construct such as an if or while statement.

Program Comments

In addition to these essential elements of a C program, most programs and supporting functions contain program comments whose purpose is to make the program more understandable to a new reader, or even to the original author after time has passed.

Program comments may contain any message starting with the character sequence /* and ending with the sequence */. The following is an example of a commented main() function:

```
/*  Program name:  whereis
 *         Author:  Peter Abbott
 *       Released:  12/31/86
 *          Input:  command name
 *         Output:  location of corresponding command
 *                  file
 *          Logic:  look through the user's value
 *                  of PATH looking for a valid,
```

```
*                        executable file and print the
*                        absolute path name of the first
*                        occurrence
*/
main()
{
        variable declarations

        program statements
}
```

Program comments may be interspersed within the program code as well as be placed at the beginning of a function. In this example, the extra asterisks preceding the program comments in lines 2 through 11 are there only to enhance the appearance of the comment; they are not necessary.

Nesting Comments

Although it might be tempting to nest comments, it is not allowed in the C language. When the compiler (actually the C preprocessor) sees the character sequence / * it ignores anything it encounters until it sees a * / including another / *.

Rules of Spacing

With few exceptions, the C compiler is not concerned with how the programmer uses spacing in a C source file. It is helpful if the programmer uses this fact to his or her advantage to make the program more readable. For example, following the standard rules of structured programming, it is customary to indent the statements within a control construct. Blank lines are also allowed and should be used to separate one logical component from the next.

VARIABLE DECLARATIONS

Before a variable is used in a C program, it must be declared. This involves notifying the compiler of the variable's name and type as follows:

```
type name;
```

where the *type* can be int if the variable is going to hold an integer value, char if this to be a character variable, or float if this is a floating-point variable.

Unlike other languages (e.g., Basic and Fortran) where the type of variable is declared implicitly from rules pertaining to the naming of the variable, *all* variables in a C program must be declared explicitly. The following is an example of a variable declaration:

```
int var_name;
```

The name of the variable is var_name and it is of type int (integer). Several variables of the same type can be declared in one statement as follows:

```
int looper, state, flags;
```

where the variable names are separated by commas. Each of these variables will be of type int.

Variable-Naming Rules

Variable names can be formed of alphabetic (upper and lower case) characters, numbers, and the underscore (_) character. The first character of the name, however, must be either an underscore or alphabetic, although using an underscore to begin a variable name is discouraged. The length of an identifier is never limited, but the number of significant characters in the name varies from machine to machine. Even different versions of the C compiler on the same machine can differ with respect to naming conventions. Check your local documentation for the variable-naming conventions for your installation.

Many new compilers and the proposed ANSI C standard compiler allow variable names to be any length, with at least 31 characters significant. This is currently the standard for UNIX System V and BSD compilers.

STATEMENTS

There are two types of statements in the C language: simple and compound. *Simple statements* consist of an expression of any kind, followed by a semicolon. Simple statements are sometimes called *expression statements*. *Compound statements* are one or more simple statements surrounded with braces and are treated as a single statement by the compiler.

Simple Statements

The following is an example of a simple statement inside a main() function:

```
main()
{
        int x, y;

        x = y + 3;
}
```

The first line within the body of this program declares two integer variables x and y. The executable portion of this example is made up of several expressions, some of which are made up of other expressions. The expressions are the value 3, y, the binary expression y + 3, and the assignment x = y + 3. In the strictest sense, the variable assignment is treated as an expression, the value of which is the value that was assigned to the variable.

Simple Statement Punctuation   A semicolon terminates all simple statements in the C language.

EXPRESSIONS

An *expression* is formed from constants, variables, and function calls, either alone or in combination with one another using any of the C operators. Each of these elements is defined below:

1. constant value: A constant expression may be of type int, char, or float and usually does not stand alone as the sole expression in a statement. (However, syntactically, it could.) It is usually combined with an operator and, perhaps, a variable or function call. The following are examples of constant expressions:

```
7
12345
123. 45
'a'
```

Constant expressions, like other expressions, have a value and a type. For example, the expression 123. 45 has a value of 123. 45 and a type of float.

2. variable: The name of a declared variable is itself an expression; it has a type and a value. Variable expressions, like constant expressions, usually do not stand alone in a statement; they are usually combined with other expressions. The following are some examples of the use of variables in forming expressions:
(a) simple variable expression

```
var
```

(b) variable as part of a more complex expression

```
var + 7

var = var + 16
```

In the second expression, the variable var is used for its current value and as the object of the assignment. The equal (=) sign, in the C language, is an operator that causes the value of the expression to the right of the operator to be assigned to the variable named to the left of the operator. Only variable expressions can appear to the left of an assignment operator.

3. function call: A function call, when standing alone, is treated as an expression. When followed by a semicolon it makes a statement. For example, the statement in line 3 below consists solely of the `printf()` function and prints the message "make backup copy now" on the terminal:

```
main()
{
    printf("make backup copy now\n");
}
```

The quotation marks in the `printf()` statement do not print; they are used by the compiler to determine where the message to be printed starts and ends. The last two characters \n in the message indicate that a newline (or carriage return) is to follow the message. If omitted, another call to the `printf()` function would continue to print on the same line.

Function calls are often combined with variable assignments. The value of a function call expression is the return value of that function call. For example, the function `rand()` returns a random number. The following statement stores the return value of the function in the variable named `rn`:

```
main()
{
        unsigned int rn;

        rn = rand();
}
```

As in the previous example, the assignment operator is used to store the value of the expression to the right of the operator (the return value of the function call) in the variable whose name appears to the left of the assignment operator.

COMPOUND STATEMENTS

A compound statement is one or more simple statements enclosed in braces. This collection is treated as a single statement by the C compiler. Using compound statements is often necessary within control constructs. For example, within an `if` construct, if the supplied condition is determined to be true, then the *statement* that follows is executed. This statement can either be a simple or compound statement. By using a compound statement within an if construct, several statements can be executed conditionally.

Compound Statement: Example

The following is an example of a compound statement in use:

```
main()
{
        int x, y, state, uid, waiting;

        /* portion of program omitted */

        if ( x == y )
        {
                state = waiting;
                uid = getuid();
        }
}
```

This code fragment tests the value of the variable x to see if it is equal to (==) the value of the variable y. If it is, the statement that follows the if condition is executed. In this case that statement is a compound statement comprised of two simple statements. The first statement within the compound statement assigns the value of the variable waiting to the variable state. The second statement assigns to the variable uid the return value of the call to the getuid() library function.

The getuid() library function may not be available on your system.

PHILOSOPHY OF BRACE PLACEMENT

Some programmers place braces differently than shown in this book; they place the initial brace of the if construct immediately after the closing parenthesis on the conditional part. This is a matter of preference; the compiler does not recognize the difference. We have chosen our convention because it makes blocks or groups of statements more easily distinguishable and makes matching braces easier. It really does not matter which method you choose, only that you are consistent.

SAMPLE PROGRAM

The following is an example of a simple, complete program that assigns a value to an arithmetic expression a + b, places the value into a variable named sum, and prints the result if the sum is not zero. The != operator tests if two expressions are not equal.

```
/*  This program assigns two values to variables,
    a and b, adds them together, puts the sum in
    a variable named sum, and then prints the result,
    in decimal, if the result is not equal to zero.
*/

main()
{
        int a, b, sum;

        a = 15;
        b = 20;
        sum = a + b;
        if ( sum != 0 )
        {
                printf( "%d\n", sum );
        }
}
```

You will notice that we have placed only one statement between the braces following the if conditional expression. According to strict C syntax the braces are not then necessary; they are used in this case to enhance the program's readability.

COMPILING AND EXECUTING C PROGRAMS

The procedures used to compile and execute C programs differ slightly among operating environments. To illustrate the process we will use the UNIX system cc command as our example. Other system's commands will be similar. When the command is invoked, the C language program is passed through the following steps:

1. C preprocessor: This program accepts C source files as input and produces a file that is passed to the compiler. The preprocessor is responsible for removing comments and interpreting special C language preprocessor directives, which can be easily identified because they begin with the # symbol. These special preprocessor statements include the following:
    (a) #include —This merges the contents of the named file with the source program being compiled. These files, called *header files,* will be discussed in Chapter 15.
    (b) #define —This directive assigns a symbolic name to a constant. Symbolic names are used to make programs more readable and maintainable.

(c) #ifdef —This directive is called *conditional compilation* and allows the programmer to write programs that are adaptable to different operating environments.

2. C compiler: This program translates the C language source code into the machine's assembly language.

3. assembler: The assembler accepts the C compiler output and creates *object code*. If the program does not contain any external function calls, this code is directly executable.

4. link editor: If a source file references library functions or functions defined in other source files, the link editor combines these functions with the main() function to create an executable program file. This program also resolves external variable references.

The compilation and execution process is shown schematically in Exhibit 2-1.

EXHIBIT 2-1

Stages of compilation and execution

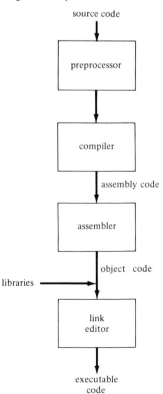

USING LIBRARY FUNCTIONS

Almost all the programs used in this text up to this point have referenced library functions. Because the C language is very small it does not include many of the traditional operations found in other languages (e.g., input and output routines). In C, these operations are found in libraries; the code for these functions is combined with your program code by the linkage editor.

Arguments to Library Functions

Some library functions, like printf(), require information to be passed to them in the form of arguments. These arguments appear between the parentheses that follow the name of the function; if more than one argument is required, they are separated by commas. For example, the following call to printf() requires two arguments:

```
main()
{

        int average;

        /* part of program omitted */

        printf( "The average is %d\n", average );
}
```

where the two arguments are: "The average is %d\n" and average. In general, function arguments represent information given to and needed by the function. C functions pass arguments via a *call by value;* only a copy of the value gets passed to the function and not the variable itself. This method of call by value has its advantages and disadvantages, as we will see in Chapter 8.

Some functions, such as the rand() function, which we have already seen, return values. The value of a function call expression is the return value of the function. This expression can be used like any other and its value can be saved through a variable assignment. For example:

```
main()
{
        int random;

        random = rand();
        printf( "The next random value is %d\n", random );
}
```

The value of the expression to the right of the assignment operator is stored in the variable whose name appears to the left. The expression on the right in this case is a function call; the value of the expression is the return value of the call.

One function call can even be used as an argument to another function. For example:

```
main()
{
        printf( "The next random value is %d\n", rand() );
}
```

This example shows one function call embedded within another. The return value of the expression rand() is given to the printf() function as its second argument. The special character sequence %d tells the printf() function that there is to be another argument and that its value is to be printed as a decimal number. If the value of the second argument were to be printed in hexadecimal, for instance, then the %d would be replaced by a %x. Again, the special sequence \n tells the printf() function to print a newline character (advance to the next line) after printing the message. The type of expression supplied as an argument is also important; you should always know (by reading the function documentation) the type of expression required.

User-Supplied Functions

In addition to the standard library functions, users can write their own functions and call them from one or more programs. Functions are defined as follows:

```
type_of_return_value name_of_function( argument_list )
definition_of_argument_list_members;
{
        local function variables;

        function executable statements;
        function executable statements;
        return( value );
}
```

For example, a function to sum two numbers and return the sum to the main program is written as follows:

```
main()
{
        int sum, a, b;

        sum = addem( a, b );
}
```

(program continues)

```
int addem( arg1, arg2 )
int arg1, arg2;
{
     int tot;

     tot = arg1 + arg2;
     return( tot );
}
```

The pieces of the function addem correspond to the structural components of a user-defined function as shown in Exhibit 2-2.

Unlike other languages, one C function cannot be defined within another function. In fact, C functions are often defined in separate source files and then combined with the program when it is compiled and link edited. User-supplied functions are described in detail in Chapters 8 and 14.

EXHIBIT 2-2

Identification of the parts of function addem

Function addem ( )	Part
int	type-of-return-value
addem	name-of-function
(arg 1, arg 2)	argument-list
int arg 1, arg 2;	definition-of-argument-list-members
{	{
int tot;	local function variables;
tot = arg1 + arg2;	function executable statements;
return (tot);	return (value);
}	}

SUMMARY

In this chapter we have provided an overview of the C language introducing many of the important features. In subsequent chapters we will look at each of these features in considerable detail. Note the distinction between an expression and a statement and the manner in which simple statements may be combined into compound statements, or blocks.

Because C is such a small language, library and user-defined functions play an important role in most programs. Through the judicious use of compound statements and functions, C programs can be properly structured for clarity, readability, and maintainability.

PART

DATA TYPES

CHAPTER

THE INTEGER

OVERVIEW

This chapter introduces the use of integers in the C
language. Topics covered include the different integer
constant representations (decimal, hexadecimal, octal), the
integer storage class, and the integer-related
operators—arithmetic, relational, logical, and bitwise.
Many of the integer operators can also be applied to
other data types; their use with these data types will be
discussed in Chapters 4 and 5.

INTEGER CONSTANTS

In the C language, integer constants are either type integer or long integer. Each of these types may be represented as a decimal, octal, or hexadecimal number.

The integer constant is stored in one word of memory, either 16 or 32 bits, depending on the machine architecture. Integer constants can represent values ranging from −32K to +32K if the host machine has a 16-bit word length or can represent values ranging from −2G (billion) to +2G if the word length is 32 bits. The following program will print your machine's word size in bits.

Do not be too concerned with the details of the program at this point.

program: size.c

```
1    main()
2    {
3         int x;
4
5         printf("word size, in bits, is %d\n", (sizeof x)*8);
6    }
```

Internal Representation of Integers and Portability

Internally, integers are stored as binary numbers, where the high-order bit represents a sign bit. Within arithmetic operations sign bit manipulation is machine dependent and operations involving the sign bit are not considered portable; they may not produce the same results on every machine. The following example was run on a machine with a 16-bit word length.

program: interint.c

```
1    main()
2    {
3         printf( "%d  %d  %d\n", 32767, 32767 + 1,
4                      32767 + 2 );
5    }
```

program output:

```
32767  -32768  -32767
```

This program prints three values (in decimal numbers): the values of 32767, 32767 + 1, and 32767 + 2. The internal representation of 32767 has all the bits turned on except the sign bit. When a one is added, all the bits become zero after the addition except the sign bit, yielding the largest negative value representable in 16 bits. Again, this is machine dependent; some machines will always protect the sign bit and yield a zero value. On machines where the word size is 32 bits, the result will be as expected, because the operation does not interfere with the sign bit.

Long Integer Constants

Long integer constants are only significant on machines where the word length is less than 32 bits. On these machines, a long-integer constant is stored in two machine words. On a 16-bit machine, a long-integer constant can represent numbers in the −2G to +2G range, while regular integer constants can only represent values between −32K and +32K. Because certain functions expect long-integer values as arguments, it is sometimes necessary to have a small number represented in 32 bits. This is possible through *explicit definition*. An integer can be defined as explicitly long by following the value with a lowercase or uppercase "l" ("el"). Exhibit 3-1 shows several integer constant examples.

In the exhibit's second example, we assume that the computer has a 16-bit word size, permitting integer values between −32K and +32K. Since the value of the constant expression is greater than the largest value an integer can hold, it is automatically stored in 32 bits. The third and fourth examples are also stored in 32 bits not because the number is too large to be stored in a word, but because the programmer has specifically asked for the 32-bit representation. Although the constant value can be followed by either an "l" or an "L", the latter is preferred for readability because the lowercase letter is often mistaken for the digit "1".

Machine Representation of Long-Integer Constants

Long-integer constants are also stored as binary numbers. The example on the next page shows the same program as before, but now the constants will be represented as long integers.

EXHIBIT 3-1

Examples of integer constants

value	type of constant
123	integer constant
79000	implicitly long integer constant (assuming 16-bit machine)
123L	explicitly long integer constant
123l	explicitly long integer constant

program: longint.c

```
1    main()
2    {
3        printf( "%d   %d   %d\n", 32767L,
4                    32767L + 1L,  32767L + 2L );
5    }
```

program output:

```
32767   32768   32769
```

HUMAN REPRESENTATION OF INTEGER VALUES

C accepts integers specified in one of three ways: decimal, hexadecimal (base 16), or octal (base 8). Of course, this representation is only for the programmer's convenience; the machine will always store the information internally in the same manner—as a series of binary digits. Operations on these constants always use binary arithmetic. Exhibit 3-2 shows some more examples of integer constants.

The 0 preceding an integer indicates that this is the desired integer's octal representation; a 0x or 0X preceding the value indicates that this number is represented as a hexadecimal number. If the number is represented in octal, only the digits 0 through 7 are valid, whereas if the number is represented as a hexadecimal number, the digits 0 through 9 and the letters a through f (or A

EXHIBIT 3-2

More integer constants

Integer	Representation	Decimal equivalent
12347	decimal	12347
−153	decimal	−153
034	octal	$28 \ (4 \times 8^0 + 3 \times 8^1)$
0xa5	hexadecimal	$165 \ (5 \times 16^0 + 10 \times 16^1)$
0Xa2	hexadecimal	$162 \ (2 \times 16^0 + 10 \times 16^1)$
123L	decimal (32 bits storage)	123
034L	octal (32 bits storage)	28
0Xa2L	hexadecimal (32 bits storage)	162

through F) are valid. When run on 16-bit machines, it is also possible to have these numbers represented internally in 32 bits by adding an l or L to the end of the constant expression.

INTEGER VARIABLES

The C language offers several integer variable varieties: the integer, the long integer, the short integer, the unsigned integer, and various combinations of the above.

The Integer

An integer variable is declared as follows:

```
int variable_name;
```

It is stored in one word of machine memory and, on a 16-bit computer, can hold values between $-32K$ through $+32K - 1$. Several integer variables can be declared at one time by separating the names of the variables with commas as follows:

```
int var_1, var_2, var_3;
```

Internally, integer variables are stored in the same manner as integer constants.

The Long Integer

The long integer is stored in 32 bits, regardless of the machine's word size. A long integer may, therefore, contain values from $-2G$ to $+2G - 1$. Long-integer variables are declared as follows:

```
long int variable_name;
```

or more simply

```
long variable_name;
```

The word int is not necessary in the variable declaration if the word long appears, but is often used to clarify the declaration. Long integers are frequently used when it is important to ensure portability from a 32-bit to a 16-bit machine environment. The following example illustrates this. Although both programs work properly on a 32-bit machine only the second program will produce correct results on a 16-bit machine.

program: wontwork.c

```
1    main()
2    {
3        int principal, flow, total;
4
5        /* useful part of program omitted here */
6        principal = 500;
7        flow = 1400;
8        total = principal * flow;
9        printf( "The total is %d\n", total );
10   }
```

program output(16 bit):

The total is -20896

program output(32 bit):

The total is 700000

program: willwork.c

```
1    main()
2    {
3        long principal, flow, total;
4
5        /* useful part of program omitted here */
6        principal = 500;
7        flow = 1400;
8        total = principal * flow;
9        printf( "The total is %d\n", total );
10   }
```

program output(16 bit):

The total is 700000

program output(32 bit):

The total is 700000

The Short Integer

The short integer is stored in 16 bits, regardless of the machine's word size and is declared as follows:

```
short int variable_name;                              •
```

or more simply

```
short variable_name;
```

The values stored in a short integer can range from −32K to +32K. As with long-integer variable declarations, the word int may be omitted if the word short appears. Both of the previous declarations are valid, but the first is more easily understood. Again, these variables can be used to make a program more portable, this time with the emphasis on space efficiency. At times, it may be necessary to decrease the memory used by a program. For example, if the program is going to be read into programmable read-only memory (PROM), it is advantageous to keep the program as small as possible. Or, if many of these variables are to be stored in a file, a substantial amount of storage space can be saved.

Unsigned Integers

Two types of unsigned integers are available: the unsigned integer and the unsigned short integer. These two variable types are declared as follows:

```
unsigned int variable_name;
unsigned short int ushort_name;
```

or can be abbreviated as

```
unsigned variable_name;
unsigned short ushort_name;
```

Unsigned integers are stored in one machine word, while unsigned short integers are stored in 16 bits, regardless of the machine's word size. The internal representation of these integers is different than that of the regular integers. The high-order bit is no longer used as a sign bit, but is used to store the number.

Arithmetic Operations

The usual integer operations found in most programming languages are also available in C. These include addition, subtraction, multiplication, and division. Other operations, like exponentiation, are available only through library functions and are not implemented directly as part of the language. Several operations available in the C language are not commonly available in other languages. Exhibit 3-3 shows the C language arithmetic operators and their descriptions.

EXHIBIT 3-3

C language arithmetic operators

Operation	Symbol	Notes
addition	+	
subtraction	−	
multiplication	*	
division	/	remainder lost
modulo	%	remainder from division
increment	+ +	placement critical
decrement	− −	placement critical

The Modulo Operator   Normally, when one integer is divided by another, the result will also be an integer and the remainder will be dropped, as in the following program:

program: divide.c

```
1     main( )
2     {
3          int x, y;
4
5          x = 14;
6          y = 4;
7          printf( "14 divided by 4 = %d\n", x / y );
8     }
```

program output:

```
14 divided by 4 = 3
```

If it is necessary to obtain the remainder of the division, then the modulo operator is used:

program: remain.c

```
1     main( )
2     {
3          int x, y;
4
5          x = 14;
6          y = 4;
7          printf( "14 divided by 4 = %d\n", x / y );
8          printf( "The remainder is = %d\n", x % y);
9     }
```

program output:

```
14 divided by 4 = 3
The remainder is = 2
```

The Increment and Decrement Operators   The C language offers two operations that increment and decrement a variable, with two possible placements of
these operators. Either operator may be placed immediately before or after a
variable name. The increment operator causes the value of the variable to be
incremented by one. The value of the expression, however, depends on the
operator's placement. For example, if the variable x has the value 5, then the
expression:

```
++x
```

has the value 6, the value of the variable x after it was incremented. If the ++
appears after the variable name, the variable is still incremented, but the value
of the expression is the value of the variable x *before* it is incremented. The
following program illustrates this:

program: increment.c

```
1       /* this program illustrates the increment operator */
2       main()
3       {
4               int x, y;
5
6               x = 5;
7               y = 5;
8
9               printf( "The value of ++x is %d\n", ++x );
10              printf( "The value of y++ is %d\n", y++ );
11
12              printf( "After the increment x is %d\n", x );
13              printf( "After the increment y is %d\n", y );
14      }
```

program output:

```
The value of ++x is 6
The value of y++ is 5
After the increment x is 6
After the increment y is 6
```

The increment operator is really a convenience and is not a necessary part
of the language. It is an historical artifact, left over from when C was primarily

used to write operating systems on the DEC PDP–11 computer. A hardware increment instruction on this machine permitted faster execution than the equivalent assignment statement. In other machines where this instruction is not available, the increment operator offers no performance improvement over the equivalent assignment statement. However, it is important because it is frequently used in the existing base of C language programs.

The decrement operator is used to decrease the value of a variable by one. The value of the expression follows the same rules as the increment operator: if the -- appears before the variable name, the value of the expression is the value of the variable after the decrement is performed (the decrement is performed before the expression is evaluated). If the decrement operator appears after the variable name, the expression is evaluated before the decrement is performed. The following program illustrates the use of the decrement operator:

program: decrement.c

```
1      /* this program illustrates the decrement operator */
2      main()
3      {
4          int x, y;
5
6          x = 5;
7          y = 5;
8
9          printf( "The value of --x is %d\n", --x );
10         printf( "The value of y-- is %d\n", y-- );
11
12         printf( "After the decrement x is %d\n", x );
13         printf( "After the decrement y is %d\n", y );
14     }
```

program output:

```
The value of --x is 4
The value of y-- is 5
After the decrement x is 4
After the decrement y is 4
```

The increment and decrement operators are the first operators we have discussed formally that have a *side effect*. In this case, the side effect is to alter the variable's value by one; in most cases, C language operators do not change the value of any variables. The other exception to this rule would, of course, be the assignment operator.

The Assignment Operators

Several assignment operators are available in the C language; one basic operator (the = operator) and several variations. These variations are part of the language simply for convenience; they all have equivalent forms using only the = operator.

The assignment operator assumes there is a variable name to its left and an expression to its right. It takes the value of the expression and stores it in the variable. To the right of the assignment operator may be an arithmetic, relational, logical, bitwise, or address expression, or another assignment. The following program illustrates the use of the assignment operator:

program: assign.c

```
1     main()
2     {
3         int x, y, z;
4
5         /* arithmetic expression */
6         x = 5 * 3;
7
8         /* another assignment */
9         z = y = 6;
10
11        printf( "The value of x is %d\n", x );
12        printf( "The value of y is %d\n", y );
13        printf( "The value of z is %d\n", z );
14    }
```

program output:

```
The value of x is 15
The value of y is 6
The value of z is 6
```

If there are multiple assignment operators in one statement, they are evaluated from right to left. As we mentioned before, a variable assignment expression has a value—the value assigned to the variable. Therefore, in the second assignment statement, the expression y = 6 is evaluated first and then the value of the expression is assigned to the variable z. The value of the expression y = 6 is 6, the value assigned to y. This is unique to C; most programming languages do not treat variable assignments as expressions, but rather as statements. Because the C language treats them as expressions, they may appear anywhere an arithmetic or relational expression could appear. This is convenient but sometimes introduces hard-to-detect errors. For example, the assignment operator is a single equal sign, but a test for equality is two equal signs placed together, making:

```
x = 5
```

an assignment expression (having a side effect and a value) and the expression:

```
x == 5
```

a simple test for equality. The following program illustrates a common C language programming error:

program: equal.c

```
1     main()
2     {
3           int x, y;
4
5           x = 6;
6           y = 6;
7
8           if ( x = 7 )
9           {
10                 printf( "First <if> successful\n" );
11          }
12          else
13          {
14                 printf( "First <if> not successful\n" );
15          }
16
17          if ( y == 7 )
18          {
19                 printf( "Second <if> successful\n" );
20          }
21          else
22          {
23                 printf( "Second <if> not successful\n" );
24          }
25    }
```

Study the output below and look back at the program:

```
First <if> successful
Second <if> not successful
```

Remember, an assignment expression has a value and can be used wherever any other expression can be used, including as the condition for an if statement. In this program, the value of the expression in the parentheses (x = 7) has a nonzero value (7). Since a nonzero value is considered to be "true" by the if statement, the statement in the then branch of the if statement was executed. Since the value of the assignment will always be 7, regardless of the previous value of x, this condition will always be true and the first branch of the if statement will always be executed. In the second if statement we see the correct conditional test; the truth value of the condition in parentheses depends on the value in the variable named y.

Other Assignment Operators   Several other assignment operators are available that combine the assignment with some other operation. Exhibit 3-4 lists these combined assignment operators.

A Word About Operator Precedence

If an expression has more than one operator, it is important to know the order in which they will be applied. For example, consider the following expression:

```
x = ++y
```

Is the value to be stored in x equal to the value of y before or after its increment? Or phrased another way, which gets done first—the increment or the assignment? In this example, it is fairly obvious the increment will be done before the variable assignment. In fact, variable assignment should always

EXHIBIT 3-4

C language combined assignment operators

Assignment operators		
shorthand	equivalent assignment	meaning
x += 5	x = x + 5	add
x −= 5	x = x − 5	subtract
x *= 5	x = x * 5	multiply
x /= 5	x = x / 5	divide
x %= 5	x = x % 5	modulo
x >>= 5	x = x >> 5	shift right
x <<= 5	x = x << 5	shift left
x &= 5	x = x & 5	bitwise "and"
x ^= 5	x = x ^ 5	bitwise "exclusive or"
x != 5	x = x | 5	bitwise "inclusive or"

EXHIBIT 3-5

C language arithmetic operator precedence rules

Order of evaluation—arithmetic expressions		
operator	meaning	associativity
++	increment	right to left
--	decrement	right to left
*	multiply	left to right
/	divide	left to right
%	modulo	left to right
+	add	left to right
-	subtract	left to right
=	assignments (all)	right to left

come last in the order of evaluation. Operator precedence is not always so obvious. If we have the following expression:

```
x = ++y  *  3
```

which operation, the increment or the multiplication, is performed first? In this case, the language's precedence rules, shown in Exhibit 3-5, must be followed.

The Relational Operators

Relational operators are used in control constructs such as `if` and `while`. They are used to form logical expressions that compare the value of one expression to another. These logical expressions have a zero value when the comparison is false and a value of one when the comparison is true. More generally, the C language considers any nonzero value to be true (we saw an

EXHIBIT 3-6

C language relational operators

Relational Operators	
Operator	Meaning
==	equal
!=	not equal
<	less than
<=	less than or equal to
>	greater than
>=	greater than or equal to

example of this with the expression x = 7), but when it generates a true value, it uses the number one. Exhibit 3-6 lists some of the relational operators available in C language.

Notice again that the test for equality is two equal signs; remember that the assignment is one equal sign and that the two should never be confused. The following program shows several relational expressions and their numeric values:

program: relation.c

```
1    main()
2    {
3
4        int x, y;
5
6        x = 15;
7        y = 20;
8
9        printf( "The value of x == y is %d\n", x == y );
10       printf( "The value of x <= y is %d\n", x <= y );
11       printf( "The value of x >= y is %d\n", x >= y );
12       printf( "The value of x != y is %d\n\n", x != y );
13
14       /* use equality operator in if statement */
15       if( x == y )
16       {
17           printf( "The expression x == y is true\n" );
18       }
19       else
20       {
21           printf( "The expression x == y is false\n" );
22       }
23
24       /* try again with assignment operator (mistake) */
25       if( x = y)
26       {
27           printf( "The expression x = y is true\n" );
28       }
29       else
30       {
31           printf( "The expression x = y is false\n" );
32       }
33
34
35       printf( "\nx is %d and y is %d\n", x, y );
36   }
```

program output:

```
The value of x == y is 0
The value of x <= y is 1
The value of x >= y is 0
The value of x != y is 1

The expression x == y is false
The expression x = y is true

x is 20 and y is 20
```

Logical Operators

The C language logical operators allow the programmer to combine simple relational expressions into more complex expressions by using logical *not*s, *and*s, and *or*s.

Logical not   The logical *not* simply reverses the truth value of the expression that follows it. For example, if the variable x has a nonzero value, then the expression:

```
x
```

has a true value, but the expression:

```
!x
```

has a false value. An exclamation point preceding the expression to be logically negated represents the logical *not*. The logical *not* can also be applied to more complex expressions; parentheses are needed to cause negation of the entire expression. For example:

```
!( x + y + rand() )
```

Logical and   The logical *and* is represented by two & signs between two expressions as follows:

```
expression1 && expression2
```

When two expressions are *and*ed the resulting expression will be true only if both of the subexpressions are true. For example, the expression:

```
(x > 5) && (y < 15)
```

will only be true if x is greater than 5 and if y is less than 15. In addition, the second expression (y < 15) will not be evaluated if the first expression is false, since the outcome of the logical expression will already be known. This is important if one of the subexpressions uses an operator that has a side effect, such as an assignment, increment, or decrement. For example, in the following expression:

```
(y < 15) && (x++ > 15)
```

the value of x is incremented only if the value of y is less than 15. Obviously then, you should be careful about using operators with side effects in logical expressions. After the logical expression is evaluated, variable values may not be what you expect. The rule for expression evaluation is as follows:

> *When evaluating a logical expression, evaluate from left to right only as far as needed to determine the logical result.*

Logical or   The logical *or* is represented by two vertical bars between two expressions:

```
expression1 || expression2
```

The logical result of the entire expression will be true if either of the two expressions surrounding the || is logically true. As with expressions involving the logical *and* operator, expressions involving a logical *or* are evaluated from left to right only until the result of the logical expression is known. Therefore, if the value of the first expression is true, then the second expression is not evaluated. The impact on variables and operators with side effects is the same as for the logical *and*.

The following program combines and illustrates the use of several logical operators:

program: boolean.c

```
1    main()
2    {
3         int minimum, maximum;
4         int sample1, sample2;
5
6         minimum = 20;
7         maximum = 2000;
8
9         /* part of program omitted */
10        sample1 = 145;
11        sample2 = 2741;
12
```

(*program continues*)

```
13          if( (sample1 < maximum && sample1 > minimum) ||
14              (sample2 < maximum && sample2 > minimum) )
15          {
16              printf( "At least one of the values is in range\n" );
17          }
18
19          if( (sample1 < maximum && sample1 > minimum) &&
20              (sample2 < maximum && sample2 > minimum) )
21          {
22              printf( "Both of the values are in range\n" );
23          }
24      }
```

program output:

```
At least one of the values is in range
```

In the first i f construct, the second part of the logical *or* expression is not evaluated; had it included an operator with a side effect, (e.g., an increment), the side effect would not have taken place. The following variation on the previous example illustrates this:

program: bool2.c

```
1     main()
2     {
3           int minimum, maximum;
4           int sample1, sample2;
5
6           minimum = 20;
7           maximum = 2000;
8
9           /* part of program omitted */
10          sample1 = 145;
11          sample2 = 2741;
12
13          if( (sample1 < maximum && sample1 > minimum) ||
14              (++sample2 < maximum && sample2 > minimum) )
15          {
16              printf( "At least one is in range\n" );
17          }
18
19          printf("The value of sample2 is %d\n", sample2);
20      }
```

program output:

```
At least one of the values is in range
The value of sample2 is 2741
```

The increment was not performed; the value of sample2 remained at 2741.

Bitwise Operators

Six bitwise operators are available in the C language enabling the programmer to manipulate integers at the bit level.

This section assumes you have some knowledge of bit manipulation; novice programmers may skip this section.

Bitwise and   The bitwise *and* operator is represented as a single ampersand (&) and is surrounded on both sides by integer expressions. The resulting expression has the value created by *and*ing each corresponding bit from the two integer expressions. (Remember not to confuse the bitwise *and* (&) with the logical *and* (&&).) For example, assume that the integer variable x has the value 0753 and the variable y has the value 0722. Bitwise *and*ing these two integers yields:

program: bitand.c

```
1     main()
2     {
3          int x, y;
4
5          x = 0753; /* octal value */
6          y = 0722;
7
8          /* print bitwise and of x and y */
9          printf( "x & y is %o\n", x & y );
10    }
```

program output:

```
x & y is 702
```

Verify this result for yourself.

Testing Flag Values   Bitwise *and*ing is often used in maintaining flags, where one integer variable can be used to hold 16 or 32 different flags. For example, to test a flag to determine if the seventh bit is turned on, we bitwise *and* the flag with an integer that has only the seventh bit set (octal 100), as follows:

program: flagtest.c

```
 1     main()
 2     {
 3          int flag;
 4
 5          /* most of program omitted */
 6          flag = 0700;
 7
 8          if ( (flag & 0100) != 0 ) /* test 7th bit */
 9          {
10               printf( "flag is set\n" );
11          }
12          /* more program omitted */
13     }
```

program output:

```
flag is set
```

It is common practice in situations like this not to embed the value of 0100 in the program text, but to define it as a symbolic constant through the #define preprocessor statement, as follows:

```
#define        RUNNABLE          0100
```

The symbolic name RUNNABLE may then appear wherever 0100 now appears. Also, note the additional parentheses in the expression:

```
(flag & 0100) != 0
```

The additional parentheses are necessary because the C language operator-precedence rules state that the nonequality test is to be done before the bitwise operation. If the parentheses were left out, then the expression would be evaluated as follows:

```
flag & ( 0100 != 0 )
```

This expression would cause octal 100 to be compared against 0, yielding a true value with the numeric value of one. The value one would then be bitwise *and*ed with the value of flag. If the low-order bit were set in the variable flag, then the expression would be true, otherwise it would be false (a valid program but probably not the one intended.)

Bitwise Inclusive or

The vertical bar (|) symbolizes the bitwise or operator and causes the corresponding bits in the two expressions surrounding it to be ored on a bit-by-bit basis. For example, if the variable x has the value 0722 and the variable y has the value 0111, then the expression x | y has the value:

program: bitor.c

```
1     main()
2     {
3         int x, y;
4
5         x = 0722;
6         y = 0111;
7
8         printf( "x | y is %o\n", x | y );
9     }
```

program output:

```
x | y is 733
```

Verify this result for yourself.

Setting Bits in a Flag   The bitwise inclusive or may be used to turn a bit on in a flag, just as bitwise *and* is used to test if a bit is already turned on in a flag. The following program illustrates the setting of a bit in a flag and the subsequent testing of that bit:

program: flagset.c

```
1     #define    RUNNABLE    0100
2     main()
3     {
4         int flag;
5
6         /* part of program omitted */
7
8         /* set RUNNABLE (7th) bit in flag */
9         flag |= RUNNABLE;
10
11        /* part of program omitted */
12
```

(program continues)

```
13              /* test to see if RUNNABLE bit is set */
14              if ( (flag & RUNNABLE) != 0 )
15              {
16                      printf( "we are in a runnable state\n" );
17              }
18      }
```

program output:

we are in a runnable state

In line 9:

flag |= RUNNABLE;

the |= operator is used instead of the equivalent statement:

flag = flag | RUNNABLE

Either is correct. This statement causes the bit to be set if it is not already set and leaves the bit on if it is already on.

Bitwise Exclusive or

The ^ character represents the bitwise exclusive *or* and will evaluate the bits of the two surrounding integer expressions on a bit-by-bit basis. In the resulting expression, a bit will be turned on only if one of the two bits in the expressions is on. If both are on, the resulting bit is set to off as shown in the following:

program: exclor.c

```
1       main()
2       {
3               int x, y;
4
5               x = 0732;
6               y = 0111;
7
8               printf( "x ^ y is %o\n", x ^ y );
9       }
```

program output:

x ^ y is 623

Verify this result for yourself.

EXHIBIT 3-7

The bitwise complement operator

x	0000011101010001
~x	1111100010101110

The Complement Operator

The bitwise complement of an integer expression is created by preceding the expression with the complement operator (~). This will reverse all the bits, turning on the "off" bits and turning off the "on" bits as shown in Exhibit 3-7.

This operator is often combined with the bitwise *and* operator to turn off a particular bit. This technique is illustrated in the following program:

program: flag.c

```
 1     #define    RUNNABLE    0100
 2     main()
 3     {
 4          int flag;
 5
 6          flag = 0;
 7
 8          /* part of program omitted */
 9
10          /* set RUNNABLE (7th) bit in flag */
11          flag |= RUNNABLE;
12
13          /* part of program omitted */
14
15          /* test to see if RUNNABLE bit is set */
16          if ( (flag & RUNNABLE) != 0 )
17          {
18               printf( "we are in a runnable state\n" );
19          }
20
21          /* reset RUNNABLE bit in flag */
22          flag = flag & ~RUNNABLE;
23
24          /* test to see if RUNNABLE bit is set */
25          if ( (flag & RUNNABLE) != 0 )
26          {
27               printf( "we are still in a runnable state\n" );
28          }
29     }
```

program output:

we are in a runnable state

The statement on line 22:

flag = flag & ~RUNNABLE;

turned off the RUNNABLE bit in the variable named flag. If any other bits were
on, they would remain on after line 22 was executed. The diagram in Exhibit
3-8 illustrates this.

These bits corresponded to other flags to be left alone by this operation.

EXHIBIT 3-8

Setting the RUNNABLE bit to off

Line	Statement	Result
11	flag | = RUNNABLE	000110000100010
	~RUNNABLE	111111111101111111
22	flag &= ~RUNNABLE	000110000000010

Shift Operators

Two shift operators, shift right (>>) and shift left (<<) appear to the right of an
integer expression and to the left of a second integer expression, as follows:

integer_expression_1 << integer_expression_2

and

integer_expression_1 >> integer_expression_2

where integer_expression_1 is the expression that is to be shifted and
integer_expression_2 is the number of bit positions to be shifted. The
following program illustrates the use of the shift operator:

program: shifty.c

```
1      main()
2      {
3              int shifty;
4
5              shifty = 0571;
6              printf( "The value of shifty is %o\n", shifty );
```

```
7
8          shifty = shifty >> 4;
9          printf( "The value of shifty is %o\n", shifty );
10
11         shifty = shifty << 6;
12         printf( "The value of shifty is %o\n", shifty );
13    }
```

program output:

```
The value of shifty is 571
The value of shifty is 27
The value of shifty is 2700
```

Exhibit 3-9 illustrates the shift operation results in the above program.

The shift operator, when combined with the bitwise operators, is useful for extracting data from an integer that holds multiple pieces of information. For example, assume there is an integer variable that represents the access permissions associated with a file. For each file there are three sets of permissions, one set for the owner of the file, one for the owner's group (or class), and permissions for everyone not associated with the owner. Next, there are four different permissions for each of these three categories: read permission, write permission, append permission, and execute permission. All these permission bits are packed into one integer; there is a different integer associated with each file on the system.

Consider the following problem: Extract only the four bits of information for the owner's group and express these permissions hexadecimally as a number between 0 and 15. The permission variable is structured as shown in Exhibit 3-10.

First we must mask out the unnecessary bits. The following statement can do this:

```
permissions = permission & 0x0F0
```

EXHIBIT 3-9

Internal representation of variable shifty in program shifty.c

After Line Number	Variable shifty
5	0000000101111001
8	0000000000010111
11	0000010111000000

EXHIBIT 3-10

The permission variable

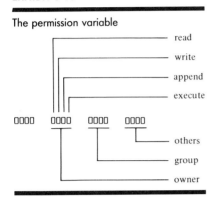

or, equivalently:

```
permissions &= 0x0F0
```

This will eliminate all but the bits that correspond to the group. Next, we need the group permissions represented as a number between 0 and 15, so we shift this variable 4 bits to the right to discard the permissions for the ''others'' category:

```
permissions = permissions >> 4
```

or, equivalently:

```
permissions >>= 4
```

The following program illustrates these steps:

program perms.c

```
1      #define    GROUPMASK    0x0F0
2      main()
3      {
4          int perms;
5
6          perms = 0xAD7;   /* 1010 1101 0111 */
7
8          perms &= GROUPMASK;
9          printf( "masked perms contains %x\n", perms );
10
11         perms >>= 4;
12         printf( "group perms contains %x\n", perms );
13     }
```

program output:

```
masked perms contains d0
group perms contains d
```

Other Integer Operations

Other integer operations involving arrays, structures, unions, and pointers will be discussed in Chapters 9 through 11.

EXHIBIT 3-11

Integer operator precedence

Order of Evaluation - Integer Operations		
Operator	Meaning	Associativity
!	logical not	right to left
~	complement	right to left
++	increment	right to left
--	decrement	right to left
*	multiply	left to right
/	divide	left to right
%	modulo	left to right
+	add	left to right
-	subtract	left to right
<<	shift left	left to right
>>	shift right	left to right
<	less than	left to right
<=	less than or equal to	left to right
>	greater than	left to right
>=	greater than or equal to	left to right
==	equal to	left to right
!=	not equal to	left to right
&	bitwise and	left to right
^	bitwise exclusive or	left to right
|	bitwise inclusive or	left to right
&&	logical and	left to right
||	logical and or	left to right
?:	conditional or	right to left
=	assignments (all)	right to left

Integer Operator Precedence

Exhibit 3-5 contains a chart showing operator precedence. Exhibit 3-11 is a more complete version of the same chart, including the operators we have just discussed.

SUMMARY

In this chapter we have discussed manipulating integers in the C language. We have seen that the C language combines the standard integer operations available in most higher-level languages with a full set of bitwise operators, usually found only in lower-level languages. This dual nature is one of the keys to the C language's power. It has a higher level language's structure and ease of use but also permits the programmer to manipulate the computer at low levels without having to escape to assembly language routines.

EXERCISES

1. What are the *decimal* values of the following numbers:

```
0xb7      0x1a
022       0x1aL
0x1a      0621
```

2. In all four statements below assume x = 100 before executing the statement. Fill in the value of x and the value of the expression after executing the statement:

	Value of x	Value of Expression
x++;		
++x;		
x--;		
--x;		

3. What will be the output of the following program?

```
main()
{
        int a, b, aa, bb, x, y;
        x = 100;
```

```
        y  =  100;
        a  =  ++x;
        b  =  y++;
        aa  =  ++x;
        bb  =  y++;
        printf("The value of a is %d\n",a);
        printf("The value of b is %d\n",b);
        printf("The value of aa is %d\n",aa);
        printf("The value of bb is %d\n",bb);
}
```

Try it, and check the actual output against your predicted output.

4.   For each statement below, assume that y = 100 before the execution of the statement. In each case what is the value of x after execution?

```
(a)     x = y;
(b)     x = --y * 4;
(c)     x = y = y++;
(d)     x = y == 100;
(e)     x = y == y++;
(f)     x = y == ++y;
```

5.   Given the following code fragment:

```
int x, y, z;
x = 10;
y = 3;
z = (x / y) * y;
```

Write a program incorporating this code that compares x and z for equality and prints out:

```
        X == Z
```

or   X < Z

or   X > Z

depending upon the value of the relationship.

6.   The octal number 0100 may be conveniently used to test if the seventh bit of a flag is "on" (set to 1). What octal number would you use to test the state of the eighth bit of a flag?, the ninth bit?, the tenth bit?

7. Rewrite the program perms. c to check "owner" permissions.

8. The following three statements:

```
y = y + 1;
z = x + y;
x = x + 1;
```

can be written as a single statement using the increment operator. Write this statement. Test your answer by writing two equivalent programs, one using the three statements, the other using your one statement equivalent. Begin each program with:

```
y = 4;
x = 3;
```

and print the values of x, y, and z at the termination of the program.

CHAPTER

THE
CHARACTER

OVERVIEW

In this chapter we introduce the character data type. We begin with character constants and their machine representation, followed by a discussion of how to use character constants and variables within C language programs. Finally, we show how character variables can be manipulated using C language operators.

CHARACTER CONSTANTS

Character constant expressions represent a single character's value. The character represented is surrounded by single quotes and has a numeric value according to the American National Standard Code for Information Interchange (ASCII) collating sequence. Most computer manufacturers adhere to mapping characters to numeric values; it is fairly standard throughout the industry. The coded characters contain numeric representations for the most commonly used icons, including characters, numbers, and special symbols, such as ! # % & *. (Appendix A shows the ASCII collating sequence.)

Examples of Character Constants

The following are examples of character constant expressions:

```
'r'
'1'
'$'
```

The value of the first character constant expression is the ASCII value of the character r, or 162 (octal). When the value is printed, the `printf()` function can output it in one of several ways, depending on the format specification supplied to it in the control string. The second expression shown above is the character 1, as opposed to the integer one. The value of the expression is the ASCII value for the character 1, or 61 (octal). The last constant expression represents the ASCII value of the dollar sign ($) character.

The following program illustrates a character constant expression's value as printed by the `printf()` function:

program: character.c

```
1    main()
2    {
3        printf( "ASCII:\t%c\t%c\t%c\n",
4                   'A', '$', '1' );
5        printf( "OCTAL:\t%o\t%o\t%o\n",
6                   'A', '$', '1' );
7        printf( "DECIMAL:\t%d\t%d\t%d\n",
8                   'A', '$', '1' );
9    }
```

program output:

```
ASCII:          A        $        1
OCTAL:          101      44       61
DECIMAL:        65       36       49
```

This program prints the values of the three character constant expressions in three ways: ASCII, octal, and decimal. The internal character representation is always the same; the printing function may cause the output to differ.

The sequence of characters \t in the preceding program represents a horizontal tab character and will advance the cursor (or print head) to the next tab stop. The sequence of characters %c requests that the value of the matching argument be printed in its ASCII representation. The matching argument should have an integer value between 0 and 177 (octal).

Special Character Constants

Some more frequently used, nonprinting characters (such as the horizontal tab character) have special character constant identifications. They are referred to as *escape sequences* and are shown in Exhibit 4-1.

The last two escape sequences let the programmer represent any character, whether or not printable, by following the backslash with either the octal or hexadecimal representation for the character, as given by the ASCII collating sequence. An example of such a representation is the character constant ' \0 ' (zero), which is used to represent a null (zero-valued) byte, and, as we shall see, is extremely useful in C.

Machine Representation

Character constants are stored in one word and can have values between 0 and 177 (octal). The word layout varies from machine to machine; some represent characters as signed entities capable of storing values from −128 to +127 (decimal) and others store them unsigned, with values ranging from 0 to 255 (decimal). If the character is stored as a signed entity, the negative values are stored in two's complement notation.

EXHIBIT 4-1

Standard C language escape sequences

Escape Sequence	Meaning
'\b'	backspace
'\f'	form feed
'\n'	newline (line feed)
'\r'	carriage return
'\t'	horizontal tab
'\v'	vertical tab
'\\'	backslash
'\''	single quote
'\"'	double quote
'\0dd'	others (octal)
'\0xdd'	others (hex)

CHARACTER VARIABLES

Although character constants are stored in one machine word, character variables are stored in a single byte. The ASCII values range from 0 to 127 (decimal); these values can fit into 7 bits without using the high-order bit. Some systems, however, use the high-order bit to extend the character set to 256 characters. Using these non-ASCII characters is discouraged because there are no standard definitions for these icons; using them produces nonportable code. Each character variable can hold one character which may be treated as a signed or unsigned entity, depending on the machine type. A character variable is declared as follows:

```
char c;
```

where c is the name of the variable and char is the variable type.

Character Input

A character may be input from the terminal by using the getchar() function. This function's return value is a character typed in from the keyboard. Exactly when the character is delivered to the program depends on the operating system on which the program is run. Some operating systems deliver the character immediately to the program; others wait until the line is completely input and the return key is depressed. On UNIX systems, the character is not delivered until the return key is depressed.

The following program illustrates using character variables in conjunction with the getchar() function:

program: char_input.c

```
1    main()
2    {
3         char c;
4
5         /* Issue prompt to terminal */
6         printf( "Please type in a character:  " );
7         c = getchar();
8
9         /* Print value of input character using
10            three different representations */
11        printf( "The character is (octal): %o\n", c );
12        printf( "The character is (decimal): %d\n", c );
13        printf( "The character is (ASCII): %c\n", c );
14   }
```

program output:

```
Please type in a character: R
The character is (octal): 122
The character is (decimal): 82
The character is (ASCII): R
```

No arguments are supplied to the getchar() function. The function re-quires no arguments; it simply reads a character from the terminal and returns it.

What, if any, would be appropriate arguments to the getchar() function? The source of this information could be supplied, instructing the getchar() function where to get the information—perhaps from a file rather than from the terminal. The getchar() function is not that sophisticated; it always gets the character from the standard input (terminal). Other functions that read characters from a file are described in Chapter 12.

The putchar() function is the complement of the getchar() function. This function simply prints the ASCII value of the expression it receives as an argument. The putchar() function may sometimes be used in place of printf() to print a single character.

The following program uses the putchar() function:

program: putch.c

```
1     main()
2     {
3            char c;
4
5            /* get a character from the terminal */
6            printf( "Please enter a character: " );
7            c = getchar();
8
9            /* print the character on the terminal */
10           putchar(c);
11           putchar('\n');
12    }
```

program output:

```
Please enter a character: P
P
```

Machine Dependencies

The signed and unsigned methods of storing characters cause machine de-pendency. Assume we have a program that reads characters until an end of file (EOF) is reached. When the end of file is encountered, the getchar() function returns the EOF value defined in the <stdio.h> header file. Currently, the EOF value is −1. On machines where characters are unsigned, it would be wiser to store the return value of getchar() in an integer first and then, if it is not end of file, store the character in a character variable. The following two programs illustrate this:

program: eof.c

```
 1    #include <stdio.h>
 2
 3    main()
 4    {
 5         char c;
 6
 7         /* prompt and accept character */
 8         printf( "Enter character (CONTROL-D to end): " );
 9         c = getchar();
10
11         if ( c != EOF )
12         {
13              printf( "The value of c is: %c\n", c );
14         }
15    }
```

program output:

```
Enter character (CONTROL-D to end): R
The value of c is: R
```

In line 1 of this program, the #include directive to the C preprocessor merges the contents of a header file named stdio.h with the source. The C preprocessor finds the file named stdio.h and merges its contents with the program; the expanded program is then compiled.

Although this program works correctly, its portability is not guaranteed. The program relies on the machine having signed characters. If it had unsigned characters, it could not have properly stored the value of EOF (−1) in the variable c. The following program corrects this problem by first placing getchar()'s return value into an integer and then, if the value is not EOF, processing it as normal input.

program: eof2.c

```
 1    #include <stdio.h>
 2
 3    main()
```

```
 4     {
 5          int character_in;
 6          char c;
 7
 8          /* prompt and accept character */
 9          printf( "Enter character (CONTROL-D to end): " );
10          character_in = getchar();
11
12          if ( character_in != EOF )
13          {
14              c = character_in;
15              printf( "The value in c is: %c\n", c );;
16          }
17     }
```

program output:

```
Enter character (CONTROL-D to end): R
The value in c is: R
```

These programs illustrate the two methods for accepting characters from the terminal.

On most terminals, entering CONTROL-D causes the <EOT> character to be sent to the program. This character is interpreted by getchar() as an end of file and getchar() then returns the defined value of EOF.

OPERATIONS INVOLVING CHARACTERS

All the operations available for integer manipulation are also available for characters. However, some operators, such as arithmetic and bitwise operators, are of little use unless a character variable is being used in place of an integer variable to save memory. (Using characters this way is discussed on page 59).

Other operators, such as logical comparisons and the assignment operator, relate more naturally to character variables. For instance, the following example tests to see if an input character is uppercase alphabetic:

program: upper.c

```
 1     main()
 2     {
 3          char c;
 4
 5          printf( "Please enter a character: " );
 6          c = getchar();
 7
```

(program continues)

```
8              /* Test to see if upper case. Assume
9                 that ASCII is contiguous between
10                A and Z inclusive */
11             if ( 'A' <= c && c <= 'Z' )
12             {
13                 printf( "character is UPPER case\n" );
14             } else
15             {
16                 printf( "character is not UPPER case\n" );
17             }
18      }
```

program output:

```
Please enter a character: P
character is UPPER case
```

program output:

```
Please enter a character: e
character is not UPPER case
```

Take a closer look at the conditional test in line 11. What would be the result if the condition was replaced with the following?

```
if ( 'A' <= c <= 'Z' )
```

The i f condition will always be true. Why?

The i f conditional expression is made up of smaller expressions that are evaluated as follows because of the rules of operator precedence and associativity:

```
if ( ( 'A' <= c ) <= 'Z' )
```

The value of the expression ('A' <= c) is evaluated first; then the value of this expression is compared with the character 'Z'. The value of the parenthesized expression is either zero or one, depending on the truth value of the expression. Either of these two values will be less than the value of 'Z', so the expression will always yield a true value.

Now, what if we wanted to test whether the character was alphabetic, not just uppercase? For this, a more complex conditional expression would be needed:

```
( 'A' <= c && c <= 'Z' ) || ( 'a' <= c && c <= 'z' )
```

This conditional expression tests to see if the character stored in the variable c is either uppercase or lowercase.

Using Characters As Small Integers

A character variable may be used as a small integer variable whose value is limited between -128 and $+127$. If the character variable is declared as an unsigned char:

```
unsigned char variable_name
```

its value may range between 0 and 255.

Character variables are often used in this manner when a software system is large relative to the size of available memory. Operating systems use this technique for storing flags and small values in variables, using, at most, half the space as comparable integer variable storage.

CHARACTER STRINGS

A *character string* in the C language is defined as a sequence of characters enclosed in double quotes. The following are examples of character strings:

```
"123 Disk Dr."
"12,300"
"I'd give my right arm to be ambidextrous"
```

Internal Character String Representation

In memory, character strings are stored contiguously starting at a particular address (memory location). The compiler stores a string-termination character (NULL or '\0') at the end of the string. For example, the string "STRING", would be stored as shown in Exhibit 4-2.

If two identical character strings are used in a program, they are stored twice at different memory locations.

Value of a Character String Expression

Character string expressions, as do all expressions in C, have values. The value of a character string expression is the starting address of where the character string is stored, and not the character string itself. The C language has few built-in facilities to manipulate strings or examine their value directly. All these

EXHIBIT 4-2

Internal representation of character string "STRING"

| S | T | R | I | N | G | \0 |

common operations are performed through library functions. These functions always expect to be passed the starting address of a string of characters. Consider the following program:

program: test_string.c

```
1     main()
2     {
3          if ( "abc" == "abc" )
4          {
5               printf( "The two are the same\n" );
6          }
7          else
8          {
9               printf( "The two are NOT the same\n" );
10         }
11    }
```

program output:

```
The two are NOT the same
```

The result of this program is perhaps not what you would expect. But consider the value of the two expressions. Since two strings are being compared, the strings, although identical, are stored twice in memory. The value of each character string expression is the starting address of the character string. Thus, the values being compared are the two addresses and not the strings at those addresses. The proper method for comparing strings is to use library functions designed expressly for this purpose. Library functions are available to compare two character strings, to compare only the first few characters in those strings, or to pattern match strings using regular expressions. The previous example should be rewritten as follows:

program: compare.c

```
1     main()
2     {
3          if ( strcmp( "abc", "abc" ) == 0 )
4          {
5               printf( "The two are the same\n" );
6          }
7          else
8          {
9               printf( "The two are NOT the same\n" );
10         }
11    }
```

program output:

The two are the same

The strcmp() function returns three possible values: 0, 1, or −1. If the two strings are identical a 0 value is returned. If the first string is lexicographically less than the second string (that is, if it would appear before the second in a sorted list) it returns a −1. A value of 1 is returned if the first string is lexicographically greater than the second.

The strcmp() function is useful because many operations within C can be used to return the address of a character string. For example, the name of an array, when used as an expression by itself, has an expression value that is the starting address of the array. So, if a string of characters is stored starting at that location, the strcmp() function can be used to compare a character string against these characters, providing the proper formatting rules have been followed (the string must be followed by the null character '\0'). Arrays of characters will be covered in detail in Chapter 10.

MORE STRING-COMPARISON AND MANIPULATION FUNCTIONS

Another version of the same function, named strncmp(), compares the two string's first few characters (the length of the comparison is specified in the argument list). In addition to these two string-comparison functions, many other string-manipulation functions exist (e.g., find the length of a string strlen(), combine two strings strcat()). These and other string-manipulation functions will be discussed in Chapter 10.

STRINGS ARE NOT CONSTANTS

Unlike some other programming languages, the C language does not consider character strings to be constants. If a particular string is repeated in several places in the same program, a copy of the character string is stored for each occurrence. Furthermore, through the use of pointer variables, it is possible to change the value of a string, although it is discouraged. A few library functions take advantage of character strings not being constant. One example is the mktemp() function which is used to create unique filenames.

This function is UNIX-system specific and may not be available on other operating systems.

The following program illustrates how this function is used:

program: temp_file.c

```
1    main()
2    {
3         char *mktemp();
4
5         printf( "The unique filename is %s\n",
6             mktemp( "/tmp/glossXXXXXX" ) );
7    }
```

program output:

```
The unique filename is /tmp/gloss000298
```

The mktemp() function requires the address of a string of characters ending in six Xs as its argument. It replaces the trailing characters with a number, resulting in a pseudorandom filename. The mktemp() function's return value is the character string address it was given. The %s control-character sequence within the printf() function (in line 5) tells printf() to expect that the matching argument is the address of a string of characters. The printf() function, instead of printing the *value* of the matching argument, will find the string at the specified address and print characters until a null character is encountered.

Line 3 of this program informs the compiler we are using a function named mktemp() that will return a character address. Function declaration is necessary whenever the function being used returns a value other than an integer. This is the first such function we have seen; the getchar() function returns an integer value. The declaration of noninteger-returning functions will be discussed in Chapter 8.

Giving programs the ability to change the value of a character string does pose some problems. Some operating systems allow multiple users of the same application program to share the constant part of the program. This would include the instructions and, potentially, some character strings. But, because users are able to modify the character strings, they cannot safely share them. This could become a problem in a large program with many character strings used frequently by many users (e.g., many text editors). Physical memory is wasted because no two users can share the same character strings.

SUMMARY

In this chapter we have seen one of the basic C language data types—the character. Characters may be constants, in which case they are enclosed in single quotes, or they may be variables of type char. Each character variable can hold only one character. All the operators we discussed in Chapter 3 may be used on characters, although some are not particularly useful.

Character string expressions are enclosed in double quotes and stored in contiguous storage ending in the special termination character \0. Perhaps, surprisingly, a character string expression's value is not the character string itself but the starting address of where the string is stored. We will see in Chapters 10 and 13 how this permits us to manipulate strings using C language pointer variables.

EXERCISES

1. Looking at the ASCII table in Appendix A, we note that the lowercase letter's ASCII values are displaced by a constant distance (decimal 32) from the upper-case letters. Use this information to write a program that accepts character input from the terminal. If the character is lowercase convert it to uppercase. Print out all input.

2. Write a program that accepts character input from the terminal and pro-cesses it as follows:
  (a) If the character is lowercase alphabetic, print it.
  (b) If the character is uppercase alphabetic, print nothing.
  (c) If the character is a digit, print the message: "A digit has been read".

3. Write a program that accepts character input from the terminal and pro-cesses it as follows:
  (a) If the character is not alphabetic, print it as is.
  (b) If the character is alphabetic (either lowercase or uppercase) print out the next successive character (e.g., if the input is "a" print "b", if the input is "D" print "E"; the letter z/Z is replaced by a/A).

4. Most personal computer software is menu-driven. Write a program to present a user with the following menu, accept a one-character response, and take the appropriate action.

         YOUR CHOICE SOFTWARE
  (a) Print the word "hello"
  (b) Print the number "2"
  (c) Print "Good choice"
  (d) Do nothing
         Enter choice: _____
If the response is invalid (i.e., anything except a, b, c, or d) print: You have selected an invalid option.

CHAPTER 5

FLOATING POINT

OVERVIEW

We conclude this section on C language data types by introducing the use of floating-point numbers. We open with a discussion of floating-point constants and their machine representations. Next, we look at floating-point variables and the C language operations that may be used with them.

We also introduce several functions that may be used with floating-point data and one function, scanf(), that is used to read data from the terminal.

FLOATING POINT CONSTANTS

Floating-point constants allow the programmer to represent numbers in a C program that approximate mathematical real numbers. The programmer represents floating-point numbers via an integral part, a decimal part, and an optional signed exponent. The actual machine representation of these numbers is hardware dependent and, consequently, is only described in general terms in this chapter.

Human Representation

In C language programs, floating-point constants may be represented in a number of ways. The floating-point constant may include the following components:

- integer part (optional)

- decimal point (required)

- fractional part (optional)

- the letters "e" or "E" and an exponent (optional). The exponent itself may be negative. If an exponent is specified, it is assumed that the number the decimal and fractional parts represent are multiplied by ten to this specified power. For example, the floating-point number

123.45e2

represents the real number

123.45 × 10²

Some examples of floating-point constants are shown in Exhibit 5-1.

EXHIBIT 5-1

Examples of floating-point constants

Floating Point Constant	Equivalent Representation
12345.	12345.00
2.1415	2.1415
2.1415e4	21415.0
0.2344e-4	0.00002344
.2344E3	234.4

EXHIBIT 5-2

Internal machine representation of floating-point numbers

sign bit	exponent (biased)	sign bit		significand

Machine Representation

The machine architecture on which the compiler is implemented defines the floating-point number representation. Exhibit 5-2 shows how floating-point numbers are usually stored.

The human and machine representations of floating-point numbers always differ. The programmer usually expresses a floating-point number as a power of 10; the machine converts this number to another number which is multiplied by a *radix* to some power. This radix is always a power of two and will differ from machine to machine. For example, on the DEC PDP-11 computer, the radix is 2, on other machines it may be 8 or 16. Increasing the radix allows larger numbers to be stored, but may result in loss of accuracy, especially when performing computations where the significands need to be aligned.

On some machines, there is an explicit sign bit in the exponent part; on others, the exponent is *biased*. This means that a constant value is added to the value of the exponent to ensure that its value will always be positive. On other machines, the exponent is kept in one's complement notation. The sizes of the exponent and significand parts also vary depending on the machine architecture. If more bits are devoted to the exponent part, then larger numbers can be stored; if more bits are dedicated to the significand, then numbers can be stored more accurately. Furthermore, the significand is usually normalized; that is, any leading zeroes are removed and the exponent part is adjusted accordingly. This allows the fractional part to be more accurately represented. This also means that the significand's first binary digit will always be one. On some machines, this first digit is omitted and assumed to be on, leaving that bit for further approximation of the number being represented. The hardware, of course, knows this and makes the necessary adjustments when evaluating the number.

The exact representation varies from machine to machine and may vary further if the machine has floating-point hardware support. Floating-point constants are usually stored in 64 bits as are double-precision floating-point variables.

FLOATING POINT VARIABLES

There are two types of floating-point variables: `float` and `double`. Typically, `float` variables are stored using 32 bits while `double` variables are stored in 64 bits. On some machines, all the extra bits in double-precision variables are attached to the significand, on others they are divided. For example, when an Intel 8087 Numeric Processor is used for floating-point arithmetic, the extra 32 bits are added in the following manner: two bits extend the exponent size and the remainder add to the significand size. On DEC computers, all extra 32 bits are added to the significand.

Floating-point variables are declared as follows:

```
float variable_name;
double variable_2;
long float variable_3;
```

where the type long float is the same as double.

OPERATIONS ON FLOATING POINT NUMBERS

The available operations for floating-point numbers are more limited than those for integers or characters. The operations include the mathematical operators shown in Exhibit 5-3 but do not include operations such as the modulous (%) operator or any of the increment operators. When a floating-point number is divided, the remainder is not lost; the fractional part becomes part of the resulting floating-point expression. Other operations normally associated with floating-point numbers (e.g., square root) are not formally part of the language; they are made available through library functions and must be linked with your program by the linkage editor.

Example: Future Value of Investment
After three years, what will be the value of $1,000 invested at an annual interest rate of 8.5 percent? The invest.1K.c program on the following page will calculate the value of the initial investment after three years:

EXHIBIT 5-3

Floating-point operators

Symbol	Operation
+	addition
−	subtraction
*	multiplication
/	division

program: invest.1K.c

```
1      main()
2      {
3              /* this program calculates and prints the
4                 future value of an invested amount; formula
5                 used is:
6
7                 future value =
8                   present( 1 + interest rate)number periods
9
10             */
11
12             double rate, months;
13             double pow();
14
15             rate = .085 / 12.0;
16             months = 36.00;
17
18             printf( "Future value = %4.2f\n",
19                   1000.00 * pow( (1.0 + rate), months ) );
20     }
```

program output:

```
Future value = 1289.30
```

In this program we have introduced a new C function, pow(). This function accepts two arguments, a number and the power to which the number is raised. It returns a double-precision floating-point value. In line 18, we see that the printf() function contains the control sequence %4.2f. This indicates that the matching expression to be printed is a floating-point number with four places preceding and two places following the decimal point. The general format of the control sequence for floating-point numbers is:

*%nnn.mmm*f

where *nnn* is the number of digits to precede the decimal point and *mmm* is the number of digits to follow.

Now, let's make the program more general by requesting three pieces of information: the current interest rate, the amount of the investment, and the length of the investment. To do this, we will need to use the scanf() function to read this information from the terminal, and the printf() function to prompt for the values:

program: invest.c

```
1     main()
2     {
3         /* this program calculates and prints the
4             future value of an invested amount; formula
5             used is:
6
7             future value =
8              present( 1 + interest rate)number periods
9
10        */
11
12        double rate, periods, savings_amount;
13        double pow();
14
15        printf( "Enter interest rate: " );
16        scanf( "%lf", &rate ); /* floating point
          input */
17        /* percentage conversion */
18        rate = rate / 100.0;
19        /* interest is compounded monthly */
20        rate = rate / 12.0;
21
22        printf( "Enter savings amount: " );
23        scanf( "%lf", &savings_amount );
24
25        printf( "Enter number of years: " );
26        scanf( "%lf", periods );
27        /* rate was converted to monthly base */
28        periods = periods * 12.0;
29
30        printf( "Future value = %.2f\n",
31            savings_amount * pow( (1.0 + rate),
              periods) );
32    }
```

Line 8 formula: future value = present $(1 + \text{interest rate})^{\text{number periods}}$

program output:

```
Enter interest rate: 8.5
Enter savings amount: 1000.00
Enter number of years: 3.0
Future value = 1289.30
```

Functions can make this program more readable and maintainable.

We provided a brief introduction to functions in Chapter 2 and will cover them in more detail in Chapters 8 and 14.

It would be advantageous to convert the calculation of a current amount's future value into a function because:

- this is a useful routine we would like to use in several programs, and

- converting this calculation into a function removes unnecessary details from the `main()` function, making the program more readable.

The modularized version of this program is shown below:

program: loan.c

```
1    main()
2    {
3        /* this program calculates and prints the
4            future amount of an invested amount; formula
5            used is:
6
7            future value =
8              present( 1 + interest rate)number periods
9        */
10
11       double rate, periods, savings_amount, f_amount;
12       double future();
13
14       printf( "Enter interest rate: " );
15       scanf( "%lf", &rate );
16
17       printf( "Enter savings amount: " );
18       scanf( "%lf", &savings_amount );
19
20       printf( "Enter number of years: " );
21       scanf( "%lf", &periods );
22
23       f_amount = future( rate, savings_amount,
             periods );
24       printf( "Future value = %.2f\n", f_amount );
25   }
26
```

(program continues)

```
27    double future( rate, amount, periods )
28    double rate, amount, periods;
29    {
30        double pow();
31        double f_amount;
32
33        /* percentage conversion */
34        rate = rate / 100.0;
35        /* interest is compounded monthly */
36        rate = rate / 12.0;
37        /* rate converted to monthly base */
38        periods = periods * 12.0;
39        f_amount = amount * pow( (1.0 + rate), periods);
40        return( f_amount );
41    }
```

Although the names of the variables holding the interest rate, the number of periods, and the future value are identical in the main() and future() functions, they are actually distinct sets of variables. Variables declared within a set of braces are local to that set of braces. The same rule applies to function arguments; they are local to the function in which they are declared.

We could have embedded the call to future() within the call to printf(), combining lines 23 and 24, by using the future() of return value as the second argument to printf() (the first argument is the control string). Similarly, we could have combined lines 39 and 40, eliminating the need for the variable f_amount.

The scanf( ) Function   The scanf() function reads input into the program. It performs printf()'s inverse function, retrieving information from the terminal according to a specified format. In this example, the first argument to scanf(), "%lf", indicates that the input will be given in the form of a double-precision floating-point number. If the matching argument were a floating-point number, we would describe it in the control string as follows:

"%f "

The second argument to scanf() is an expression that tells the function *where* the variable is located so that it may store the input there. The expression consists of the variable name preceded by an ampersand as follows:

&variable_name

This expression has the value of the variable's memory address. The ampersand operator may only precede variable names; it may not precede a constant expression. This is the second type of expression we have seen whose value is a starting address; the character string was the first.

Accuracy Problems

In C, as in other programming languages, floating-point numbers *approximate* mathematical "real" numbers; they do not represent them exactly. The following program illustrates the use of single- and double-precision variables to approximate the value of a floating point number:

program: accurate.c

```
1      main()
2      {
3              float fpoint;
4              double lfpoint;
5
6              fpoint = 123.45;
7              printf( "%f\n", fpoint );
8              fpoint /= 3.30;
9              fpoint *= 3.30;
10             printf( "%f\n", fpoint );
11
12             lfpoint = 123.45;
13             printf( "%f\n", lfpoint );
14             lfpoint /= 3.30;
15             lfpoint *= 3.30;
16             printf( "%f\n", lfpoint );
17     }
```

program output:

```
123.449997
123.449989
123.450000
123.450000
```

Example: Internal Floating Point Storage

C has an interesting library function, frexp(), that we can use to show a floating-point number's internal representation. The return value from the function call is the significand; the value of the exponent is stored in the variable whose address is given to frexp() as its second argument.

program: showfloat.c

```
1    main()
2    {
3         double significand, sample, frexp();
4         int exponent;
5
6         printf( "Enter floating point number: " );
7         scanf( "%lf", &sample );
8         significand = frexp( sample, &exponent );
9
10        printf( "original number = %f\n", sample );
11        printf( "significand = %f\n", significand );
12        printf( "exponent = %d\n", exponent );
13   }
```

program output:

```
Enter floating point number: 123.45
original number = 123.450000
significand = 0.964453
exponent = 7
```

This program was run on a machine with a radix of 2. So, using the following formula:

floating point = significand $*$ radix^{exponent}

and inserting the values printed by the program, we can calculate the original value from the returned values:

$123.45 = 0.964453 * 2^7$

Actually, there is another library function, ldexp( ), that expects a significand and an exponent as its arguments and performs the calculation. Added to the previous example, this routine will accurately bring us back to our original number:

program: showfloat.c

```
1    main()
2    {
3         double significand, sample, frexp(), ldexp();
4         int exponent;
5
```

```
6               printf( "Enter floating point number:  " );
7               scanf( "%lf", &sample );
8               significand = frexp( sample, &exponent );
9
10              printf( "original number = %f\n", sample );
11              printf( "significand = %f\n", significand );
12              printf( "exponent = %d\n", exponent );
13              printf( "original number = %f\n",
14                  ldexp( significand, exponent ) );
15      }
```

program output:

```
Enter floating point number: 123.45
original number = 123.450000
significand = 0.964453
exponent = 7
original number = 123.450000
```

SUMMARY

Floating-point numbers may be represented either as single or double precision. Since floating-point numbers are always, at best, an approximation of true mathematical representation, it is best to declare floating-point variables as `double` or `long float` if accuracy is important and memory is not at a premium.

Unlike other programming languages that have an exponentiation operator, C language programs must use the `pow( )` library function. The `pow( )` function must be declared as `double` because it returns a double-precision value.

In this chapter we also introduced the important and useful `scanf( )` function and had our first view of the & operator. The & operator, when placed before a variable name, yields the variable's address, as opposed to its value. Chapter 9 discusses the & operator in detail.

EXERCISES

1. Use the `pow( )` function to print out the square and cube of any value read from the terminal. Use the `scanf( )` function to accept numeric input.

2. Conversion from Fahrenheit to Celsius (or vice versa) is given by the formula:

$$\frac{F - 32}{C} = \frac{9}{5}$$

where:

F = temperature in degrees Fahrenheit
C = temperature in degrees Celsius.

Write a program to convert Fahrenheit to Celsius.

3. An object starting at rest and accelerating at a constant rate a will travel a distance s as given by the formula:

$$s = \frac{at^2}{2}$$

where t is time (in seconds).

Write a program to calculate distance traveled as a function of acceleration and time. Use the scanf ( ) function to accept arbitrary values of a and t from the terminal.

4. Modify program invest. c to account for different interest rates as a function of length of investment. Assume the following:

Length of Investment (years)	Interest Rate (%)
1	6.2
2	7.0
3	7.7
4	7.92

PART

CONTROL FLOW

CHAPTER 6

CONDITIONAL EXECUTION

OVERVIEW

The C language provides two basic methods for executing a statement or series of statements conditionally: the `if` statement and the `switch-case` statement. In previous chapters we used the `if` statement in some sample programs. In this chapter, we will introduce the `if` statement and the `switch-case` statement formally and show examples of their use.

In addition to the `if` and `switch-case` statements, we will discuss two `if` statement variants—the `if-else` and the `if-else-if` statements. We will also cover the conditional operator and the `assert()` function, as well as the `goto` statement (briefly).

THE if STATEMENT

As we have seen before, the i f statement allows the programmer to execute a statement or series of statements conditionally. If the condition supplied to the statement is logically true (has a nonzero value), the statement that follows it is executed. The i f statement syntax is:

```
if ( condition )
        statement;
```

(The control flow for the i f statement is shown in Exhibit 6-1).

The condition may be any valid C language expression including constants, variables, logical comparisons, binary arithmetic expressions, bitwise expressions, or return values from function calls. It is important not to follow the right parenthesis with a semicolon. The semicolon will be interpreted as a valid statement and will itself be conditionally executed. For example, the following code fragment:

```
if ( condition );
        statement;
```

is interpreted by the compiler as:

```
if ( condition )
        ;
statement;
```

EXHIBIT 6-1

Control flow of the i f statement

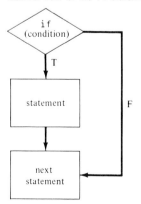

The semicolon standing alone is interpreted as a null statement. The statement *statement* will be executed unconditionally.

The statement part of the i f construction can either be a simple statement as shown in the first illustration or a compound statement (or block):

```
if ( condition )
{
        statement;
        statement;
}
```

If the value of the expression denoted by *condition* is true, then all the statements in the compound statement are executed. The statements within the compound statement may be simple statements or may themselves be compound statements. This is illustrated in the following program:

program: nested.if.c

```
1       #include    <stdio.h>
2
3       main()
4       {
5           int month, day, year, maxday;
6
7           /* useful part of program here */
8           month = 2;
9           year = 1984;
10
11          if ( month == 2 )
12          {
13              maxday = 28;
14
15              /* check for possible leap year */
16              if ( (year % 4) == 0)   /* crude check */
17              {
18                  /* assume leap year */
19                  printf( "Leap year\n" );
20                  maxday = 29;
21              }
22              printf( "February \n" );
23          }
24
25          printf( "max days in this month: %d\n", maxday );
26
27          /* useful part of program here */
28      }
```

program output:

```
Leap year
February
max days in this month:  29
```

Inside the compound statement that follows the first i f statement (lines 12 through 23), there is a simple statement (line 13), another i f statement (line 16), a compound statement (lines 17 through 21), and a third simple statement (line 22).

For readability, statements within i f constructs are usually indented. As we mentioned in Chapter 2, the compound statement's opening brace placement is done either as shown here or follows the i f statement's closing parenthesis. Either is acceptable to the compiler; you should use the method you think is more readable.

The if-else Construct

The i f - e l s e construct is an extension of the i f statement, and has the form shown on page 83.

EXHIBIT 6-2

Control flow of the i f - e l s e construct

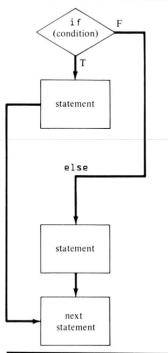

```
if ( condition )
        statement;
else
        statement;
```

If the condition within the parentheses is true, then the statement immediately following it is executed; otherwise the statement following the else clause is executed. As before, these statements may be simple or compound. Exhibit 6-2 shows the if-else construct's control flow.

Now the previous example may be rewritten more readably and efficiently as follows:

program: if.else.c

```
 1     #include    <stdio.h>
 2
 3     main()
 4     {
 5          int month, day, year, maxday;
 6
 7          /* useful part of program here */
 8          month = 2;
 9          year = 1985;
10
11          if ( month == 2 )
12          {
13               if ( (year % 4) == 0)   /* crude check */
14               {
15                    printf( "Leap year\n" );
16                    maxday = 29;
17               }
18               else
19               {
20                    printf( "Not a leap year\n" );
21                    maxday = 28;
22               }
23               printf( "February \n" );
24          }
25
26          printf( "max days in this month: %d\n", maxday );
27
28          /* useful part of program here */
29     }
```

program output:

Not a leap year
February
max days in this month: 28

The if-else-if Construction

Occasionally, multiple if-else statements are required to check several mutually exclusive conditions (i.e., only one of the conditions may be true.) The
following pseudocode illustrates this:

```
if ( variable a is a first range )
{
        appropriate action 1;
}
else if ( variable a is in a second range )
{
        appropriate action 2;
}
else if ( variable a is in a third range )
{
        appropriate action 3;
}
else
{
        default action;
}
```

Usually, a variable is checked against several conditions, resulting in the
execution of a single action. In this pseudocode the second if statement is
actually the statement that belongs to the "else" part of the first if statement.
According to our former rules of indentation we could indent the second if
statement one tab stop to the right of the first and the third, one tab stop to the
right of the second, and so on. Since several conditions are usually checked in
one of these constructs, we do not recommend indentation because the construct would almost certainly run off the right-hand side of the page. The
control flow for the if-else-if construct is shown in Exhibit 6-3.

The sample program on page 86 is a more formal example of the
if-else-if construct and how it is used within a C program:

EXHIBIT 6-3

Control flow for the if-else-if construct

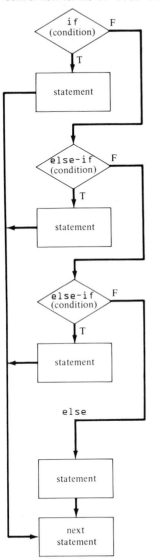

program: ifelseif.c

```
1     #include <stdio.h>
2
3     main()
4     {
5         int input_character;
6
7         printf( "Enter character: " );
8         input_character = getchar();
9
10        if ( input_character == EOF )
11        {
12            printf( "End of file encountered\n" );
13        }
14        else if ( input_character >= 'a' &&
15                  input_character <= 'z' )
16        {
17            printf( "lowercase character\n" );
18        }
19        else if ( input_character >= 'A' &&
20                  input_character <= 'Z' )
21        {
22            printf( "UPPERcase character\n" );
23        }
24        else if ( input_character >= '0' &&
25                  input_character <= '9' )
26        {
27            printf( "DIGIT\n" );
28        }
29    }
```

program interaction:

```
Enter character: D
UPPERcase character
```

THE switch-case STATEMENT

The switch-case statement is used when an expression's value is to be checked against several values; if a match takes place, the appropriate action is taken. The switch-case syntax is as follows:

```
switch ( expression )
{
        case constant:
                statement;
                statement;
                break;
        case constant:
                statement;
                statement;
                break;
        default:
                statement;
                statement;
                break;
}
```

In this construct, the *expression* whose value is being compared may be any valid expression, including the value of a variable, an arithmetic expression, a logical comparison (rare), a bitwise expression, or the return value from a function call, but not a floating-point expression. The expression's value is checked against each of the specified cases and, when a match occurs, the statements following that case are executed. When a break statement is encountered, control proceeds to the end of the switch-case statement. The break statement should be included in each case. If the break is omitted, then the statements for the subsequent cases will also be executed, even though a match has already taken place. The control flow is represented schematically in Exhibit 6-4.

The values that follow the keyword case may only be constants; they cannot be expressions. They may be integers or characters, but not floating-point numbers or character strings. If it is necessary to check the value of an expression against another expression, then the if-else-if construct should be used. Case constants may not be repeated within a switch statement.

The last case in this example has the special keyword default instead of the keyword case. The statements following this case are executed if none of the other cases are matched. The default case may or may not be included, depending on the program's needs. If it is included, it should always follow all other cases. If the default case is not included in a switch statement and the expression is not matched by any of the other cases, nothing happens.

The sample program switchcase.c on the next page is part of a larger program that determines the type of a file (data file or command file). Upon finding a data file, the program frees the file while keeping track of how many files it has freed. If it finds a program file, it prints a message describing its contents. If it cannot determine the file type, an appropriate message is printed.

EXHIBIT 6-4

Control flow of the switch-case statement

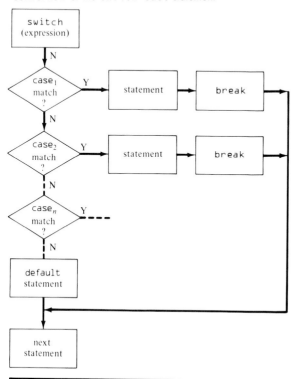

program: switchcase.c

```
1    main()
2    {
3        int freed, file_type;
4
5        /* part of program omitted */
6        file_type = 'd';
7
8        switch ( file_type )
9        {
10           case 'd':
11               printf( "File type is 'data'\n" );
12               /* part of program omitted that
13                    frees up data file */
14               freed++;  /* count number of freed
15                          files */
16               break;
```

```
17
18              case 'c':
19                  printf( "File type is 'commands'\n" );
20                  break;
21
22              default:
23                  printf( "Unknown type\n" );
24          }
25
26          /* part of program omitted */
27      }
```

program output:

```
File type is 'data'
```

The break statement is not included in the default case, where it is not needed, since the break simply tells the program to transfer control to the end of the switch-case statement. If there were no default case, the last valid case would not need a break; it is advisable, however, to include it. If the program needs to be modified later and another case is added, then the existing cases will not have to be modified; they will work correctly as is.

The following is another example showing switch-case statement use:

program: dropcase.c

```
1       #include <stdio.h>
2       main()
3       {
4           int input_character;
5
6           /* part of program omitted here */
7
8           printf( "Enter character: " );
9           input_character = getchar();
10
11          switch( input_character )
12          {
13              /* check to see if input character
14                 is a vowel  */
15              case 'A':
16              case 'E':
17              case 'I':
18              case 'O':
19              case 'U':
```

(program continues)

```
20                  printf( "uppercase " );
21            case 'a':
22            case 'e':
23            case 'i':
24            case 'o':
25            case 'u':
26                printf( "vowel entered\n" );
27                break;
28
29            case EOF:
30                printf( "end of file\n" );
31                break;
32
33            default:
34                printf( "not a vowel\n" );
35                break;
36        }
37    }
```

program interaction:

```
Enter a character: D
not a vowel
```

program interaction:

```
Enter character: A
uppercase vowel entered
```

program interaction:

```
Enter character: e
vowel entered
```

Here we see an example of multiple cases causing execution of one statement. If the character is an uppercase vowel, then the word uppercase will be printed, followed by a space. The program will then continue to execute statements until a break is reached, printing vowel entered also. If the character is a lowercase vowel, then the first statement executed in the switch-case statement will print vowel entered. If an end-of-file (EOF) character is typed in, a relevant message will print, but if the character typed in is neither a vowel nor an EOF, then the message not a vowel will print.

ASSERTIONS

Often, in a program, a mistake is made that causes the program to "bomb," not at the point of error, but at some point later in the program. Problems like these are very hard to find. A library function, assert(), is included in C. It is a debugging aid to help the programmer track down these elusive bugs.

While creating a program, the programmer makes assumptions about the possible values of variables and other expressions. The assert() function checks the validity of these assumptions. It accepts a single logical expression as its argument; if the expression is not true, an error message is printed with the line number at which it failed and the program's execution is stopped. During the testing phase of program development it is useful to include assertions about variable's expected or relative values. The following is an example of the assert() function's use:

program: assert.c

```
1      #include <stdio.h>
2      #include <assert.h>
3
4      main()
5      {
6           int x, y;
7
8           x = 6;
9           y = x++,   /* intentional error, should be ++x */
10          /* part of program omitted */
11
12          /* We assume that, at this point,
13               the two MUST have the same value */
14          assert( x == y );
15
16          if ( y == 6 )
17          {
18               printf( "How did we get here?\n" );
19          }
20          else
21          {
22               printf( "We shouldn't have gotten here\n" );
23          }
24     }
```

program output:

```
Assertion failed: file assert.c, line 14
```

When using the assert() function, it is necessary to include both the stdio.h and assert.h files in the same order as shown in the example.

When a final version of the program is prepared, the assertions may be taken out through a compiler command line option, although it is not bad practice to leave them in.

THE CONDITIONAL OPERATOR

The conditional operator forms an expression that will have one of two values, depending on the truth value of another expression. This expression's syntax is:

```
condition ? expression1 : expression2
```

This expression's value depends on the subexpression's truth value, labeled here as *condition*. If the value of the expression is true, then the value of the entire expression is the value of *expression1*; otherwise it is the value of *expression2*. The following program uses this construct to compute the absolute value of a number.

program: absolute.c

```
1      main()
2      {
3          int input_number, absolute;
4
5          printf( "Enter a signed number:  " );
6          scanf( "%d", &input_number );
7
8          absolute = (input_number < 0) ? -input_number :
9                              input_number;
10         printf( "Absolute value = %d\n", absolute );
11     }
```

program interaction:

```
Enter a signed number: -12
Absolute value = 12
```

program interaction:

```
Enter a signed number: 15
Absolute value = 15
```

In this example, the conditional expression's value is assigned to the variable absolute and then printed.

The conditional operator is a notational convenience; it always has an equivalent if statement. For example, the following two constructs are equivalent:

```
x = y < 10 ? -y : y;
```

and

```
if ( y < 10 )
{
    x = -y;
}
else
{
    x = y;
}
```

THE *goto* STATEMENT

Like many other programming languages, the C language provides a method to transfer control to a labeled point in the program. The goto statement does this. The goto statement requires a destination label, declared as:

```
label:
```

The label is a word (permissible length is machine dependent) followed by a colon (:). The goto statement is formally defined as

```
goto statement-label
```

The next program illustrates the use of the goto statement:

program: goto.c

```
1     main()
2     {
3          int x, y;
4
5          x = 6;
6          y = 12;
7
8          /* part of program omitted */
9
```

(*program continues*)

```
10          if ( x == y )
11          {
12              x++;
13          }
14          else
15          {
16              goto error;
17          }
18
19          /* part of program omitted */
20
21          error:
22              printf( "Fatal error; exiting\n" );
23      }
```

program output:

```
Fatal error; exiting
```

This program could have been written better using the assert() function. In fact, whenever a goto is used, there is probably a better way to achieve the same result.

SUMMARY

In this chapter we have introduced several statements for causing conditional execution within a program. The three constructs if, if-else, and if-else-if, test a logical condition and the switch-case statement tests an expression against a series of constant values. Although it is always possible to use an if-else-if construct rather than a switch-case statement, the latter is preferred for its simplicity when a comparison is to be made against several constant values.

One school of thought contends that, for clarity, every if statement should have an else branch even if this branch is empty. This is not required and is a matter of personal style.

Last, and certainly least, we discussed the goto statement, which permits unconditional branching. Its use is not recommended except perhaps for handling error conditions.

EXERCISES

1. Using the scanf() function introduced in Chapter 5, modify program if.else.c to accept an arbitrary year as input and print out its result as:

```
"year" is/is not a leap year
```

2. We know that the program developed in problem 1 calculates leap years incorrectly for certain centennial years. Modify the program to take into account the following rule:

Centennial years (years divisible by 100) are leap years only when they are also divisible by 400.

3. Write a program to read in four numbers and print out:
    (a) the smallest number of the four
    (b) the largest number of the four

4. Write a program to read in a number from the terminal. If the number is even, multiply it by 100 and print it. If the number is odd, print it as is.

5. Read in two numbers from the terminal. If the larger of the two numbers is more than twice as large as the smaller, print it. Otherwise, print the smaller number.

6. To test a student's keyboard skills, devise the following program:
    (a) Print out an alphabetic character for the student to type, for example:

```
Please type in an a
```

(Use the rand() *function and the ASCII table in Appendix A to generate a random letter.)*

    (b) Read the student's response and give the student feedback as follows:

If the student responded correctly type:

```
Excellent!
```

If you asked for a lowercase letter and the student typed the correct letter but in uppercase type:

```
Sorry, correct letter but I wanted lowercase.
```

Same as above except student types lowercase when you wanted uppercase.

If student types in totally incorrect letter:

```
Not even close, try taking your mittens off!
```

CHAPTER 7

ITERATION

OVERVIEW

This chapter describes how iterative constructs available
through the C language are used. This includes `while`,
`do-while`, and `for` statements. We give examples of
each of the three statement types and discuss the
circumstances under which each construct is appropriate.

ITERATION

Variables, conditional execution, and looping, or iteration, are the three critical elements of a programming language. Iteration is a statement's or group of statements' repeated execution as a function of the state of a condition.

THE while STATEMENT

The while statement is the first method of iteration we will discuss. This construct allows us to repeat a statement or a series of statements while a condition remains true. The while statement syntax is:

```
while ( condition )
       statement;
```

The condition, as it is labeled, can be any valid C language expression including the value of a variable, a unary or binary expression, an arithmetic expression, or the return value from a function call. The statement can be a simple or compound statement. A compound statement appears in a while statement as:

```
while ( condition )
{
       statement;
       statement;
}
```

EXHIBIT 7-1

Control flow of the while statement

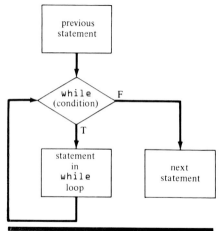

As with the if statement, it is important that no semicolon follow the closing parenthesis, otherwise the compiler will assume the loop body consists of a single null statement. This usually results in an infinite loop because the value of the condition will not change within the body of the loop. Exhibit 7-1 shows the control flow of the while statement.

The following program uses the while construct to produce a list of random numbers:

program: random.c

```
1      main()
2      {
3          /* this program generates a series of
4             random numbers used as test data for
5             another program by using the rand()
6             function */
7
8          int loop_control;
9
10         loop_control = 0;
11
12         while ( loop_control <= 9 )
13         {
14             printf( "%d\n", rand() );
15             loop_control++;
16         }
17     }
```

program output:

```
16838
5758
10113
17515
31051
5627
23010
7419
16212
4086
```

In this example, the condition tested is:

```
loop_control <= 9
```

The program begins with the loop_control value equal to 0 and evaluates the expression. Because it is true (has a nonzero numeric value) the random value is printed and the variable's value is incremented. The expression is continually reevaluated each pass through the loop; while it remains true, the statement is executed. When the condition becomes false, the program continues with the next statement following the while construct.

The next program counts the number of lines in its input that begin with a period. The program will be used in conjunction with a document typesetting system, where control commands are placed on a line beginning with a period (.), followed by the command itself. Typical input to the program is:

```
.P
This is the beginning of the document
.P
This would start a new paragraph.  I don't need to worry about
wraparound because the typesetting system will do it for me.  If
I want to include a table, I could use the .TS macro:
.TS
table specifications
table data
.TE
```

The commands in the file are those lines that begin with a period. The rest of the lines are considered to be part of the document's text. We need to know how many of these commands are in the input file:

program: begin.dot.c

```
1      #include <stdio.h>
2
3      main()
4      {
5          /* a clumsy solution */
6
7          int dot_lines, input_char;
8          char previous_char;
9
10         previous_char = ' ';
11         dot_lines = 0;
12
13         /* get first character */
14         input_char = getchar();
15
16         while ( input_char != EOF )
17         {
18             if ( input_char == '.' &&
19                 previous_char == '\n' )
```

```
20                    {
21                          dot_lines++;
22                    }
23                    previous_char = input_char;
24                    /* read next character */
25                    input_char = getchar();
26              }
27
28              printf( "Format lines = %d\n", dot_lines );
29        }
```

program output:

```
Format lines = 3
```

There are a few problems with this program. For instance, the program unnecessarily accepts input in two places. This can be easily resolved by combining lines 14 and 25 and adding them into the condition on line 13, as follows:

program: bdot.2.c

```
1       #include <stdio.h>
2
3       main()
4       {
5            /* a more graceful but inaccurate solution */
6
7            int dot_lines, input_char;
8            char previous_char;
9
10           previous_char = ' ';
11           dot_lines = 0;
12
13           while ( (input_char = getchar()) != EOF )
14           {
15                if ( input_char == '.' &&
16                        previous_char == '\n' )
17                {
18                     dot_lines++;
19                }
20                previous_char = input_char;
21           }
22
23           printf( "Format lines = %d\n", dot_lines );
24      }
```

program output:

```
Format lines = 3
```

The extra parentheses are needed in the conditional part of the `while` statement because, according to our precedence rules, the test for equality is performed before the assignment is made. If the conditional part were written as

```
while ( input_char = getchar() != EOF )
```

then the expression would be evaluated as follows:

1.   execute the `getchar()` function and retrieve a character from the terminal

2.   check `getchar()`'s return value (the value of that function call expression) against the EOF value as defined in the file `stdio.h`

3.   assign the comparison value (the truth value) to the variable named `input_char`

The value of the entire expression is the value assigned to `input_char`, either a one (if the character typed in was not EOF) or a zero if it was. Either way, it will not contain the input character's value. Including the parentheses as shown causes the expression to be evaluated as follows:

1.   execute the `getchar()` function and retrieve a character from the terminal

2.   assign the value of the character to the variable `input_char`; the value assigned becomes the value of the expression

```
(input_char = getchar())
```

3.   check this value against the character EOF and use the comparison's truth value as the entire expression's value

The input portion is improved, but the program still does not function properly. We can see that the file begins with a line that starts with a period. This program will not count it, because when it reads the first character, the previous character is not a newline. This can be fixed by initializing the value of the `previous_char` variable to `'\n'`, but that would make the program harder to understand. To solve this problem we restructure the program as follows:

program: bdot.3.c

```
1      #include <stdio.h>
2
3      #define START_OF_LINE 0
4      #define IN_LINE 1
5
6      main()
7      {
8          int state, dot_lines, input_char;
9          char previous_char;
10
11         state = START_OF_LINE;
12         dot_lines = 0;
13
14         while ( (input_char = getchar()) != EOF )
15         {
16             if ( state == START_OF_LINE )
17             {
18                 if ( input_char == '.' )
19                     dot_lines++;
20                 state = IN_LINE;
21             }
22
23             if ( input_char == '\n' )
24                 state = START_OF_LINE;
25         }
26
27         printf( "Format lines = %d\n", dot_lines );
28     }
```

program output:

Format lines = 4

Unlike the previous two programs, this solution does not remember the previous character; instead it keeps track of where it is on the input line. Two symbolic constants are defined, START_OF_LINE and IN_LINE, which describe the two possible program states. We initialize the program to START_OF_LINE. When a character is read, the program checks its current state. If it is START_OF_LINE it checks to see if the first character is a period. If it is, then the counter is incremented; regardless of its value the state is changed to IN_LINE. If the state is already IN_LINE, the program doesn't even bother to check for a period. It will check only for a newline and upon encountering one it will flip its state back to START_OF_LINE.

The previous program is an example of a *finite-state machine,* a name given to programs that are always in one of several defined states and react differently to input depending upon the current state.

What if the two i f statements (lines 18 and 23) were combined into one i f-e l se statement?

In that case, the empty lines would not be processed properly.

THE do-while STATEMENT

The do-while statement's function is similar to the while construct's—a logical expression controls iteration through the loop. The loop executes as long as the condition remains true. However, unlike the while statement, the check is made at the bottom of the loop instead of at the top. Consequently, the body of the loop is always executed at least once. The do-while construct syntax is:

```
do
        statement;
while ( condition );
```

EXHIBIT 7-2

Control flow of the do-while statement

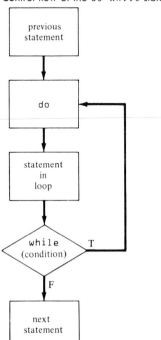

Unlike the while construction, the do-while requires a semicolon to follow the statement's conditional part.

If more than one statement is to be executed in the body of the loop, then these statements may be formed into a compound statement as follows:

```
do
{
        statement;
        statement;
}
while ( condition );
```

Exhibit 7-2 shows the control flow for the do-while statement.

This construction is useful when the loop controls input to the program and the input itself determines whether or not to continue with the loop. The following program demonstrates this:

program: lines.vowels.c

```
1      #include <stdio.h>
2
3      main()
4      {
5          int lines, vowels, input_char;
6
7          lines = vowels = 0;
8
9          do
10         {
11             input_char = getchar();
12             switch ( input_char )
13             {
14             case '\n':
15                 lines++;
16                 break;
17
18             case 'A':
19             case 'E':
20             case 'I':
21             case 'O':
22             case 'U':
23             case 'a':
24             case 'e':
25             case 'i':
26             case 'o':
27             case 'u':
```

(program continues)

```
28                    vowels++;
29                    break;
30
31              default:
32                   ;  /* nothing */
33              }
34         }
35      while ( input_char != EOF );
36
37         printf( "Number of lines = %d\n", lines );
38         printf( "Number of vowels = %d\n", vowels );
39   }
```

program output:

```
Number of lines = 398
Number of vowels = 3824
```

THE for STATEMENT

The for statement is the third, and probably most widely used iteration construct. Like the while statement, testing of the condition is done at the top of the loop. The for statement syntax is:

```
for ( expression1; condition; expression3 )
      statement;
```

where the *statement* is either a simple or compound statement. The first expression is known as the *initialization expression* and usually is an assignment of some variable that will be used to control the loop's execution. It is executed once before the loop begins. The third expression is known as the *increment expression* and is executed after each pass through the loop and before the conditional expression is reevaluated. The for statement has an equivalent restatement in terms of a while as follows:

```
expression1;
while ( condition )
{
      statement;
      expression3;
}
```

EXHIBIT 7-3

Control flow of the for statement

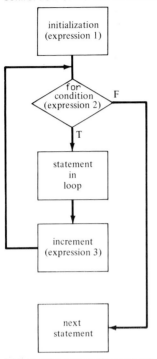

The *condition* expression has the same meaning it did in the while statement. It usually consists of a relational expression or a truth value returned by a function call. Exhibit 7-3 shows the control flow for the for statement.

The random.c program that appeared at the beginning of this chapter could be rewritten as follows using the for statement:

program: forandom.c

```
1    main()
2    {
3         int control;
4
5         for ( control = 0; control <= 9; control++ )
6         {
7              printf( "%d\n", rand() );
8         }
9    }
```

program output:

16838
5758
10113
17515
31051
5627
23010
7419
16212
4086
2749

It is permissible to leave any of the three expressions out of a for statement, but if left out, the delimiting semicolons must still remain. The for
statement is generally used in circumstances where there is a one-time initialization and a value that is incremented each time through the loop. By using the
for statement, all the controlling expressions for the loop are kept together,
making the program more readable. If the controlling expressions are not
closely related it is probably better to use a while statement.

In this next example, the program prints the square roots of the integers 0
through 8, inclusive:

program. sqrt.c

```
1    #include <math.h>
2
3    main()
4    {
5         int sub;
6         double temp;
7
8         printf( "x\tsqrt(x)\n\n" );
9         for ( sub = 0; sub < 9; sub++ )
10        {
11             temp = sub; /* type conversion */
12             printf( "%d\t%f\n", sub, sqrt(temp) );
13        }
14   }
```

program output:

```
x     sqrt(x)

0     0.000000
1     1.000000
```

```
2      1.414214
3      1.732051
4      2.000000
5      2.236068
6      2.449490
7      2.645751
8      2.828427
```

Assigning the value of sub to a temporary variable (temp) in line 11 may seem unnecessary. However, it is needed because the sqrt() function has to have a double-precision floating-point value as its argument, and not an integer. Alternatively, we could have used *type casting*. Type casting allows us to transform an expression into an expression of the same value but represented as a different type. For example, the previous argument to sqrt() could have been:

(double)sub

This expression has the same value as sub but is represented as a double-precision floating-point number. The type of the variable sub is not changed; it temporarily functions as a double. Using type casting, the previous program could be changed as follows:

program: sqrt2.c

```
1      #include <math.h>
2
3      main()
4      {
5          int sub;
6
7          printf( "x\tsqrt(x)\n\n" );
8          for ( sub = 0;  sub < 9;  sub++ )
9          {
10             printf( "%d\t%f\n", sub,
11                          sqrt( (double)sub ) );
12         }
13     }
```

THE break AND continue STATEMENTS

Two statements allow the programmer to alter effectively the path through a looping construct. The break statement, which we have seen before in the switch-case statement, transfers control to the end of the construct. In looping constructs, it transfers control to the next statement after the construct. The continue statement, on the other hand, transfers control back to the beginning of the looping construct. In the for statement, continue transfers control to the *increment* part of the loop, which is evaluated. The loop then continues its normal procedure.

The break and continue statements are often used for error processing. The problem solution, however, can often be reformulated so that these statements are not necessary. In some circumstances, their use makes the program more understandable.

Exhibit 7-4 shows the control flow when a break statement is inserted into a while loop. In the case depicted, we test for a condition using an if statement within the loop. If the condition is true we break out of the loop. In Exhibit 7-5 we have substituted a continue statement for the break statement. In this case, control is returned back to the top of the while loop. Notice that the statement(s) following the if statement is(are) not executed when the if condition is true.

The following program illustrates typical use of the break and continue statements. The program breaks up its input strings into individual words, one word per output line. It is part of a larger spelling-check program that compares

EXHIBIT 7-4

Control flow for while statement with embedded if and break

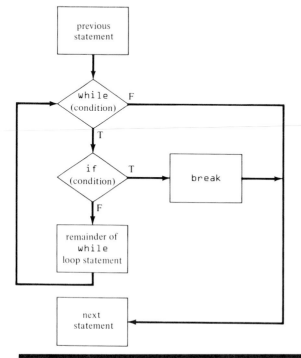

the output from this program against a series of correctly spelled words and looks for words in the input that are not in the dictionary.

program: copygraph.c

```
1     #include <stdio.h>
2     #include <ctype.h>
3
4     main()
5     {
6         int c;
7
8         while ( ( c = getchar() ) != EOF )
9         {
10            /* non ASCII character; stop copy */
11            if ( isascii(c) == 0 )
12            {
13                printf( "Non ASCII character; " );
14                printf( "not continuing\n" );
15                break;
16            }
17
18            /* if it is a punctuation character of any
19               kind, print newline character instead of
20               actual character */
21            if ( ispunct(c) || isspace(c) )
22            {
23                putchar('\n');
24                continue;
25            }
26
27            /* non-printing character; do not print */
28            if ( isprint(c) == 0 )
29                continue;
30
31            /* print alphanumeric character */
32            putchar(c);
33        }
34    }
```

program input:

```
A few short lines ^G;
With^N several control
characters in it.
```

program output:

```
A
few
short
lines
with
several
control
characters
in
it
```

This program processes the input as follows:

1. If the character entered is non-ASCII, then the input is probably not com-
ing from a terminal, but from a data file. An error message is printed and
the break statement branches to the end of the while statement and thus
to the end of the program.

   To check for non-ASCII characters we have used the isascii()

EXHIBIT 7-5

Control flow for while statement with embedded if and continue

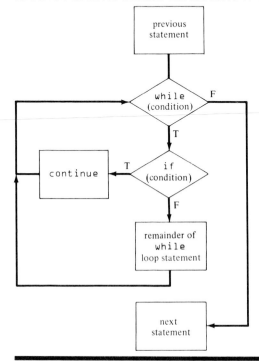

function (line 11). This function checks the value of its argument and returns a true or false value. To use the isascii() function it is necessary to include the file ctype.h.

2. If the character is a punctuation character or a space, a newline character is printed. This conditional statement is the program's main purpose, that is, to separate its input into a list of words, one on each line, and discard any punctuation characters. After the newline character is printed, the continue statement is encountered and the program returns to read in the next character.

3. If the character read is a nonprinting character (usually entered while holding down the control key on the terminal keyboard), it is ignored. The continue statement will return the program back to line 8 to retrieve the next input character.

4. If the character is none of the above, it is considered a standard alphanumeric character and printed.

SUMMARY

In this second chapter on control flow we introduced several important C language statement types. This chapter's iterative constructs combined with the previous chapter's conditional constructs provide the C language with all of the "modern" control statements necessary to form well-structured programs.

Although the three iterative constructs function very similarly, there are subtle differences in their use. Remember that the for and while constructs test the condition at the top of the loop while the do-while construct checks the condition at the bottom of the loop. Also, the for construct has an increment expression "built in" to the construct, whereas within the while constructs you must remember explicitly to include a statement that affects the condition test. An infinite loop is frequently the penalty for neglect.

EXERCISES

1. The expression:

   rand() % 100

always generates a number between 0 and 99. Generate 1000 such numbers and print out the number of numbers in each decile (0 to 9, 10 to 19, etc.)

2. Write a program to read letters typed in at the keyboard until an end-of-terminal input is encountered. Print out the number of:
   (a) vowels
   (b) consonants

(c) uppercase letters

(d) lowercase letters

that were encountered. (The sum of the four categories will be double the number of letters entered since each letter will fall into two categories.)

3. Write a program to read in characters typed in at the keyboard. Keep reading characters until the third period is encountered. Then print the number of characters read before the first period, the number between the first and second periods, and finally the number of characters between the second and third periods.

4. Use the scanf ( ) function to read in integer numbers from the terminal until an end of input is encountered. Then print the following:

(a) number of negative integers

(b) number of positive integers

(c) sum of negative integers

(d) sum of positive integers

(e) sum of even values (positive and negative)

(f) sum of odd values (positive and negative)

5. Write a program to print all prime numbers between 1 and 100.

6. Twin primes are defined as two consecutive odd numbers that are both prime (e.g., 17 and 19). Print all twin primes between 1 and 100.

7. In Chapter 5, Exercise 2, you wrote a program to convert from Fahrenheit to Celsius using the formula:

$$\frac{F - 32}{C} = \frac{9}{5}$$

In our experience the value of the Fahrenheit number is usually larger than its equivalent Celsius temperature. However, the scales do converge and eventually cross, yielding values of Fahrenheit that are lower than their Celsius equivalent. Write a program to determine where the two scales converge. Start with an arbitrary value of Celsius (e.g., 100 degrees) or Fahrenheit and iterate until the two numbers are equal. You should test early on to make sure you are iterating in the correct direction (i.e., the numbers are converging not diverging).

8. Write a program to read in a sequence of alphabetic characters from the terminal. Valid input is all upper- and lowercase characters plus the blank space. Define a word as a sequence of letters between two blanks. Print out the number of five letter words in the sequence. Terminate the program upon encountering a period. Remember to account for the boundary conditions (i.e., first and last words).

9. Write a program that reads in a positive integer number and prints it out backwards. For example, 12345 becomes 54321.

CHAPTER 8

FUNCTIONS I

OVERVIEW

In this chapter we will take a closer look at C language functions. We will see how they are defined and how they can be organized into separate source files and libraries. We will also discuss methods for passing information to functions and returning information back to the calling function. We have deferred discussion of some more advanced topics using functions until Chapter 14.

USING FUNCTIONS

In previous chapters, we have called many standard library functions and occasionally defined a function of our own. Within these examples have been functions that returned integer or floating-point values, and functions that returned no value, but performed some useful task.

Some programming languages make a distinction between subroutines and functions; the C language does not. All subprocedures are combined into the category called "functions."

Using Noninteger-Returning Functions

Whenever a function returns a value other than an integer, the calling function must declare the return value of the function. The pow() function, which returns a double-precision value, is an example of such a function. In general, return values of functions are declared in the calling function as follows:

```
main()
{
        double pow();
        char    *calloc();

        variable declarations;

        executable statements;
}
```

CALL BY VALUE

The C language uses *call by value* to pass information from a calling function to a called function. This means that the supplied variable's value is passed to the function, and not the variable itself. The programmer can assume that a function will never change the value of one of the supplied arguments, unless the argument is the address of a variable rather than the value of the variable. We will see this illustrated in Chapter 14.

WRITING FUNCTIONS

A function is defined as follows:

```
return_type   function_name( arg1, arg2 )
type arg1;
type arg2;
{
        variables local to function;

        function executable statements;
        return( return value );

}
```

The return value type is specified in the first line of the function. This value can be any of the basic types (char, int, or float), pointers to any of these types, structures, or unions. The ability to return a structure or union is a recent addition to the language and may not be available on all compilers. If the function does not return any value, the specified return value should be void.

Next, the function's name is given. The naming conventions for function names are similar to those for variables. The first character can be alphabetic (upper- or lowercase) or an underscore, and the remaining characters can be either of those, or numbers. The function name can be any length, but some compilers treat only the first few characters of the name as significant. Following the function name is the argument name list, enclosed in parentheses and separated by commas. These are the names that the function will attach to the values it is passed. Within the function, these arguments can be treated in the same manner as local variables defined within the function itself.

Following the argument name declaration is their type definition. Except for arrays, argument types are defined in the same manner as variable declarations. (We will discuss arrays in Chapter 14.)

After all the linkage information has been defined, the body of the function is specified. User-defined functions have the same format as the main( ) function: local variable declarations followed by executable statements.

The following example illustrates each of these parts:

program: simplefunc.c

```
 1    main( )
 2    {
 3         int x, y, z;
 4
 5         x = 4;
 6         y = 5;
 7         z = 6;
 8
 9         simplefunc( x, y, z );
10
11         print_ints( x, y, z, (x + y + z) );
12    }
13
```

                                                    (*program continues*)

```
14    simplefunc( a, b, c )
15    int a, b, c;
16    {
17        int total;
18
19        total = ++a + ++b + ++c;
20        print_ints( a, b, c, total );
21    }
22
23    print_ints( n1, n2, n3, n4 )
24    int n1, n2, n3, n4;
25    {
26        printf( "%d %d %d %d\n", n1, n2, n3, n4 );
27    }
```

program output:

```
5 6 7 18
4 5 6 15
```

The print_ints() function is called from the main() and simplefunc() functions. It requires four arguments that it names n1, n2, n3, and n4. These are private copies of the values passed to it from its calling (parent) function; they can be manipulated in the same manner as the local (automatic) variables it declares.

The call to the simplefunc() function does not change the values of x, y, and z. This is because the *values* of these variables are passed to the function and not the variables themselves. The function simply alters the values of its copies of the variables.

In this example, the two functions, simplefunc() and print_ints(), are shown in the same file as the main() function. In larger programs, it is often better to put auxiliary functions in different source files and then compile them with the main() function, creating one executable file.

The return Statement

The simplefunc.c file contains two functions that do not return values. The return statement, when included in a function, permits the programmer to return a value to the calling function. In the calling function, the return value becomes the value of the expression function(), where function is the name of the function being called. Although not strictly required, by convention the value returned is usually enclosed in parentheses. The following program illustrates the return statement.

program: returnval.c

```
 1    main()
 2    {
 3          int identification, getunique();
 4
 5          identification = getunique();
 6
 7          printf( "ID: %d\n", identification );
 8    }
 9
10    getunique()
11    {
12          int temp;
13
14          temp = getpid();
15          return( temp );
16    }
```

program output:

```
ID:  319
```

The value of the expression:

```
getunique()
```

in the main() function is the value returned from the getunique() function. This value is then assigned to the variable identification in line 5.

To enhance portability, the call to getpid() is placed within a function rather than within main(). Because getpid() is operating-system dependent, functions like getunique() are best placed in a separate source file labeled as machine specific. If isolated in a file by itself, we can change the function easily when we move this program to another machine or to a different operating system.

SUMMARY

In general, functions break a large programming task into a collection of small, manageable units. All C language programs contain a main() function, which will often contain calls to user-defined and library functions. The main() function usually contains few programming details; the called functions contain the bulk of the activity. These functions may in turn be broken into general and detailed pieces, depending on the nature and complexity of the task.

Using functions also permits us to break up the source code into separate files, each of which can contain related functions. For example, one file can contain the main() function, another the I/O functions, a third the file maintenance routines, and so on. These source files can be treated as libraries and shared across programs.

EXERCISES

1. To convert from kilometers to miles (or vice versa) we use the formula:

1 kilometer = 5/8 miles

Write a program containing two functions, one that converts kilometers to miles, the other that converts miles to kilometers. Accept, as input, a floating-point number and the character "k" or "m" (indicating the value is kilometers or miles, respectively), perform the appropriate conversion, and print out the result.

2. Rewrite the absolute.c program in Chapter 6, converting the absolute value calculation into a function.

3. Rewrite Exercise 2 in Chapter 5, placing the Fahrenheit to Celsius conversion into a function.

4. Write a program that reads characters from the terminal and has four functions that check the character's attributes as follows:
    (a) Is the character alphabetic?
    (b) Is the character numeric?
    (c) If alphabetic, is the character uppercase?
    (d) If alphabetic, is the character lowercase?
Print out the character's attributes.

5. The series of numbers:

1, 1, 2, 3, 5, 8, 13, 21, . . .

is known as the Fibonacci series. Each number is the sum of the two preceding numbers. Write a program that reads in an arbitrary number between 1 and 100, then calls a function check_fib() that checks if the number is part of the Fibonacci series. The main() function should then print:

"Number" is/is not part of the Fibonacci series.

6. Write a program containing two functions bignum() and littlenum(). This program should accept values typed in at the terminal until an end-of-input is encountered. Function bignum() should then print out the largest number read and function littlenum() should print out the smallest.

7. Write a program that contains a function isbigger() that compares values as they are read from the terminal against the previous value read. Only those values that are bigger than the previous value are printed.

PART 4

DERIVED
VARIABLE TYPES

CHAPTER

POINTERS I

OVERVIEW

In this book the discussion of pointers is divided into two parts. This chapter introduces the subject; Chapter 13 covers more sophisticated pointer operations.
We begin this chapter discussing the distinction between a variable and its address. Next, we cover the declaration of pointer variables and the use of some simpler pointer operations. We also demonstrate how pointers may be used within the scanf() *function to accept input from the terminal.*

ADDRESSES

In the C language, each variable and character string is stored in memory and has an address that describes its location. So far, we have seen two expressions that have an address as their value—the character string expression and an expression made up of a variable name preceded by an ampersand, as follows:

```
&variable_name
```

We used these expressions in conjunction with functions that expected the value of an address as one of their arguments. For example, the `printf()` function expects the starting address of a character string as its first argument. When the following function call is made:

```
printf( "Hello, there\n" );
```

two things happen:

1. at compile time, memory is allocated and the character string is stored;

2. when the program executes, the character string's starting address is passed to the `printf()` function.

The `printf()` function then looks at the passed location to find the character string. The characters in the character string are not passed to the function; instead, the string's starting location is passed and the function reads at the location to find the information.

The `scanf()` function is another function we have already seen that requires a variable's address as one of its arguments. For example, the following code fragment is used to prompt for and receive a floating-point value from the terminal:

```
float rate;

printf( "Enter floating-point number: " );
scanf( "%f\n", &rate );
```

EXHIBIT 9-1

Variable rate with value 50.3 stored in memory location 1000

rate		&rate
memory location	value	value
1000	50.3	1000

The expression &rate does not yield the value of the contents of the variable rate; it has the value of the address, or memory location of the variable. This is illustrated in Exhibit 9-1. The scanf() function, instead of returning a value, stores the input information at the address supplied to it. It functions this way because many pieces of information can potentially be entered at one time. For example:

program: mult.input.c

```
1      #include <stdio.h>
2
3      main()
4      {
5           int x, y;
6           char c;
7           float f;
8
9           printf( "Enter two integers, a character, " );
10          printf( "and a floating-point number\n" );
11          scanf( "%d %d %c %f", &x, &y, &c, &f );
12
13          printf( "The values entered were\n" );
14          printf( "%d\t%d\t%c\t%f\n", x, y, c, f );
15     }
```

program output:

```
Enter two integers, a character, and a floating-point number
13345 4372 J 6540.70e-4
The values entered were
12345    4372    J    0.654070
```

Since a function may have only one return value, scanf() uses this alternate method to store information. Therefore, it is very important to give the scanf() function the proper control information. The following program illustrates this:

program: test.input.c

```
1      main()
2      {
3           /* incorrect version */
4
5           float smaller;
6           double larger;
```

(program continues)

```
7
8          printf( "Enter floating-point number: " );
9          scanf( "%f", &smaller );
10
11         printf( "Enter floating-point number: " );
12         scanf( "%f", &larger );
13
14         printf( "smaller = %f, larger = %f\n", smaller, larger );
15     }
```

program output:

```
Enter floating-point number: 123.45
Enter floating-point number: 123.45
smaller = 123.449997, larger = 0.000000
```

In line 12 of this program, scanf() reads a floating-point number and stores it in the 32 bits that start with location:

&larger

Unfortunately, the item at this address starts a 64-bit variable. The scanf() function is not aware of this discrepancy and stores the number in the wrong format. To fix the program we simply make the following change to line 12:

program: test.input.c

```
1      main()
2      {
3          /* correct version */
4
5          float smaller;
6          double larger;
7
8          printf( "Enter floating-point number: " );
9          scanf( "%f", &smaller );
10
11         printf( "Enter floating-point number: " );
12         scanf( "%lf", &larger );
13
14         printf( "smaller = %f, larger = %f\n", smaller, larger );
15     }
```

program output:

```
Enter floating-point number: 123.45
Enter floating-point number: 123.45
smaller = 123.449997, larger = 123.450000
```

POINTER VARIABLES

Formally, pointers are variables that contain addresses and are declared as follows:

*type *variable_name*

The address contained in a pointer may be the address of a variable or a character string. For example, a pointer to a character variable is declared as follows:

```
char *cptr;
```

where the variable's name is `cptr` and the value it holds is a character's address. The asterisk preceding the variable name informs the compiler that this variable will hold the character's *address* and not a character. A variable that contains an integer's address is declared as follows:

```
int *iptr;
```

where `iptr` is the name of the variable. Pointers to other types of variables are similarly declared—by preceding the variable name with an asterisk. Several pointers can be declared at one time and can even be declared along with other variable declarations, as in this example:

```
int x, y, *iptr, *another_pointer;
```

where x and y are regular integers and `iptr` and `another_pointer` are pointer variables.

To obtain a variable's address we can use the & operator. Previously, we have seen the & operator used only within functions:

```
scanf("%f",&variable)
```

Additionally, the & operator may also be used within assignment statements. For example, the following code fragment:

```
int z, *ptrtoz;
```

```
ptrtoz = &z;
```

places the address of variable z in the pointer variable ptrtoz. The following example further illustrates this point:

program: inputter.c

```
1     main()
2     {
3          int x, *intptr;
4
5          intptr = &x;
6
7          printf( "Enter an integer: " );
8          scanf( "%d", intptr );
9
10         printf( "The value entered is %d\n", x );
11    }
```

program output:

```
Enter an integer: 1234
The value entered is 1234
```

In line 3, we declare two variables; an integer named x and a pointer to an integer named intptr. In line 5, we set the variable intptr equal to the address of the variable x. In line 8, we pass the value of the pointer variable to the scanf() function; in previous examples, we passed it an expression:

```
&x
```

where the value of the expression was the "address of x". The two expressions are equivalent. The scanf() function will read an integer from the terminal and place it in the variable named x located at address &x. Exhibit 9-2 illustrates this example. We assume that variable x is at memory location 2000. Note also that intptr, since it is also a variable, has its own memory location.

Pointer Dereferencing

If a pointer variable contains a second variable's address, we can find the second variable's value by using the dereferencing operator. For example, given the following code fragment:

```
int x;
int *pointer;

pointer = &x;
```

we can obtain the value of x through either of the following two expressions:

```
x
*pointer
```

The second expression has the value of the integer whose address is stored in the variable pointer. We know it is an integer because pointer was declared as a pointer to an integer. Exhibit 9-3 shows an example of the relationship between values and memory locations.

If, by mistake, we assign the address of the variable x to a pointer to a character, for example:

```
cpointer = &x
```

then the value of the expression *cpointer will be the 8 bits that start at the address. If we apply the dereferencing operator to a pointer variable whose value has not yet been initialized, then a runtime error will occur and the program will fail. The deref.c program (on page 131) illustrates dereferencing operator use:

EXHIBIT 9-2

Value assignments and storage locations in program inputter.c

After line 3:

x	
memory location	value
2000	?

intptr	
memory location	value
3000	?

After line 5:

x	
memory location	value
2000	?

intptr	
memory location	value
3000	2000

After line 8:

x	
memory location	value
2000	1234

intptr	
memory location	value
3000	2000

EXHIBIT 9-3

The effect of the & and * operators

C Language Statements

```
(1)    int a, *ptr, b, c, *d ;
(2)    a = 25;
(3)    ptr = &a;
(4)    b = a;
(5)    c = *ptr;
(6)    d = ptr;
```

Corresponding Values in Memory

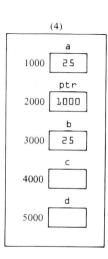

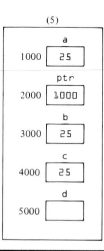

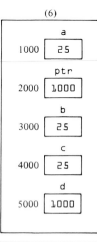

program: deref.c

```
1     main()
2     {
3           int x;
4           int *pointer;
5
6           pointer = &x;      /* pointer "points to " x */
7
8           x = 15;
9           printf( "The value of x = %d\n", x );
10          printf( "The value of *pointer = %d\n", *pointer );
11
12          *pointer = 32;
13          printf( "\nThe value of x = %d\n", x );
14          printf( "The value of *pointer = %d\n", *pointer );
15    }
```

program output:

```
The value of x = 15
The value of *pointer = 15

The value of x = 32
The value of *pointer = 32
```

Machine Representation of Pointers

Internally, a pointer is stored in one machine word, regardless of the variable type to which it points. The following program illustrates pointer variable sizes:

program: sizeof.c

```
1     main()
2     {
3          char x, *pointer;
4
5          printf( "The size of x is %d\n", sizeof x );
6          printf( "The size of pointer is %d\n",
7                     sizeof pointer );
8     }
```

program output:

```
The size of x is 1
The size of pointer is 2
```

The sizeof *operator forms an expression whose value is the size, in bytes, of the variable whose name follows it.*

Another use of pointer variables is illustrated below. Consider the following printf() statement:

```
printf( "%d\t%d\t%d\t%d\t%d\t%d\t%d\t\n", ... )
```

(The periods here indicate that the rest of the argument list is omitted; at this point we are only interested in the first argument to printf().) What is the value of the character string expression contained within the double quotes? It is the starting address of where the character string:

```
"%d\t%d\t%d\t%d\t%d\t%d\t%d\t\n"
```

is stored. Thus, since a pointer variable may also contain a character string's starting address, an alternate method for specifying a control string is shown in lines 11 and 12 in the program below:

program: longer.c

```
1     main()
2     {
3          char *format;
4          int x, y, z;
5
6          x = 10;
7          y = 15;
8          z = 20;
9          printf( "x = %d; y = %d; z = %d\n", x, y, z );
10
11         format = "x = %d; y = %d; z = %d\n";
12         printf( format, x, y, z );
13    }
```

program output:

```
x = 10; y = 15; z = 20
x = 10; y = 15; z = 20
```

In this program, there are two character strings, each containing the same information. (There are two because, even if the strings contain identical information, the compiler will store them separately.) The second character string (line 11), however, is recyclable. If the character string is needed again, the pointer can be supplied, eliminating the need for an additional character string. Exhibit 9-4 shows how this is represented in memory.

EXHIBIT 9-4

Memory representation for program `longer.c`

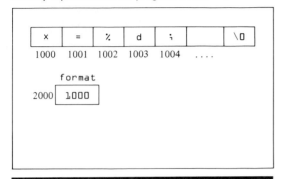

Operations on Pointer Variables

So far, we have seen only one operator applied to a pointer variable—the dereferencing operator. Other operations are available, including comparison of pointers and pointer arithmetic. We have deferred a discussion of these operations until Chapter 13.

SUMMARY

In this chapter we introduced one of the C language's most powerful features—pointers. As we will see in subsequent chapters, the C language uses pointers extensively for string, array, and structure handling, and for passing data among functions.

Although other languages use pointers, the C language is known for its rich set of pointer operations. We will cover these in Chapter 13.

EXERCISES

1. Given five integer variables:

   a = 100;
   b = 200;
   c = 300;
   d = 400;
   e = 500;

set each variable equal to the succeeding variable's address (set e to the address of a) and print out each variable's value and address.

2. Define four variables:

a character
an integer
a floating point
a double-precision floating point

and pointers to each of them. Print out the size (in bytes) of each variable and all four pointers.

3. Given two floating-point numbers a and b initialized as follows:

a = 122.5;
b = 10.7;

and two pointer variables c and d initialized as follows:

c = &a;
d = &b;

(a) Print the values of a, b, c, and d.
(b) Swap the values of a and b, and print a, b, c, and d.
(c) Swap the values of c and d, and print a, b, c, and d.
(d) Use the expressions *c and *d to swap the values of a and b, and print a, b, c, and d.

CHAPTER 10

ARRAYS

OVERVIEW

In this chapter we introduce the array, the most common C language derived variable type. Arrays are frequently used for accepting input from the terminal and for storing strings of characters. We will discuss several string manipulation functions and the gets() and puts() functions which are used for terminal input and output. We will also show several array applications including some searching and sorting routines.

ARRAYS

Single and multidimensional arrays are available in the C language and are used to group sets of like objects. A single dimensional array is declared as follows:

type array_name[n];

where *array_name* is the name of an array of *n* elements of the type specified. The size of an array must be an integer constant. Any of an array's elements can be accessed through subscripting. For example:

```
array[20] = 1234;
```

In the C language, subscripting begins with zero. Any integer C language expression can appear between the brackets that follow the array name; thus, the subscript value could result from a subscripting variable, a unary expression, a binary expression, or the return value from a function call.

INTERNAL REPRESENTATION OF ARRAYS

Arrays are declared as containing a certain data type (just like variables) and internally they are stored as a contiguous set of these data types. The following program illustrates this:

program: show.array.c

```
1     main()
2     {
3          int sub, array[10];
4
5          printf( "sizeof(int) is %d\n\n", sizeof(int) );
6
7          for ( sub = 0; sub < 10; sub++ )
8          {
9               printf( "&array[%d] = %x\n", sub,
10                   &array[sub] );
11         }
12    }
```

program output:

```
sizeof(int) is 2

&array[0] = ff32
&array[1] = ff34
```

```
&array[2]  =  ff36
&array[3]  =  ff38
&array[4]  =  ff3a
&array[5]  =  ff3c
&array[6]  =  ff3e
&array[7]  =  ff40
&array[8]  =  ff42
&array[9]  =  ff44
```

As we can see, this program was run on a machine with a word length, and hence, integer size, of 16 bits. Exhibit 10-1 shows the array's organization in memory. Line 5 combines type casting with the `sizeof` operator. The `sizeof` operator examines the type of an expression and prints its size in bytes. In this case, the expression is null, but its value has been forced to look like an integer.

The & operator can be applied to any variable, including an array element. An array element can be treated like any other variable; its value can form an expression, it can be assigned a value, and it can be passed as an argument (or parameter) to a library function. In this example we see that the array elements' addresses are exactly two bytes apart. We are guaranteed that array elements will always be contiguous in virtual memory. We will see the importance of this when we use arrays in conjunction with pointer variables.

MULTIDIMENSIONAL ARRAYS

The C language also provides for arrays of arbitrary dimensions. A two-dimensional array of size *n* rows by *m* columns is declared as follows:

type array_name[n][m];

Elements in a two-dimensional array can be accessed this way:

`twodim[3][10]`

This will access the element in row number 3 (the fourth row) and in column number 10 (the eleventh column) of the array. Arrays with more than

EXHIBIT 10-1

Storage of array `array` in memory

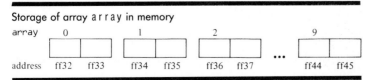

EXHIBIT 10-2

Organization of two-dimensional array with two rows, three columns

[0] [0]	[0] [1]	[0] [2]
[1] [0]	[1] [1]	[1] [2]
[2] [0]	[2] [1]	[2] [2]

two dimensions are declared similarly. Arrays are stored in memory in row-major order. This is shown in Exhibit 10-2.

ARRAY NAME AS AN EXPRESSION

If an array name is used by itself as an expression, then the value of the expression is the array's starting address. For example:

program: array.name.c

```
1    main()
2    {
3         int array[100];
4
5         printf( "The value of \"array\" is %x\n", array );
6         printf( "The value of \"&array[0]\" is %x\n",
7                 &array[0] );
8    }
```

program output:

```
The value of "array" is fe80
The value of "&array[0]" is fe80
```

This can be used to our advantage when we combine it with some functions we have already seen. For example, the scanf() function reads information from the terminal and stores it at the supplied address. So far, we have seen how to enter a character, an integer, and a floating-point number using scanf(). By using the %s option to the scanf() function, we can enter character strings from the terminal and have these strings placed in an array of characters. The following program illustrates this:

program: char.input.c

```
1      #include <stdio.h>
2
3      main()
4      {
5           char carray[256];
6           int sub;
7
8           printf( "Enter character string\n" );
9           scanf( "%s\n", carray );
10
11          printf( "The array contains: %s\n", carray );
12
13          for ( sub = 0; (sub < 256) && (carray[sub] != '\0');
14              sub++ )
15          {
16              putchar( carray[sub] );
17          }
18          putchar('\n');
19     }
```

program output:

```
Enter character string
Hello
The array contains: Hello
Hello
```

The starting address of the array named carray, an array of characters, is the value passed as the second argument to the scanf() function in line 9. The scanf() function reads the string of characters from the terminal and stores it starting at this location. After it has read in all the characters, it places one more character in the array, the null character. Remember, this character terminates all character strings and any function that processes a character string expects this termination character, including the printf() function (see line 11 of this program). This is illustrated in Exhibit 10-3.

Before moving on, let's look at a stylistic problem with this program. The size of the array is declared to be 256; later this value is used to control looping through the array. While this is not a problem here, it could lead to problems in larger programs. For example, in a program with 15 arrays, each of the same size (100 elements), the number 100 will appear in the declaration of each of these arrays, and then many more times throughout the program (for controlling loops, etc.) If, for some reason, the size of one of these arrays needs to be altered it would be necessary to search the entire program for all of the 100s

EXHIBIT 10-3

Array c a r r a y after execution of statement 9 in program c h a r . i n p u t . c

carray	[0]	[1]	[2]	[3]	[4]	[5]	
	H	e	l	l	o	\0	

that relate to the array in question and change them, while ignoring all 100s not related to the array size.

To make the program more easily maintainable, the previous example should be rewritten as follows:

program: char.2.c

```
1       #include <stdio.h>
2       #define CARRAY_SIZE 256
3
4       main()
5       {
6           char carray[CARRAY_SIZE];
7           int sub;
8
9           printf( "Enter character string\n" );
10          scanf( "%s", carray );
11
12          printf( "The array contains: %s\n", carray );
13
14          for ( sub = 0; (sub < CARRAY_SIZE) &&
15              (carray[sub] != ' '); sub++ )
16          {
17              putchar( carray[sub] );
18          }
19          putchar( '\n');
20      }
```

program output:

```
Enter character string
Hello
The array contains: Hello
Hello
```

In line 2 we have used the #define to associate the symbolic name CARRAY_SIZE with the value 256. Whenever we need to refer to the array size we use CARRAY_SIZE. If the array size needs to be changed, we need only change line 2.

■■■■■■■■■
APPLICATIONS USING ARRAYS

Often, we need to store information in arrays in sorted order. The following examples demonstrate two simple sorting techniques. The first example shows an *insertion sort* and the second a *bubble sort*. For data in fully random order these two methods are very inefficient when compared to other sorting techniques. We use them primarily to illustrate how arrays are handled in the C language.

Sorting: Insertion Sort

This method of sorting accepts numbers from an input source and places them into an array, while keeping the array sorted at all times. The insertion sort is not an "in-place" sort (unlike the bubble sort). In this example the input source is the terminal and the array name is array.

The logic for this sorting method is as follows:

```
insert_one_element_into_the_array( )
{
        read number from terminal;
        for ( each element in the array )
        {
                if( table entry > input number )
                {
                        make room for that number by
                            "pushing down" all remaining
                            elements in the array;
                        store number in correct position;
                }
                else if ( at dynamic end of array )
                {
                        put input number at dynamic end;
                }
        }

        extend the size of the array (dynamic end) by 1;
}
```

The following program implements the previous pseudocode while printing the sort results after each entered number:

program: show.insrt.c

```
1      #include <stdio.h>
2      #define ARRAY_SIZE 100
3
4      main()
5      {
6          int input, array[ARRAY_SIZE], sub, i, virtual_end;
7
8          virtual_end = 0;   /* array is empty */
9
10         while ( scanf( "%d", &input ) != EOF )
11         {
12             for( sub = 0; sub <= ARRAY_SIZE; sub++ )
13             {
14                 /* at dynamic end of data in table */
15                 if ( sub == virtual_end )
16                 {
17                     array[sub] = input;
18                     printf( "array[%d] = %d (end)\n",
19                         sub, input );
20                     virtual_end++;
21                     break;
22                 }
23                 else if ( input < array[sub] )
24                 {
25                     /* from end of table to my
26                         current position */
27                     for ( i = virtual_end; i > sub; i-- )
28                     {
29                         printf( "array[%d] = array[%d]\n",
30                             i, i - 1 );
31                         array[i] = array[i-1];
32                     }
33                     array[sub] = input;
34                     printf( "array[%d] = %d (inserted)\n",
35                         sub, input );
36                     virtual_end++;
37                     break;
38                 }
39             }
40
41             /* print sorted array after each inserted item */
42             printf( "SORTED LIST AT END OF %d INSERTIONS\n",
43                 virtual_end );
```

```
44                for ( sub = 0; sub < virtual_end; sub++ )
45                    printf( "array[%d] == %d\n", sub,
46                        array[sub] );
47                printf( "\n" );
48            }
49
50     }
```

program input:

```
16838
5758
10113
17515
31051
5627
```

program output:

```
array[0] = 16838 (end)
SORTED LIST AT END OF 1 INSERTIONS
array[0] == 16838

array[1] = array[0]
array[0] = 5758 (inserted)
SORTED LIST AT END OF 2 INSERTIONS
array[0] == 5758
array[1] == 16838

array[2] = array[1]
array[1] = 10113 (inserted)
SORTED LIST AT END OF 3 INSERTIONS
array[0] == 5758
array[1] == 10113
array[2] == 16838

array[3] = 17515 (end)
SORTED LIST AT END OF 4 INSERTIONS
array[0] == 5758
array[1] == 10113
array[2] == 16838
array[3] == 17515
```

```
array[4] = 31051 (end)
SORTED LIST AT END OF 5 INSERTIONS
array[0] == 5758
array[1] == 10113
array[2] == 16838
array[3] == 17515
array[4] == 31051

array[5] = array[4]
array[4] = array[3]
array[3] = array[2]
array[2] = array[1]
array[1] = array[0]
array[0] = 5627 (inserted)
SORTED LIST AT END OF 6 INSERTIONS
array[0] == 5627
array[1] == 5758
array[2] == 10113
array[3] == 16838
array[4] == 17515
array[5] == 31051
```

The following are some comments on important statements within the
program:

Line	Comments
10	If CONTROL-D is entered at the terminal, scanf() returns EOF as defined in stdio.h
12	For each number input, execute the loop ARRAY_SIZE number of times or until the dynamic end is reached.
15–22	The entered number is larger than any other in the array. Place this number at the virtual end and extend the virtual end.
24–38	Push all other elements in the array down to make room for the number entered.
44–47	Print sorted list after each new entry is inserted/appended.

The following is a less wordy version of the same program:

program: insertion.c

```
1       #include <stdio.h>
2       #define ARRAY_SIZE 100
3
4       main()
5       {
6           int input, array[ARRAY_SIZE], sub, i, virtual_end;
7
8           virtual_end = 0;   /* array is empty */
9
10          while ( scanf( "%d", &input ) != EOF )
11          {
12              for( sub = 0; sub <= ARRAY_SIZE; sub++ )
13              {
14                  if ( sub == virtual_end )
15                  {
16                      array[sub] = input;
17                      virtual_end++;
18                      break;
19                  }
20                  else if ( input < array[sub] )
21                  {
22                      for ( i = virtual_end; i > sub; i-- )
23                      {
24                          array[i] = array[i-1];
25                      }
26                      array[sub] = input;
27                      virtual_end++;
28                      break;
29                  }
30              }
31          }
32
33          /* print sorted array */
34          for ( sub = 0; sub < virtual_end; sub++ )
35              printf( "%d\n", array[sub] );
36      }
```

program input		program output	
16838	23010	2749	16212
5758	7419	4086	16838
10113	16212	5627	17515
17515	4086	5758	23010
31051	2749	7419	31051
5627		10113	

Sorting: Bubble Sort

The following program illustrates a bubble sort. It looks at all adjacent pairs of
the array, swapping them if the first is greater than the second, for the entire
array. Several passes are made through the array, until the array is sorted.

program: bubble.c

```
1    #define ARRAY_SIZE    6
2    #define UNSORTED      0
3    #define SORTED        1
4
5    main()
6    {
7        int state, sub, x[ARRAY_SIZE], temp;
8
9        /* fill the array with random numbers */
10       for ( sub = 0; sub < ARRAY_SIZE; sub++ )
11       {
12           x[sub] = rand();
13       }
14
15       /* print unsorted array */
16       printf( "UNSORTED LIST\n" );
17       for ( sub = 0; sub < ARRAY_SIZE; sub++ )
18       {
19           printf( "%d\n", x[sub] );
20       }
21
22       state = UNSORTED;
23       while ( state == UNSORTED)
24       {
25           state = SORTED;   /* now prove
26                               that it is not */
27           for ( sub = 0; sub < ARRAY_SIZE - 1; sub++ )
28           {
29               /* look at adjacent pairs; swap
30                   if second smaller than first */
31               if ( x[sub] > x[sub + 1] )
32               {
33                   /* swap values */
34                   temp = x[sub];
35                   x[sub] = x[sub + 1];
36                   x[sub + 1] = temp;
37                   state = UNSORTED;
38               }
39           }
40       }
```

```
41
42          /* print sorted array */
43          printf( "\nSORTED LIST\n" );
44          for ( sub = 0; sub < ARRAY_SIZE; sub++ )
45          {
46              printf( "%d\n", x[sub] );
47          }
48     }
```

program output:

```
UNSORTED LIST
16838
5758
10113
17515
31051
5627

SORTED LIST
5627
5758
10113
16838
17515
31051
```

Exhibit 10-4 shows several intermediate steps in the sort process.

I/O Using gets() and puts()

In previous examples we used the scanf() function to read an array of characters from the terminal. This function reads a sequence of characters termi-
nated by either a space or a newline. To read input a line at a time we can also
use the gets() function, which expects the address of an array of characters
as its argument. The gets() function retrieves a line of characters (as opposed
to a string of characters) from the terminal and stores it in an array. For
example, the following code fragment:

```
char input_here[LENGTH];

gets(input_here);
```

EXHIBIT 10-4

Status of array x after first pass through for and while loops in program bubble.c

Step 0 (unsorted)

```
x[0] ==  16838
x[1] ==   5758
x[2] ==  10113
x[3] ==  17515
x[4] ==  31051
x[5] ==   5627
```

Step 4 (after first pass through for loop)

```
x[0] ==   5758
x[1] ==  16838
x[2] ==  10113
x[3] ==  17515
x[4] ==  31051
x[5] ==   5627
```

Step 5 (after first complete pass through while loop)

```
x[0] ==   5758
x[1] ==  10113
x[2] ==  16838
x[3] ==  17515
x[4] ==   5627
x[5] ==  31051
```

reads a line of characters from the terminal and stores it in the input_here array. The following program combines the insertion sort technique with the gets() function to sort lines of input. Several new functions are introduced in this program. They are defined immediately following the program.

program: sortlines.c

```
1    #include <stdio.h>
2    #define NUMBER_LINES 20
3    #define LINE_LENGTH 80
4
5    main()
6    {
7        int sub, i, virtual_end;
8        char input_line[LINE_LENGTH];
9        char paragraph[NUMBER_LINES][LINE_LENGTH];
```

```
10
11          virtual_end = 0;   /* array is empty */
12
13          while ( gets( input_line ) != NULL )
14          {
15              for( sub = 0;  sub <= NUMBER_LINES;  sub++ )
16              {
17                  if ( sub == virtual_end )
18                  {
19                      strcpy( paragraph[sub], input_line );
20                      virtual_end++;
21                      break;
22                  }
23                  else if ( strncmp( input_line,
24                      paragraph[sub], LINE_LENGTH ) < 0 )
25                  {
26                      for ( i = virtual_end;  i > sub;  i-- )
27                      {
28                          strcpy( paragraph[i],
29                          paragraph[i - 1] );
30                      }
31                      strcpy( paragraph[sub], input_line );
32                      virtual_end++;
33                      break;
34                  }
35              }
36          }
37
38          /* print sorted array of sentences */
39          for ( sub = 0;  sub < virtual_end;  sub++ )
40              puts( paragraph[sub] );
41      }
```

program input:

```
a bowl of spaghetti
this is a line of input
nostalgia is not what it used to be
fgets() returns a NULL on end-of-file
UNIX is a trademark of AT&T Bell Laboratories
```

program output:

```
UNIX is a trademark of AT&T Bell Laboratories
a bowl of spaghetti
```

```
fgets() returns a NULL on end-of-file
nostalgia is not what it used to be
this is a line of input
```

Note that the sentence beginning with the word "UNIX" appears before the sentence starting with the word "a". This is because capital letters come before lowercase letters in the ASCII collating sequence.

This program introduces several new C language features that are worth discussing in some detail.

The gets() and puts() Functions

The gets() function reads one line of characters from the terminal and stores it in an array. The puts() function is the complement function of gets(); it prints the string whose address is supplied on the terminal. Since gets() does not store the trailing newline character in the input array, the puts() function adds one to its output. Formally, the two functions are defined as follows:

Function Name

```
(char *)gets( array )
```

Description

This function gets a character string from the terminal and stores it in an array. It does not store the newline character, but does end the string properly with the string termination character '\0'.

Argument List

(char *)array	The starting address of an array of characters. String will be stored here. No checks are made to make sure that the array is large enough. If this is important, the fgets() function should be used.

Return Values

char *	Upon successful completion, the character string address is returned.
NULL	Returned upon end-of-file or if there was an error in reading from the standard input.

Function Name

```
(int) puts( string )
```

Description

This function puts a character string to the standard output followed by a newline character. The function assumes that the string is formed properly and will print characters until a null character is reached.

Argument List

(char *)string   This is the address of an array of characters. It is assumed that a null-terminated string of characters is at this address.

Return Values

EOF   Returned if there was an error while printing string.

The strcpy() and strcmp() Functions

These two string manipulation functions are used to copy and compare character strings.

The strcpy() function is used in lines 19, 28, and 31 of sortlines.c to copy a character string from one location to another. The two arguments to the function define the starting locations of the source string and the destination array. For example, in line 19, the expression input_line yields the starting address of the character string that was read in from the terminal. This string is copied to the location beginning at the address defined by paragraph[sub], which yields the location of a subarray within the character array paragraph. (This technique is discussed more fully below.)

In line 23, the strcmp() function does a character-by-character comparison of the two character strings beginning at input_line and paragraph[sub].

These two functions are formally defined as follows:

Function Name

(char *)strcpy(s1, s2)

Description

This function copies a string of characters into an array of characters, preserving the string termination character '\0'.

Argument List

(char *)s1   The destination. This should be declared as an array of characters sufficient in size to hold the string being copied.

(char *)s2   The string to be copied. This can be any expression that yields the starting address of a string of characters, either an array name, a character string expression, or a pointer to a character that begins a character string. It is assumed that the string ends with a '\0' character.

Return Values

char *   The address of the destination string if the copy was successful. This function will not fail if the destination array is not sufficiently long. Instead, it will overwrite whatever memory follows the destination array. Therefore, it is wise to be certain that the destination array is sufficiently large to hold any possible input.

Function Name

(int)strncmp(s1, s2, n)

Description

This function compares the first *n* characters of two character strings, a character at a time, for lexicographical (alphanumeric) positioning using the ASCII collating sequence.

Argument List

(char *)s1   The starting address of a string of characters.
(char *)s2   The starting address of a string of characters.
(int)n   The number of characters to compare. It will compare this many characters or terminate the comparison at the end of the character string if it comes first.

Return Values

< 0   The return value will be less than zero if the first string is lexicographically less than the second character string.
== 0   The two character strings are identical in the first *n* places.
> 0   The first string is lexicographically greater than the second.

WARNING: This function is often used to compare two strings for equality. If the two are the same, then the return value from st rncmp() is 0, or false. A call to this function to test equality should be made in the following manner:

```
if ( strncmp( s1, s2 ) == 0 )
{
        assume the two are the same
}
```

Addressing Strings Within Multidimensional Arrays

As we have seen, we can obtain an array's starting address by using the array name without subscripting. This same technique can be used to obtain the starting address of locations within the array. For example, a five-row, 20-column, two-dimensional integer array is declared as:

```
int twodim[5][20];
```

We can also view two-dimensional arrays as being arrays of arrays. In this case we have an array of five arrays, each of which contains 20 integers. We can address any one of these arrays by using only the first dimension of the array. For example, to address the 20 elements of the third array we can write:

```
twodim[2]
```

This expression describes the name of an array and therefore has the value of the starting address (first element) of the array. Exhibit 10-5 shows the value of the expressions.

This technique was used in several locations in program sortlines.c to obtain the starting address of strings within the array paragraph. This is shown in Exhibit 10-6.

EXHIBIT 10-5

Value of expressions representing subarrays of array twodim[5][20]

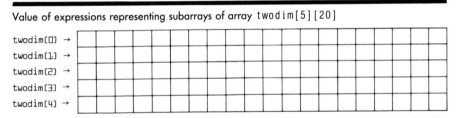

EXHIBIT 10-6

Location of subarrays within array paragraph[20][80]

		column					
row	[0]	[1]	[2]	[3]	[4]	[5] •••
paragraph[0] → [0]	a		b	o	w	l
paragraph[1] → [1]	t	h	i	s		i
paragraph[2] → [2]	n	o	s	t	a	l
paragraph[3] → [3]	f	g	e	t	s	C
paragraph[4] → [4]	U	N	I	X		i

Other String Manipulation Functions

In the previous example, we saw how we could test to see whether one character string was equal to, less than, or lexicographically greater than another. Several other functions exist that permit us to process character strings, check for a character in a string, or use regular expressions (patterns) to pattern match character strings.

Finding a Character

The following function determines if a character string contains a particular character:

Function Name

```
(char *)strchr( string, c )
```

Description

This function tests to see if a particular character appears within a character string and returns its position in the string.

Argument List

(char *)string	The starting address of a string of characters—either the name of a character array, a character string, or a pointer to a character variable.
(char)c	A character expression. The specified string will be searched for this character.

Return Values

char *	The address of the matched character within the character string if the return value is greater than zero.

(char *)NULL   The specified character is not found in the char-
                           acter string.

The following program uses the strchr() function to find and print all
lines in its input that contain a BELL character:

program: findbell.c

```
1       #include <stdio.h>
2       #define BELL '\07'
3       #define ARRAY_SIZE 80
4
5       main()
6       {
7           char input[ARRAY_SIZE];
8           char *strchr(), *gets();
9
10          /* continually read lines from
11              terminal */
12          while ( gets(input) != NULL )
13          {
14              /* line with bell character */
15              if ( strchr( input, BELL ) > 0 )
16              {
17                  puts( input );
18              }
19          }
20      }
```

program input:

```
data data data data
data data data data
ERROR MESSAGE ^G FILE TOO LARGE
data data data data
data data data data
ERROR MESSAGE ^G NOT ENOUGH MEMORY
data data data data
ERROR MESSAGE ^G CANNOT READ FILE
```

program output:

```
ERROR MESSAGE ^G FILE TOO LARGE
ERROR MESSAGE ^G NOT ENOUGH MEMORY
ERROR MESSAGE ^G CANNOT READ FILE
```

- *In this example we have represented the* BELL *character with the symbol* ^G.
- *On some systems, the* strchr() *function is named* index().

Pattern Matching Using regcmp() and regex()

Often, we need to see if a character string contains either another character string or a particular pattern of characters (regular expression). Both of these operations can be performed through the regcmp() and regex() functions. The regcmp() function takes a supplied regular expression and prepares it for use by regex(), which actually does the comparison. These two functions are defined as follows:

Function Name

(char *)regcmp(string1, string2, ..., 0)

Description

This function compiles a regular expression into a character string that the function regex() uses for string comparison. This regular expression can be either a simple character string or a pattern containing regular characters and/or the special characters shown in Exhibit 10-7.

A character class matches a single character, if that character is listed in the character class. For example, the following character class matches a single character *if* it is lowercase alphabetic:

[abcdefghijklmnopqrstuvwxyz]

This can be abbreviated using a dash, to indicate a range of characters:

[a-z]

Argument List

(char *)string   The starting address of a character string that contains the pattern to be compiled.

0   Denotes the end of the list of regular expressions.

Return Values

char *   The address of the compiled regular expression. At runtime, the regcmp() function dynamically allocates the memory to store this compiled regular expression. The programmer is not required to declare an array for this purpose.

EXHIBIT 10-7

Special regular expression characters

Character	Meaning to regcmp
.	matches any character
^	beginning of string anchor
$	end of string anchor
*	zero or more occurrences of preceding character
+	one or more occurrences of preceding character
[list]	character class—matches a single character from specified list or range
(re)	group—used together with * or + to form repeated groups

Function Name

```
(char *)regex( re, string )
```

Description

This function compares a character string against a compiled regular expression and returns the address of the first position in the string not matched by the regular expression.

Argument List

(char *)re	The pointer to a compiled regular expression; return value from regcmp().
(char *)string	The address of a character string that will be inspected to see if it matches the supplied regular expression.

Return Values

char *	If the match is successful, then this is the address (within the character string) of the first character after the matched expression.
(char *)0	The return value if match is not successful.

The following program illustrates these two functions, using the character string "UNIX" as a regular expression.

program: findUNIX.c

```
 1    #include <stdio.h>
 2    #define ARRAY_SIZE 80
 3
 4    main()
 5    {
 6        char *cpointer, input[ARRAY_SIZE];
 7        char *regcmp(), *regex();
 8
 9        /* compile regular expression */
10        cpointer = regcmp( "UNIX", 0 );
11
12        /* continually read lines from terminal  */
13        while ( gets(input) != NULL )
14        {
15            /* line with word "UNIX" */
16            if ( regex( cpointer, input ) > 0 )
17            {
18                puts( input );
19            }
20        }
21    }
```

program output:

```
The UNIX operating system,
as they did in the UNIX editor 'ed.'
```

This example uses the simplest form of a regular expression—a sequence of characters. The function regex() searched for a substring in the same way that strchr() searches for a single character. Regular expressions, however, are considerably more powerful than simple character matches. Exhibit 10-8 shows some more complex examples of regular expressions and the character strings they match.

SUMMARY

In this chapter we have seen that arrays are frequently used in the C language for character string manipulation. The gets() and puts() functions permit us to read and write lines of characters. Numerous functions for searching and manipulating character strings are in the C language libraries.

An array name, when used by itself, forms an expression whose value is the starting address of the array. In multidimensional arrays we can access

EXHIBIT 10-8

Examples of regular expressions

Regular expression	Will match line that:
^frog	begins with word "frog"
frog$	ends with word "frog"
fr.g	contains a sequence of 4 characters where first two are "fr" and the last is "g"
fr.*g	contains a sequence of characters of any length that begins with "fr" and ends with "g" including the string "frg"
fr.+g	contains a sequence of four or more characters that begin with "fr" and end with "g"
fr[aeiou]g	contains a sequence of 4 characters where first two are "fr", the third is a vowel and the last is the letter "g"
fr[aeiou]+g	contains a sequence of characters where first two are "fr", followed by one or more vowels, followed by the letter "g"
^[a-z]$	contains only lowercase letters

subarrays through a similar technique. In Chapter 13 we will see how pointers and pointer arithmetic can be used to access the elements of any array.

EXERCISES

1. Write a program to multiply two two-dimensional arrays. The arrays may be of any size up to 50 rows by 50 columns.

2. Write a program to input a line of characters from the terminal and remove all blanks and punctuation.

3. Extend the above program to read in two lines of characters. Compare the two lines for equality. Consider the two lines the same if they differ only in blanks and punctuation.

4. Write a program to compute the sum of the rows, columns, and diagonals of a two-dimensional array.

5. Print the size of the array `array[10]`, which is declared in program `show.array.c`.

6. Modify the insertion sort program `insertion.c` to sort the list in descending order.

7. Program `bubble.c` can be made somewhat more efficient if we realize that, after the first complete iteration of the `for` loop (lines 27–39), the largest value is now at the end of the array. Similarly, after the second complete iteration the second largest value will be the next to last element, etc. Therefore, in each successive pass through the `while` loop (lines 23–40), it is unnecessary to check the lastmost element(s). Rewrite the program to take advantage of this.

8. As defined in this chapter, the `strncmp()` function compares the first n characters of two character strings. Write a program that emulates `strncmp()`, but ignores case (i.e., `Word` would be considered equivalent to `woRd`.)

9. Write a program that reads in two sentences and compares them. Define a word as any string of characters separated on the left and right by at least one blank (except for the beginning and end of sentence, of course). Test the two sentences to see if one sentence is a subset of the other (i.e., the larger sentence contains all of the words in the smaller sentence plus, optionally, some more).

10. Use `rand()%100` to generate 1,000 random numbers between one and 100. Count the number of occurrences of each number and print them out in order of frequency of occurrence.

11. Read in a character string. Count the number of one, two, three, four, and five or more character words. Output the results.

12. Modify the above program to print out its results in the form of a histogram, as follows:

```
Word Length                         Frequency
    1                               * * * * * * *
    2                               * * * *
    3                               * * * * * * * * *
    4                               * *
    5+                              * * * * * * * *
```

13. Read in a line of characters, then a number n. Delete the n rightmost words from the string and print it.

14. Write a regular expression that searches strings for the occurrence of a substring in the form of a telephone number:

$$xxx-yyy-zzzz$$

where: x, y, and z are all digits
and   the first three digits and following hyphen are
            optional

Using `regcmp()` and `regex()` write a program incorporating this regular expression.

CHAPTER 11

STRUCTURES AND UNIONS

OVERVIEW

This chapter discusses collections of unlike objects—structures and unions. In other programming languages, structures are called "records" and usually store large volumes of information in data files. Since they serve a similar purpose in the C language, they are closely associated with the standard I/O package, which permits us to open, close, read from, and write to files. The standard I/O package will be discussed in detail in Chapter 12.

In this chapter we also introduce the C language's typedef facility. It is a method of declaring synonyms for data types.

STRUCTURES

Structures are collections of unlike data types, just as arrays are collections of like data types. By defining a structure, the programmer derives a new data type composed of a collection of already-known data types and their names. This derivation allows us to treat related but unlike data types in an organized manner.

Structure Definition

In general, a structure within a C program is defined as follows:

```
struct  struct_type
{
        member_type        member_name;
        member_type        member_name;
        member_type        member_name;
        member_type        member_name;
};
```

Unlike the *declaration* of a variable or array, *defining* a structure causes no storage to be reserved. By defining a new structure, we increase the number of available data types beyond the built-in data types.

Assume, for example, that we need to keep information about 10,000 business accounts. The information is mixed in type; for each account we need:

account number   (`int`)

account type   (`short`)

name   (30 `char` array)

street address   (30 `char` array)

city/state/zip   (30 `char` array)

balance   (`long`)

last payment
date   (`long`)

For each account we will have one of these structures, defined as follows:

```
struct account
{
        int      acct_no;
        short    acct_type;
        char     name[30];
        char     street[30];
        char     city_state[30];
        long     balance;
        long     last_payment;
};
```

A variable of the new type is declared like this:

```
struct account input;
```

where the variable name is input and the data type is struct account.

To keep track of this information for 10 different accounts, we declare an array of 10 of these structures as follows:

```
struct account  vendors[10];
```

This allocates 10 of these structures; each structure is accessed like any array, by subscripting. Exhibit 11-1 shows a pictorial representation of vendors.

It is also possible to define a structure and declare a variable of that type at the same time:

```
struct account
{
        int      acct_no;
        short    acct_type;
        char     name[30];
        char     street[30];
        char     city_state[30];
        long     balance;
        long     last_payment;
} vendors;
```

This defines a new structure type, account, and declares a variable of that type named vendors. Other structures of the same type can also be declared. Defining a structure type and declaring a variable at the same time is not recommended because it detracts from the program's readability.

If wanted, the structure type may be omitted if the variable is declared when it is defined. However, the structure definition will not be available for declaring other variables of the same type.

EXHIBIT 11-1

Array vendors[]

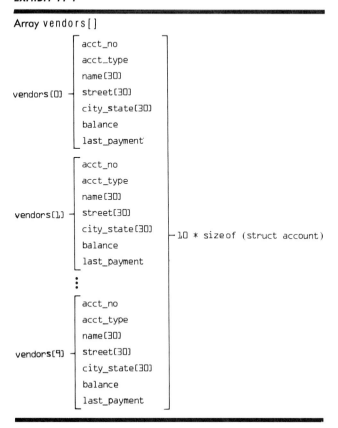

Referencing Structure Members

Individual structure members can be referenced with the dot (.) operator. For example, in the previous declaration of the variable input, the structure member named acct_no can be referred to as:

```
input.acct_no
```

On its left, the dot operator expects the name of a declared structure and on its right the name of one of the members of that structure. The three parts combine to form an expression whose value is the value of the structure member. To avoid ambiguity, the member name must be qualified with the variable name because there may be several structures declared of the same type. If an array of structures is declared:

```
struct account array[10];
```

then the account number in the third structure, for example, can be referenced through the following expression:

```
array[2].acct_no
```

where the name of the structure is:

```
array[2]
```

and the member name is:

```
acct_no
```

This is shown in Exhibit 11-2.

EXHIBIT 11-2

Referencing a structure member

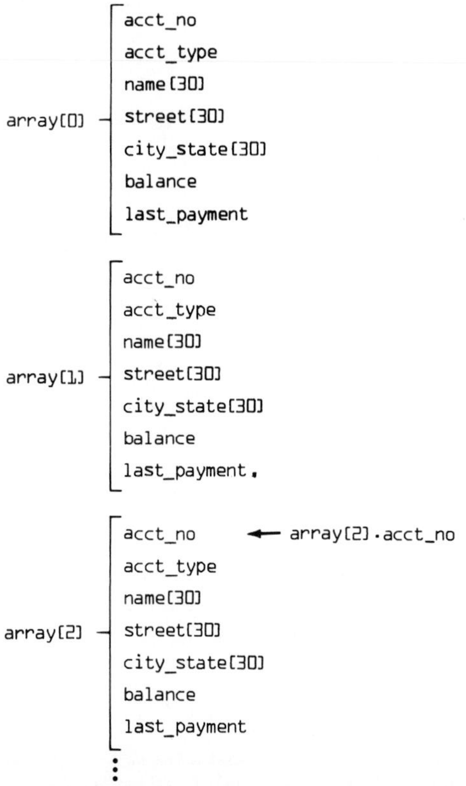

The following program illustrates the definition of a structure, the declaration of a structure variable, and the referencing of a member of the declared structure variable:

program: vendor.c

```
1    main()
2    {
3         /* define new variable type */
4         struct account
5         {
6             int      acct_no;
7             short    acct_type;
8             char     name[30];
9             char     street[30];
10            char     city_state[30];
11            long     balance;
12            long     last_payment;
13        };
14
15        /* declare variable of type
16            "struct account" */
17        struct account vendor;
18
19        printf( "Enter account number: " );
20        scanf( "%d", &vendor.acct_no );
21        printf( "Account number is %d\n",
22            vendor.acct_no );
23
24        /* part of program omitted */
25    }
```

program output:

```
Enter account number: 765
Account number is 765
```

In line 20 of this program, we see the address of (&) operator combined with a structure-member expression yielding the address of the member within that structure. This is passed to scanf() which populates the variable.

NESTED STRUCTURES

The C language allows one structure to be included inside another; these are known as *nested structures*. They usually exist only in more complicated programs or systems where the size of structures can be very large, or where an array of structures is desired inside one structure definition. To illustrate this, we will extend the structure type `account` to include information about the last three payments made to this vendor. We will keep the following information on each of these transactions:

invoice number   (int)

invoice date   (long)

amount of purchase   (long)

date paid   (long)

We can add this information to the `account` structure as follows:

```
struct history
{
        int     inv_no;
        long    inv_date;
        long    inv_amt;
        long    inv_paid;
};

struct account
{
        int     acct_no;
        short   acct_type;
        char    name[30];
        char    street[30];
        char    city_state[30];
        long    balance;
        long    last_payment;
        struct  history payments[3];
};
```

The structure type `account` has been redefined to contain an integer, a short integer, three character arrays, two long integers, and an array of three structures of type `history`. The names of these members are `acct_no`, `acct_type`, `name`, `street`, `city_state`, `balance`, `last_payment`, and `payments`. To access one of the members inside one of the `payments` structures, we first have to address the proper structure and then the proper member of that structure. For example, if we declare a variable of type `struct account` with the name `vendors`, as follows:

```
struct account vendors;
```

we can reference the invoice number of the most recent invoice through the following expression:

```
vendors.payments[0].inv_no
```

In this expression, the dot operator is used twice, and in each case, a structure name appears to the left of the operator and a member name appears to the right. Inside the structure named vendors is the member named payments. To look at the first member of payments[0], we reference the variable name inv_no. This expression represents the value of an integer and is illustrated by Exhibit 11-3.

MACHINE REPRESENTATION

The representation of a structure within the computer is machine dependent. Because of memory alignment restrictions for certain computers, integers and other data types may need to be aligned on a full- or half-word boundary. Thus,

EXHIBIT 11-3

Accessing members of nested structures

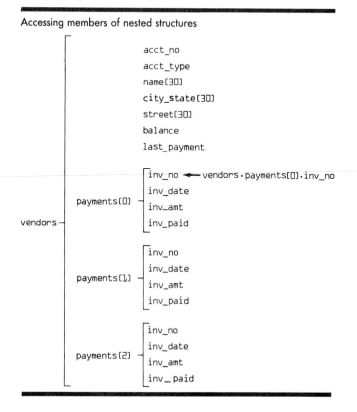

the size of the structure may not be equal to the sum of the sizes of its parts. The following program illustrates this:

program: sizeof.c

```
1     main()
2     {
3         struct sample
4         {
5             char      a;
6             int       b;
7             char      c;
8             float     d;
9         };
10
11        struct sample variable;
12
13        printf( "sizeof char=%d, int=%d, float=%d\n",
14            sizeof(char), sizeof(int),
15            sizeof(float) );
16
17        printf( "sizeof struct sample=%d\n",
18            sizeof(struct sample) );
19    }
```

program output:

```
sizeof char=1, int=2, float=4
sizeof struct sample=10
```

It is often necessary to reference a structure's size (e.g., when writing or reading a structure from a file). It is not usually correct to sum the sizes of each of the members and hard-code this number into the program. Use the sizeof operator, as in line 18 of the previous example.

TYPE DEFINITIONS

In the C language, a facility called typedef, exists for assigning synonyms to types. For example, the following statement creates a synonym;

```
typedef char *c_addr;
```

named c_addr that refers to a pointer to a character. From this statement on, pointers to characters can be declared as follows:

```
c_addr cptr1, cptr2, aptr;
```

This is not the same as using the C preprocessor to define a string. For example, if we assign a synonym with the following statement:

```
#define C_ADDR char *
```

and then use C_ADDR to declare three pointers to characters:

```
C_ADDR a, b, c;
```

the results will not be as intended. Since the C preprocessor only does text-string substitutions, after the substitution, the line will appear as:

```
char *a, b, c;
```

and will declare one pointer to a character and two other characters, instead of three pointers to characters.

Type Definitions: Purpose

Type definitions are used to increase program readability. The name chosen as the synonym can be more descriptive than just the type of the variable.

In general, type definitions appear as follows:

```
typedef already_known_data_type    new_type
```

where *already_known_data_type* is a previously defined data type, including the built-in data types (int, long, etc.), or defined structures, or even other newly created types that were defined through an earlier typedef. In the following example we define a new, more descriptive, type through a typedef statement:

```
typedef char *filename;

filename input, output;
```

By adding this type synonym, whoever reads the program is informed that input and output relate to filenames. A tradeoff does exist—we are leaving out information about the nature of the variable; this may or may not be important to the reader.

Type-Defining Structures

The typedef facility is often used to assign synonyms to structure types. The following code fragment illustrates this:

```
struct payments
{
        long inv_date;
        long inv_amt;
        int  inv_no;
};

typedef struct payments pay_t;

pay_t array_name[20];
```

This code assigns a synonym to the structure type payments and then declares an array of these structures named array_name. This is exactly equivalent to, and may be used interchangeably with

```
struct payments array_name[20];
```

The suffix added to the end of the typedef is a naming convention to inform the reader that pay_t is a typedef. If the reader needs to know the variable's exact structure, the typedef and the structure definition must be located. Others use the convention of capitalizing all synonyms. The typedef may also be assigned when the structure is defined. For example:

```
typedef struct payments
{
        long inv_date;
        long inv_amt;
        int  inv_no;
} pay_t;

pay_t array_name[20];
```

This simultaneously defines the new structure type (struct payments) and assigns a synonym (pay_t) for the type. From this point on the programmer can refer to either struct payments or pay_t; they have the same meaning.

OPERATIONS

The set of operations available for structures is limited. We have already seen the dot operator, used for referencing members of structures. The other operation that can be applied to structures is assignment. A relatively new addition to the language, structure assignment takes the contents of one structure and stores it in another structure of the same type. The following program illustrates this:

program: assign.c

```
 1     main()
 2     {
 3         struct sample
 4         {
 5             int a;
 6             float b;
 7             char c;
 8         };
 9
10         struct sample struct1, struct2;
11
12         struct1.a = 100;
13         struct1.b = 555.32;
14         struct1.c = 'G';
15
16         struct2 = struct1;
17
18         printf( "a = %d, b = %f, c = %c\n",
19                 struct2.a, struct2.b, struct2.c );
20     }
```

program output:

```
a = 100, b = 555.320007, c = G
```

Arithmetic, unary, bitwise, and relational operators are not permitted in an expression with a structure name; they are, however, permitted in the same expression as a member of a structure if the member is not, in turn, another structure.

BIT FIELDS

In Chapter 3, we saw how we could use bitwise operators to set, reset, or test an integer's bit pattern. It is possible to define a structure containing bit fields (variables that are less than the size of an integer). For example, to store five different flags in a structure, we can either declare five separate integers or use five 1-bit wide fields, as follows:

```
struct packemin
{
        int flag1 : 1;
        int flag2 : 1;
        int flag3 : 1;
```

```
          int flag4 : 1;
          int flag5 : 1;

          int invoice_no;
          float balance;
};
```

The first five fields will be stored together in the same integer, but are address-able separately. When any of these bit fields are referenced in an expression, they are treated as an integer. The general syntax for declaring bit fields within structures is:

```
struct struct type
{
          type bitfield_name :  length;
};
```

The following code, an excerpt from a real estate program, stores the results of a housing survey. This survey was conducted nationwide; the information is to be transmitted from one local office to another via telephone lines. Since signifi-cant amounts of data are to be transmitted, we will try to reduce transmission costs by reducing the size of the structure containing the information.

program: resurvey.c

```
 1     #define TRUE 1
 2     #define FALSE 0
 3
 4     main()
 5     {
 6         struct real_estate /* one per property */
 7         {
 8             int gas_heat : 1;
 9             int dishwasher : 1;
10             int garbage_disp : 1;
11             int garage : 1;
12             int central_air : 1;
13             int carpet : 1;
14
15             long value;
16             char street[40];
17             char city_state[40];
18             long zip;
19         };
20
```

(program continues)

```
21          int answer;
22          struct real_estate house;
23
24          /* part of program omitted */
25
26          printf( "gas heat? (y or n): " );
27          answer = getchar();
28          getchar(); /* throw away newline */
29          if ( answer == 'y' )
30          {
31              house.gas_heat = TRUE;
32          }
33
34          printf( "central air? (y or n): " );
35          answer = getchar();
36          if ( answer == 'y' )
37          {
38              house.central_air = TRUE;
39          }
40
41          /* part of program omitted */
42
43          printf( "GAS HEAT: %s\n",
44              house.gas_heat == TRUE ? "YES" : "NO" );
45          printf( "CENTRAL AIR: %s\n",
46              house.central_air == TRUE ? "YES" : "NO" );
47      }
```

program output:

```
gas heat? (y or n): y
central air? (y or n): n
GAS HEAT: YES
CENTRAL AIR: NO
```

Even small storage savings can result in large cost savings when many structures are transmitted. By using bit fields instead of integers we have reduced the size of the structure by more than five words.

UNIONS

Unions and structures have two common attributes: they are defined similarly, and they both define new variable types. However, unions and structures serve somewhat different purposes. Unlike structures, which contain a collection of different data types, unions contain one of several data types. The size of a structure is at least the sum of the sizes of all of the elements. The size of a union is the size of the largest of the elements contained in it. A union is defined as:

```
union union_type
{
        member_type member_name;
        member_type member_name;
        member_type member_name;
};
```

and a variable of this type is declared as:

```
union union_type variable_name;
```

A union is a mutually exclusive collection of variables of which only one should be used at any given time, because the variables share the same physical storage. For example, suppose we have two arrays, one needed at the beginning of the program and one at the end. As long as we do not need to use both of them at the same time, we can define a union consisting of the two arrays, as shown below:

```
union carrays
{
        char beginning_array[50];
        char ending_array[30];
};
```

and we can declare a variable of this type named `array_name` as follows:

```
union carrays array_name;
```

This union requires 50 bytes of storage, the length of the longest member. In this example, the members of the union are arrays; they could be integers, characters, floating-point variables, defined structures, or even other unions. Unions save some memory space compared to the alternative, separately declared members. Their use may help us fit larger programs into smaller machines, but little more than that. Unions are most helpful when they are used to conserve space in data files by reducing the size of a structure that appears many times in the file.

For example, unions may appear inside structures and can be used in the following manner:

```
struct add
{
        char a_address[2][30];
        long a_phone;
};
struct change
{
        char c_old_addr[2][30];
        char c_new_addr[2][30];
        long c_old_phone;
        long c_new_phone;
};

struct delete
{
        long d_phone;
};

struct transaction
{
        char t_type;
        int acct_no;
        char name[30];
        /* redefined based on transaction type
            'a' _ struct add
            'c' _ struct change
            'd' _ struct delete          */
        union info
        {
                struct add i_add;
                struct change i_change;
                struct delete i_delete;
        } t_info;
};

struct transaction input;
```

This could be a transaction file's layout. In each structure stored in the file, there is some fixed information: the name of the account, the account number, and the transaction type. How the rest of the record is viewed depends on the transaction type's value. If the transaction type is 'a', then the structure named i_add defines the rest of the structure; if the value of the transaction type is 'c', then the rest of the structure looks like a structure of type struct change and is accessed through the member name i_change. Similar results stem from a transaction type of 'd'.

Union members are accessed in the same manner as structure members. For example, if the transaction type is 'd', we access the structure i_delete by using the following expression:

```
input.t_info.i_delete
```

In this expression, we are using the dot operator twice. Each time, a structure or union name appears to its left and a member name appears to its right. This is only a reference to the structure i_delete. If we need to access the field inside i_delete, we reference it by again applying the dot operator as in the following expression:

```
input.t_info.i_delete.d_phone
```

The type of this expression is long integer; its value is the phone number of the account to be deleted.

SUMMARY

In this chapter we discussed two additional methods for organizing data—structures and unions. Unlike arrays, which are collections of objects of a single type, structures and unions are collections of objects of different types. Of the two data types, structures are more commonly used; unions are primarily a method of saving memory and must be used carefully.

In other programming languages, structures are called records and, as the name implies, are closely related to the process of reading from and writing to files. To access the members of a structure (or union) we introduced a new operator, the dot (.) operator. In Chapter 13 we will see how pointers can be used to access structure members.

EXERCISES

1. Write a program that uses a structure to emulate a simple library card catalog. Entries are stored by:
Title (80 characters)
Author's last name (20 characters)
Author's first name (20 characters)
Date of publication (mm/dd/yy)
Populate 10 instances of the structure by prompting for the information at the terminal.

2. Expand the above program to print out a book title when given an author's last name. (Remember to account for invalid inquiries.)

3. Expand the program from Exercise 2 to account for the following situations:
   a. One author has multiple titles that may be distinguished by requesting the year of publication. (Only prompt for year of publication if an author has multiple publications.)
   b. Two authors have the same last name and must be distinguished by first name.

4. Using the "library" structure, expand the program to search for all books with a given keyword in the title.

5. Expand the program to search for all books published in a given year.

6. We are interested in keeping weather information for the three most recent days. At the end of each day we input the weather data for that day. The data for each of the two previous days is "bumped down" in the array of structures. The data from three days ago is lost. Write a program to implement this algorithm. Keep the following data for each day:
   Date
      Month
      Day
      Year
   High temperature
   Low temperature
   Maximum wind speed
   Precipitation (inches)
   Notes (80 characters)

7. Using the above array of structures, write a program to print out the date with the highest temperature.

5

MORE ON I/O, POINTERS, FUNCTIONS, AND VARIABLES

CHAPTER 12

THE STANDARD I/O PACKAGE

OVERVIEW

Within the C language are several functions used to read from and write to files. These functions are not formally part of the C language, but reside in a separate library, the standard I/O package. In this chapter we will discuss functions for opening and closing files, functions that read from and write to a file sequentially, and functions that permit random access to a file.

THE STANDARD I/O PACKAGE

So far, all our sample programs have written data to the standard output and read data from the standard input (in both cases, the terminal). As long as we are only accessing small amounts of data in the form of simple variables and character strings this type of I/O is sufficient. However, large amounts of data are generally stored in files. To perform I/O from and to files we need the services of the functions in the *standard I/O package*.

Access to files generally requires four basic operations:

open	This allows access to a file and establishes the position, or offset, in the file.
close	This ends access to the file. When access to a file is complete, it should be closed. The number of files that a running program can have open at any time is limited; by closing files properly these limited facilities can be used more intelligently.
read	This gets information from the file, either in the form of character strings, or in the form of data (combined integers, characters, floating-point numbers, and structures).
write	This adds information to the file or replaces information already in the file.

Opening a File: fopen( )

The standard I/O package function used to open a file is named `fopen()`. It returns a pointer to a structure that has been type-defined in the header file `stdio.h`. This structure contains information about the opening of the file and buffering information that is used while the file is open. The return value must be saved; all the other functions in the package require it as an argument. The `fopen()` function is formally defined as follows:

Function Name

`(FILE *)fopen( file_name, mode)`

Description

   This function opens a file and establishes a current offset within the file. This must be done before attempts are made to read from or write to the file.

Argument List

`(char *) file_name`   The starting address of a character string describing the name of the file. This can be either a character string, an array name, or a character pointer return value of a library function.

(char *) mode   This describes the actions to be performed on the file and governs the initial offset in the file. The modes for opening a file are:

r   Opened for reading. Positioned at the beginning of the file.

w   Opened for writing. The assumption is that the file is to be created. If the file does not exist, it is created; if it does exist, it is truncated (size of file is reduced to zero). Positioned at the beginning of the file.

a   Opened for writing. Same rules apply as for mode w except that initial positioning is at the end of the file and the file is not truncated.

r+   Opened for update. File is available for reading and writing but is not truncated. Initial positioning is at the start of the file.

w+   Opened for update. File is available for reading and writing and is truncated if the file exists. If the file does not exist, it is created. Initial positioning is at the start of the file.

a+   Opened for update. File is available for reading and writing, is not truncated, and initial positioning is at the end of the file.

Return Values

FILE *   Returned for successful open. Value is pointer to a structure that contains file opening and buffering information. The return value is used to identify the file for performing input and output.

(FILE *)NULL   Returned if the file cannot be opened. Occurs if the file does not exist and is being opened other than for writing, or if the user is opening a new file for writing, but does not have permission to create a file with the supplied filename.

The return value from the function is always kept and usually checked for errors as illustrated on the next page:

```
FILE *read_ptr;

read_ptr = fopen( "frog", "r" );
if ( read_ptr == (FILE *)NULL )
{
        /* error processing for failure to
           open file */
}
```

where f rog is the name of the file being opened for reading. You should note that both arguments are represented here by character string expressions, but they can also come from array names or pointers to character strings.

Closing a File: fclose()

When a program has completed its use of a file, the file should be closed using the fclose() function. This function is defined formally as follows:

Function Name

(int) fclose(stream)

Description

    This function closes the specified file and releases any overhead used in maintaining the file, permitting the memory that held this information to be used for opening another file. If a program exits without closing a file, the system will automatically close the file through proper calls to fclose().

Argument List

(FILE *) stream   This is the return value from fopen() and is used to identify which file is to be closed.

Return Values

0   This means a successful file closing.

EOF   This means an error was encountered when closing the file, possibly because the file had already been closed or an improper argument was supplied.

    The following program illustrates how these two library functions are used:

program: openclose.c

```
1    #include <stdio.h>
2
3    main()
4    {
5        FILE *ioptr;
6
7        ioptr = fopen( "tempfile", "w" );
8        if ( ioptr == (FILE *)NULL )
9        {
10           printf( "Cannot open tempfile\n" );
11           exit(1);
12       }
13
14       /* part of program omitted */
15
16       close( ioptr );
17   }
```

In C language programs you will often see the file opening embedded within the condition of the i f statement; it is separated here for clarity.

Reading from a File

Through the getchar(), scanf(), and gets() functions, we have already seen several methods of reading information from the terminal. Analogous functions read information from open files. These functions are fgetc(), fscanf(), and fgets(). There are, however, subtle differences between these functions and their terminal counterparts of which you should be aware. For example, the gets() function does not include the terminating newline character, but the fgets() function does. This is illustrated in Exhibit 12-1. At least one additional argument is required for each of these calls—the identification of the file from which the information is being read. This identification is the fopen() function call's saved return value.

The following program uses the fgets() function to read lines from a file and then print them on the standard output (the terminal) followed by a count of the number of lines in the file:

program: icat.c

```
1    #include <stdio.h>
2
3    main()
```

(*program continues*)

```
 4     {
 5          char input_line[256], filename[256];
 6          int counter;
 7          FILE *ioptr;
 8
 9          printf( "Enter filename: " );
10          gets( filename );
11
12          /* open input file */
13          ioptr = fopen( filename, "r" );
14          if ( ioptr == (FILE *)NULL )
15          {
16              printf( "Cannot open %s\n", filename );
17              exit(1);
18          }
19
20          counter = 0;
21          /* read lines from input file; write them to
22              terminal */
23          while ( fgets( input_line, 256, ioptr ) != (FILE *)NULL )
24          {
25              printf( "%s", input_line );
26              counter++;
27          }
28
29          printf( "\nTOTAL LINES = %d\n", counter );
30          close( ioptr );
31     }
```

EXHIBIT 12-1

Using the functions gets() and fgets() to read input into arrays char and fchar, respectively

Reading from terminal with gets ( ):

	w	o.	r	d	\0
char	[0]	[1]	[2]	[3]	[4]

Reading from file with fgets ( ):

	w	o	r	d	\n	\0
fchar	[0]	[1]	[2]	[3]	[4]	[5]

program output:

```
Enter filename: frog
This is the contents of the file named
"frog." It doesn't contain much useful
information but it lets us test our
file printing program.

TOTAL LINES = 4
```

A few points should be noted about this example. Two functions request string input: gets() and fgets(). The first gets a character string from the terminal; the second gets the string from a file. Furthermore, the fgets() function requires the size of the destination array as an argument. It will store a maximum of that many characters, even if the input exceeds the array size. For this reason, it is safer to use fgets() than gets(). But what if the application requires using a terminal for input? If terminal input is necessary, it is still possible to use the fgets() function. Assign the name stdin to the stream argument. The name stdin as well as stdout and stderr (for error message output) are defined in the included file stdio.h. Thus, the function call on line 10 could be rewritten as follows:

```
fgets( filename, 256, stdin );
```

To reference the name stdin, it is necessary to include the file stdio.h, as in line 1 of the program icat.c.

Writing to a File
In the previous section we read from files using functions analogous to those used for terminal input. Similarly, three functions for writing to files exist and are directly analogous to functions used for terminal output. These functions are fputc(), fprintf(), and fputs(). Like the input functions, they require an additional argument—an output file identification. The fputs() function does not append a newline to its output (as does puts()), because its complementary function, fgets(), has already stored the newline character in the string. This is illustrated in Exhibit 12-2.

Reading and Writing Structures
File input and output frequently involves reading and writing structures. The two library functions fread() and fwrite() do this. They read and write a fixed number of bytes from or to a file. They are defined formally as follows:

Function Name

```
(int) fread( dest, size, items, stream )
```

EXHIBIT 12-2

Using the two functions puts ( ) and fputs ( )

Writing array chars (see Exhibit 12-1) to
the terminal using puts ( ) yields:

line 1:	w o r d
line 2:	← cursor located here because
	puts ( ) adds \ n to output

on the terminal.

Writing array fchar (see Exhibit 12-1) to
a file using fputs ( ) yields:

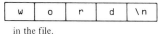

w	o	r	d	\ n

in the file.

Description

This function reads a fixed number of bytes from a file and stores it into a structure whose address is supplied to the function.

Argument List

(char *) dest	This is the destination structure's address. It should be a pointer to a structure type cast to look like a pointer to a character, if necessary.
(int) size	This is the size of the structure to be read. It is multiplied by the number of items to calculate the number of bytes to be read from the file.
(int) items	This is the number of structures to be read. Multiple structures may be read through one call to fread ( ). It is the programmer's responsibility to ensure that the destination is large enough to hold the information.
(FILE *) stream	This is the return value from the fopen ( ) function call identifying the file from which the data is to be read.

Return Values

int	If successful, this is the number of items actually read. This number may be less than the requested number of items; if it is, then the number of structures in the file was less than the number requested and it may be assumed that another read is not necessary.

0   This is the end-of-file return value. No items were read from the file.

Function Name

```
(int) fwrite( ptr, size, items, stream )
```

Description

This function writes a fixed number of bytes to a file. It is normally used to write a structure or an array of structures to an output file.

Argument List

```
(char *) ptr
```
                   This is the address of the source for the output—the address in memory of the structure or array of structures being written to the file.

```
(int) size
```
                   This is the size of one of the structures being written out to the file. This number will be multiplied by the number of items to calculate the number of bytes to be written to the file.

```
(int) items
```
                   This is the number of structures to be written to the file.

```
(FILE *) stream
```
                   This is the output file's identification. It is the return value from the call to `fopen()`, or may be `stdout` or `stderr`.

Return Values

```
int
```
                   If successful, it is the number of items written to the file.

0   This means an unsuccessful write. It may be caused by one of several operating system problems, including a full disk.

The following program represents a continuation of the real estate program (`re.survey.c`) introduced in Chapter 11. Assume the program has been previously revised to create a file named `housefile` and to write its results to this file using `fwrite()`. The program below opens `housefile` for input, reads the stored structures using `fread()`, and prints the information on the terminal:

program: print.c

```
1    #include <stdio.h>
2    #define YES 1
3    #define NO 0
4
5    main()
6    {
7        FILE *inptr;
8        struct property
9        {
10           int gas_heat : 1;
11           int air_cond : 1;
12           int dishwash : 1;
13           int wash_dry : 1;
14           int block    : 8; /* 8 bits */
15           char lot[6];
16       };
17
18       struct property input;
19
20       inptr = fopen( "housefile", "r" );
21       if ( inptr == (FILE *)NULL )
22       {
23           printf( "Cannot open housefile\n" );
24           exit(1);
25       }
26
27       while ( fread( &input, sizeof(struct property),
28               1, inptr ) != 0 )
29       {
30           printf( "BLOCK: %d LOT: %s\n",
31               input.block, input.lot );
32
33           printf( "GAS HEAT: %s   CENTRAL AIR: %s\n",
34               input.gas_heat == YES ? "YES" : "NO",
35               input.air_cond == YES ? "YES" : "NO" );
36
37           printf( "DISHWASHER: %s   WASHER-DRYER %s\n",
38               input.dishwash == YES ? "YES" : "NO",
39               input.wash_dry == YES ? "YES" : "NO" );
40
41           printf( "**********\n" );
42       }
43   }
```

program output:

```
BLOCK: 23  LOT:  5a
GAS HEAT: YES    CENTRAL AIR: YES
DISHWASHER: NO   WASHER-DRYER YES
* * * * * * * * *
BLOCK: 33  LOT: 22a
GAS HEAT: NO   CENTRAL AIR: YES
DISHWASHER: YES   WASHER-DRYER YES
* * * * * * * * * *
BLOCK: 44  LOT: 15c
GAS HEAT: NO    CENTRAL AIR: NO
DISHWASHER: NO   WASHER-DRYER YES
* * * * * * * * * *
```

Random Access: fseek()

It is possible to access any position randomly within a file using the fseek() function. This function expects three arguments and is defined formally as follows:

Function Name

```
(int) fseek( stream, offset, where )
```

Description

This function changes the current position within a file by changing the offset associated with the opening of the file. Positioning can be specified as a number of bytes from the beginning of the file, from the end of the file, or from the current position in the file. If a file is positioned past the actual end of the file and a write is performed, then the size of the file will be extended and a (logical) gap will be placed in the file. If a read is attempted past the end of the file, an error will occur.

Argument List

(FILE *) stream	This identifies the file in which the current offset is to be changed. Should be the saved return value from the file's fopen().
(long) offset	The offset, in bytes, either from the start of the file, the end of the file, or from the current position.
(int) where	Defines the context for the second argument. Legal values are 0, 1, or 2 indicating from the beginning, from the current position, or from the end of the file, respectively.

Return Values

0   This means a successful seek.

!= 0   This means we couldn't seek to the specified lo-
                           cation in the file. Possibly out of range or an argu-
                           ment was incorrectly specified.

The current offset in the file can be determined using the ftell() function.
This function expects only one argument, the return value from the fopen()
of the file whose offset is needed.

These functions can be used to form a type of relative structure addressing
in a file. For example, if we have a file where several thousand structures of a
particular type are stored, and we need to access the 234th structure in this file,
then we can use the following program fragment:

```
new_offset = 234 * sizeof(struct mystruct);

if ( fseek( ioptr, new_offset, 0 ) == 0 )
{
        /* seek was successful; doesn't necessarily
           mean that record is there or that it has
           valuable information in it */

        if ( fread( myarray, sizeof(struct mystruct),
                       1, ioptr ) != 0 )
        {
                /* successful read.  must now perform
                   validity check on the structure */
        }
}
```

Just because we can seek to the desired location does not necessarily imply that
we are still in a valid part of the file. It is possible that we have "seeked" past
the end of the file. If so, attempting a write will create a logical gap in the file. If
we then try to read from this gap, we will read a null-filled structure. Thus, after
reading a structure, we should perform some validity checking on the structure's contents itself. This is usually done using a flag within the structure; the
flag is set if the structure contains valid information.

SUMMARY

Functions to read from and write to files are not formally part of the C language
but reside in an external library called the standard I/O package. This library,

however, is so standardized across all implementations of C language that, for all practical purposes, it can be thought of as part of the language. It is the responsibility of the command used to compile programs and the link editor to link the source program with these I/O functions. Since many of these functions reference defined symbolic constants, it is necessary to include their definitions through the

```
#include <stdio.h>
```

preprocessor directive. The C language libraries have facilities for reading, writing, and appending files. The mode of access is specified when the file is opened.

We introduced the `fgets()` and `fputs()` functions which are analogous to the terminal I/O functions `gets()` and `puts()` with subtle differences. The `fgets()` function stores the newline character as part of the string, while `gets()` does not. Consequently, `fputs()` does not append a newline character when it is writing, whereas `puts()` does.

We also defined the file I/O functions `fread()` and `fwrite()`. They have the important task of reading and writing structures.

EXERCISES

1. Generate 100 random numbers between one and 100 and store them in a file. Print the file.

2. Print the above file in descending sorted order.

3. Print the above file in ascending sorted order but with all duplicate numbers removed. How many of the 100 numbers were unique?

4. Create a file where each record in the file contains a character string of one to 80 characters. Read in the file and print it out right justified.

5. A concordance is a method for analyzing a piece of text. One aspect of a concordance is a list of the frequency with which words appear in the text. Write a program to read in a file containing a block of text and print out the frequency (sorted lowest to highest) of occurrence for each word in the text.

6. Another method for analyzing text is to determine the length of the sentences in the text. (This is one measure of readability level.) Using the text file from above, count the number of words in each sentence and print out a frequency distribution of the number of sentences by length. What is the average sentence length?

7. Using the same file as in Exercises 5 and 6, remove all four-letter words from the file and write the result to a new file.

8. Create a file containing 25 strings. Write a program to randomly select strings and print them until all strings are printed. No string may be printed more than once.

9. The standard deviation of a sample is given by the following formula:

$$S = \sqrt{\frac{\Sigma(x_i - \bar{x})^2}{n - 1}}$$

where:

    x_i are the individual sample values

    $\bar{x}$ is the sample mean

    n is the number of values in the sample

Create a file of 50 random numbers between one and 100 and calculate the standard deviation of the numbers. (You will need to read through the numbers twice, first to calculate the mean, then to find the differences from the mean.)

10. There is a second method for calculating standard deviation that does not require reading the numbers twice. Using the same file as in the previous exercise recalculate the standard deviation using the formula:

$$S = \frac{1}{n - 1} \sqrt{n\Sigma x_i^2 - (\Sigma x_i)^2}$$

Note that the mean is never calculated.

CHAPTER 13

POINTERS II

OVERVIEW

In previous chapters we have discussed addresses, pointer variables, arrays, and structures. In this chapter we will integrate these topics by discussing arithmetic operations on pointer variables. Using pointer arithmetic we will demonstrate techniques for manipulating arrays using pointer variables.

We also introduce the arrow operator as a method for accessing structure members using pointers. Finally, we show how arguments may be passed to a program through the invoking command line.

REVIEW: POINTERS AND ADDRESSES

In previous chapters, we have seen several expressions whose value is an address: a character string, the name of an array, and a variable name preceded by the & operator. We introduced a variable type that holds addresses, the pointer variable, and encountered several functions whose argument must be an address.

Pointer variables are declared by preceding the variable name with an asterisk, as follows:

```
char *cpointer, another_character, *xpointer;
```

This declaration declares two pointers to characters and a character variable.

In Chapter 9 we discussed the pointer dereferencing operator. This operator, when applied to a pointer variable, creates an expression with the value of the variable whose address is in the pointer variable, and not the value of the pointer itself. The following short program uses the dereferencing operator:

program: simple.ptr.c

```
 1    main()
 2    {
 3          int number, *i_pointer;
 4
 5          number = 5;
 6
 7          i_pointer = &number;
 8          printf( "The value of 'number' is %d\n",
 9                    *i_pointer );
10    }
```

program output:

```
The value of 'number' is 5
```

Exhibit 13-1 illustrates the relationship between number and *i_pointer.

EXHIBIT 13-1
___

Using the dereferencing operator

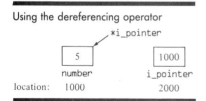

location: 1000   2000

POINTER OPERATIONS

In Chapter 9 we learned that declaring the pointer type properly is important; a pointer to a character is different from a pointer to an integer. We illustrate this in the following program by printing the type and size of three expressions that use the dereferencing operator:

program: sizeof.star.c

```
1    main()
2    {
3         int *i_pointer, i;
4         char *c_pointer, c;
5         double *d_pointer, d;
6
7         i_pointer = &i;
8         c_pointer = &c;
9         d_pointer = &d;
10        *i_pointer = 12;
11        *c_pointer = 'x';
12        *d_pointer = 123.45;
13
14        printf( "sizeof( *char_pointer ) is %d\n",
15                 sizeof (*c_pointer) );
16
17        printf( "sizeof( *int_pointer ) is %d\n",
18                 sizeof (*i_pointer) );
19
20        printf( "sizeof( *double_pointer ) is %d\n",
21                 sizeof (*d_pointer) );
22    }
23
```

program output:

```
sizeof( *char_pointer ) is 1
sizeof( *int_pointer ) is 2
sizeof( *double_pointer ) is 8
```

However, remember that all pointer variables are themselves one word long.
    Be careful when declaring the pointer type.

- The pointer type affects the size and type of the resulting dereferenced expression.

- The pointer type affects computations performed on the pointer itself.

If we add 2 to a pointer variable's value, then the C language adds 2 times the size of the variable pointed to by the pointer. The following example illustrates this.

program: point.add.c

```
 1   main()
 2   {
 3        double array[10], *d_pointer;
 4
 5        d_pointer = array;
 6
 7        printf( "initial value of d_pointer = %x\n",
 8                d_pointer );
 9
10        d_pointer += 1;
11
12        printf( "incremented value of d_pointer = %x\n",
13                d_pointer );
14   }
```

program output:

```
initial value of d_pointer = fef8
incremented value of d_pointer = ff00
```

In line 5 of this example, we set the pointer variable equal to the starting address of the array named array; in line 10, we add 1 to the pointer variable's value. The pointer's value (the address it contains) has now been incremented by 8, the size of a double-precision variable. (This is illustrated in Exhibit 13-2.) The pointer now points to the next element in the array (we are guaranteed that

---

EXHIBIT 13-2

The effect of scaling in pointer arithmetic

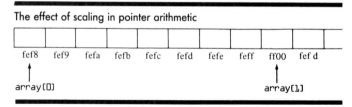

arrays are stored contiguously in memory). In fact, using square brackets in an array reference is only a notational convenience; when the compiler encounters the expression:

```
array[subscript]
```

it translates it into the following expression:

```
*(array + subscript)
```

This works properly because the expression

```
array
```

when used by itself has the *value* of the starting address of the array and has a *type* equal to that of a pointer to one of its elements. The only difference between an array name expression and a pointer variable is that the name of an array cannot appear on the left side of an assignment statement whereas a pointer variable can.

This is an extremely powerful feature of the C language and is worth stating again:

> *When performing arithmetic on a pointer, or on an expression with the same type as a pointer, the arithmetic is scaled by the size of what the object points to.*

In general, pointer arithmetic is restricted to only a few basic operations:

- *adding a constant value to a pointer*
  This is useful when processing arrays of objects. Each increment of the pointer variable causes the variable to point to the next of the objects in line, or to the next element in the array.

- *subtracting a constant value from a pointer*
  This has the opposite effect of adding a constant to a pointer.

- *subtracting the value of one pointer from another of the same type*
  This is used to find out how *many* elements are in memory between the two pointers. For example, if we have two pointers, one pointing to the beginning of an array and another pointing to the end of the array, we can determine how many elements are in the array by subtracting one from the other.

Array Processing Using Pointers

We now see there are two methods for accessing an array's elements—standard array notation and pointer arithmetic. Array notation is a form of *relative addressing.* The compiler treats the subscript as a relative offset from the beginning of the array. When we set a pointer variable equal to the start of an array and increment it to find the next element, we are using *absolute addressing*—we are supplying the element's exact location and not its relative position from the beginning of the array. As a consequence, accessing arrays through pointers is marginally faster than using array notation. But this is not the primary reason we use pointers. Pointers are used because they give us better control over array processing. They also allow us to perform certain functions that are extremely difficult with array notation. Some of these will be discussed later in this chapter.

The following program uses pointers to populate an array of numbers and then array notation to print the values from the array:

program: fill.array.c

```
 1    main()
 2    {
 3         double *d_pointer, *e_pointer, d_array[6];
 4         double sqrt();
 5         int loop_cntl;
 6
 7         /* fill using pointers */
 8         d_pointer = d_array;
 9         e_pointer = &d_array[5];
10         loop_cntl = 0;
11
12         while ( d_pointer <= e_pointer )
13         {
14              *d_pointer = sqrt( (double)loop_cntl );
15              loop_cntl++;
16              d_pointer++;
17         }
18
19         /* print using array notation */
20         for ( loop_cntl = 0; loop_cntl < 6; loop_cntl++ )
21         {
22              printf( "x = %d, sqrt(x) = %lf\n",
23                   loop_cntl, d_array[loop_cntl] );
24         }
25    }
```

program output:

```
x = 0,  sqrt(x) = 0.000000
x = 1,  sqrt(x) = 1.000000
x = 2,  sqrt(x) = 1.414214
x = 3,  sqrt(x) = 1.732051
x = 4,  sqrt(x) = 2.000000
x = 5,  sqrt(x) = 2.236068
```

Array Processing: Example—Selection Sort

The selection sort is one of the simpler (and least efficient) methods for sorting numbers stored in an array into increasing order. The array is scanned and the smallest number in the array is moved to the first position in the array, swapping it with the value currently there. Then the second smallest number is found and swapped with the array's second element, and so on. The logic flow for this sort is:

```
for ( each element in the array )
{
          look at all which follow element
                   for the smallest value;
          swap the element with the smallest
                   value;
}
```

A C program to implement this sorting method is shown below:

program: select.c

```
1     #include "array.h"
2
3     main()
4     {
5          int sub, array[ARRAY_SIZE], temp, saved, swap;
6          int *iptr, *jptr, *eptr, *sptr;
7
8          randomize( array );
9
10         printarray( "UNSORTED LIST", array );
11
12         /* selection sort */
13         eptr = &array[ARRAY_SIZE - 1];
14
```

(program continues)

```
15          for( iptr = array; iptr <= eptr; iptr++ )
16          {
17              swap = NO;
18              saved = *iptr;
19              for ( jptr = iptr + 1; jptr <= eptr; jptr++ )
20              {
21                  if( *jptr <= saved )
22                  {
23                      swap = YES;
24                      saved = *jptr;
25                      sptr = jptr;
26                  }
27              }
28              if ( swap == YES )
29              {
30                  temp = *iptr;
31                  *iptr = *sptr;
32                  *sptr = temp;
33              }
34          }
35
36          /* print sorted array */
37          printarray( "SORTED LIST", array );
38      }
```

program output:

```
UNSORTED LIST     SORTED LIST
16838             5627
5758              5758
10113             10113
17515             16838
31051             17515
5627              31051
```

In this example, several program elements are placed in include files and functions. The #define statements are put in an include file named array.h located in the same directory as the C source file(s). The contents of this file are:

```
#define ARRAY_SIZE       6
#define NO               0
#define YES              1
```

It defines the three values used in the `main()` function. Two routines, `randomize()` and `printarray()`, which populate the array with random values and print the array, have been turned into functions and stored in a separate source file. These functions will be explained more fully in Chapter 14 when we discuss the relationship among pointers, arrays, and functions.

We use pointer variables to reference elements in the array. The pointer `iptr` scans slowly through the array and the pointer `jptr` checks for elements in the array that have a lower value than the element `iptr` points to. When we find an element with a lower value than `*iptr`, we save both its value (for later comparisons) and its location in the "save pointer" named `sptr`.

We could have written an equivalent program using array notation. In fact, most problems can be solved by either method; it's up to the programmer to choose which method is preferable. Some other kinds of problems are, however, much harder to solve using array notation. This will become more evident when we talk about dynamic memory allocation later in this chapter.

The Relationship of Pointers to Arrays

Single-dimensional arrays   As we have seen, for every array notation expression there is an equivalent expression using pointers. In general any expression of the type:

```
array_name[subscript]
```

is translated by the compiler into an expression of the type:

```
*(array + subscript)
```

The parentheses are necessary here to force the addition of the two operands before applying the pointer dereferencing operator.

Two-dimensional arrays   If we have a two-dimensional integer array declared:

```
int  twodim[5][20];
```

and we only reference the first dimension:

```
twodim[5]
```

as an expression, then we are referring to a single-dimensional array of 20 integers. If this expression is used in an arithmetic expression, the arithmetic is scaled by the size of an integer. If we use the expression:

```
twodim
```

within an arithmetic expression, its value is the starting address of the two-dimensional array and the arithmetic is scaled by the size of one of the single-dimensional arrays. So, the expression

```
( twodim + 1 )
```

refers to the starting address of the second array of 20 integers and the expression:

```
*( twodim + 1 )
```

refers to the array itself. If *this* expression is used within an arithmetic expression, then the arithmetic is scaled by the size of an integer. This expression is the same as the following array notation:

```
twodim[1]
```

Given the two equivalent expressions:

```
twodim[1]          *(twodim + 1)
```

both expressions have the array's starting address as their value. We can reference an element in the two-dimensional array in at least four possible ways:

```
*( *(twodim + 1) + 3 )
```

or by using a mixture of the two notations:

```
*( twodim[1] + 3 )      or      *(twodim + 1)[3]
```

or by using strict array notation:

```
twodim[1][3]
```

All these expressions are equivalent. Some may be more readable than others, but the choice of notation is up to the programmer who should choose the notation that is most understandable.

Pointers and Dynamic Memory Allocation

Pointers may be used profitably in conjunction with the calloc() library function. This function allocates storage at run time assuming that the programmer will format it using pointers. The function is defined as follows:

Function Name

```
(char *) calloc( number_elements, element_size )
```

Description

This function allocates space dynamically for an array described by its arguments. The space allocated is cleared.

Argument List

unsigned int number_elements	This will be multiplied by the size of an element to determine the amount of storage to allocate. It should be used in the application program as the upper boundary for the dynamically allocated array.
unsigned int element_size	This is the size of an element. The sizeof operator is usually used here to ensure portability and that the size of a structure is correctly represented.

Return Values

char *	This is the newly allocated memory's starting address. It should be saved in a pointer to a character variable and then converted to a pointer of the proper type. This value is also needed if the programmer wishes to deallocate the memory using the free() library function.
(char *) NULL	This is returned if the process has already used up all available memory. How this is determined depends on the hardware and the operating system.

The following program illustrates the use of calloc() function:

program: dmemory.c

```
1
2   #include <stdio.h>
3
4   main()
5   {
6        char *cpointer, *calloc();
7        int *spointer, *epointer, *current;
8
9        /* allocate memory for an array of 7
10            integers */
11       cpointer = calloc( 7, sizeof(int) );
12       spointer = (int *)cpointer;
13       epointer = ( spointer + 7 );
```

(program continues)

```
14
15          /* fill the array with random numbers */
16          for ( current = spointer; current < epointer ;
17               current++ )
18          {
19               *current = rand();
20               printf( "%d\n", *current );
21          }
22
23          /* free allocated memory */
24          free ( cpointer );
25          }
```

program output:

```
16838
5758
10113
17515
31051
5627
23010
```

Why have we chosen to use `calloc()` rather than declare an array of seven integers? We see that the array's size is represented as an argument to `calloc()` rather than as a constant expression at compile time. It is therefore possible to "declare" an array of arbitrary size at run time by allocating the memory for it dynamically.

Changing the Size—realloc()

To change a piece of dynamically allocated memory's size we use the `realloc()` library function. The `realloc()` function is defined as follows:

Function Name

```
(char *) realloc( ptr, size )
```

Description

This function changes the size of an allocated block of memory that was allocated using `calloc()` or a previous call to `realloc()`.

Argument List

`char * ptr`   This is the return value from the last call to `calloc()` or `realloc()`. This block may still

be in use or it may have been deallocated using
free(). If it has been deallocated, it is manda-
tory that no other calls to one of the allocation
functions were made between the time the block
was freed and this call.

unsigned int size

This is the size of the new region in bytes. This
field should be an unsigned integer.

Return Values

char *

This is the block of memory's starting address.
This address may have changed if the block size
has increased. It is guaranteed that the block will
be contiguous in memory. The return address is
also guaranteed to be aligned so that any object
(int, char, struct) can be stored at that address.

(char *) NULL

realloc() has failed because either the first
argument was supplied incorrectly or no more
memory is available on the system.

The following program illustrates the use of realloc() to increase the
size of an allocated block of memory:

program: expand.c

```
1    #include <stdio.h>
2
3    main()
4    {
5        char *cpointer, *calloc(), *realloc();
6        int *spointer, *epointer, *current, *newpointer;
7
8        /* allocate memory for an array of 7
9            integers */
10       cpointer = calloc( 7, sizeof(int) );
11       spointer = (int *)cpointer;
12       epointer = ( spointer + 7 );
13
14       /* fill the array with random numbers */
15       for ( current = spointer; current < epointer;
                current++ )
16       {
17           *current = rand();
18           printf( "%d\n", *current );
19       }
```

(program continues)

```
20
21          /* free old block: not necessary */
22          free( cpointer );
23
24          printf( "REALLOCATE LARGER BLOCK OF MEMORY\n" );
25          newpointer = realloc( cpointer, 20 );
26          spointer = (int *)newpointer;
27          epointer = ( spointer + 10 );
28
29          for ( current = spointer; current < epointer;
30              current++ )
31          {
32              printf( "%d\n", *current );
33          }
34
35     }
```

program output:

```
16838
5758
10113
17515
31051
5627
23010
REALLOCATE LARGER BLOCK OF MEMORY
16838
5758
10113
17515
31051
5627
23010
2600
0
0
```

When increasing the size of a dynamically allocated block, never assume that the additional area will be cleared (as does the `calloc()` function). You can assume, however, that the contents of the previously allocated memory will remain intact. You can see both of these assumptions illustrated in the previous example's output.

Whenever `realloc()` is used to enlarge a block of memory, do not

EXHIBIT 13-3

Reallocating a block of memory

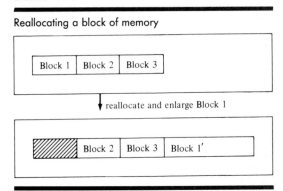

assume that the larger block will be at the same memory location as the smaller block. This is because the block of memory whose address is returned must be contiguous. The process is illustrated in Exhibit 13-3. If we have several pointers that point into the region this can present some problems. If the region is moved, then we will need to adjust all the pointers by the difference in the return addresses of calloc() and realloc(). The following program shows this:

program: adjust.c

```
 1    #include <stdio.h>
 2
 3    main()
 4    {
 5        char *cpointer, *calloc(), *realloc();
 6        int  *spointer,
 7             *epointer,
 8             *smallest,     /* pointer to smallest member */
 9             *current,
10             *newpointer;
11        int sm_value;
12
13        /* allocate memory for an array of 7 integers */
14        cpointer = calloc( 7, sizeof(int) );
15        spointer = (int *)cpointer;
16        epointer = ( spointer + 7 );
17
18        /* fill the array with random numbers */
19        for ( current = spointer; current < epointer;
20              current++ )
21            *current = rand();
```

(*program continues*)

```
22
23      /* find smallest member—store address in
24          "smallest" */
25      sm_value = *spointer;
26      for ( current = (spointer + 1); current < epointer;
27              current++ )
28      {
29          if ( *current < sm_value )
30          {
31                sm_value = *current;
32                smallest = current;
33          }
34      }
35
36      printf( "BEFORE realloc(): SMALLEST NUMBER IS %d\n",
37              *smallest );
38      free( cpointer );
39
40      newpointer = realloc( cpointer, 20 );
41
42      smallest += (newpointer—cpointer); /* scaled */
43      printf( "AFTER realloc(): SMALLEST NUMBER IS %d\n",
44              *smallest );
45
46    }
```

program output:

```
BEFORE realloc(): SMALLEST NUMBER IS 5627
AFTER realloc(): SMALLEST NUMBER IS 5627
```

An alternative to readjusting all pointers when the block is enlarged is to keep offsets from the beginning of the block instead of pointers into the block. When the block's starting address changes, the offsets are still valid and nothing has to be adjusted. The following program illustrates this technique:

program: offset.c

```
1     #include <stdio.h>
2     #define ARRAY_SIZE 7
3     #define NEW_SIZE 20
4
```

```
5    main()
6    {
7         char *calloc(),   *realloc();
8         int  *cpointer,    /* start of small array      */
9               *newpointer; /* start of large array      */
10        int  smallest,     /* offset of smallest member */
11        sm_value,          /* value of smallest member  */
12        current;
13
14        /* allocate memory for an array of ARRAY_SIZE integers */
15        cpointer = (int *)calloc( ARRAY_SIZE, sizeof(int) );
16
17        /* fill the array with random numbers */
18        for ( current = 0; current < (ARRAY_SIZE -1); current++ )
19        {
20             *(cpointer + current) = rand();
21        }
22
23        /* find smallest member-store address in "smallest" */
24        sm_value = *(cpointer + 0);
25        for ( current = 1; current < (ARRAY_SIZE -1); current++ )
26        {
27             if ( *(cpointer + current) < sm_value )
28             {
29                  sm_value = *(cpointer + current);
30                  smallest = current;
31             }
32        }
33
34        printf( "BEFORE realloc(): SMALLEST NUMBER IS %d\n",
35             *(cpointer + smallest) );
36        free( (char *)cpointer );
37
38        newpointer = (int *)realloc((char *)cpointer, NEW_SIZE);
39
40        printf( "AFTER realloc(): SMALLEST NUMBER IS %d\n",
41             *(newpointer + smallest) );
42
43   }
```

program output:

```
BEFORE realloc(): SMALLEST NUMBER IS  5627
AFTER realloc(): SMALLEST NUMBER IS 5627
```

Exhibit 13-4 contrasts the two methods of maintaining pointers into the reallocated block.

EXHIBIT 13-4

Two methods of addressing an element in an allocated block

program: adjust.c

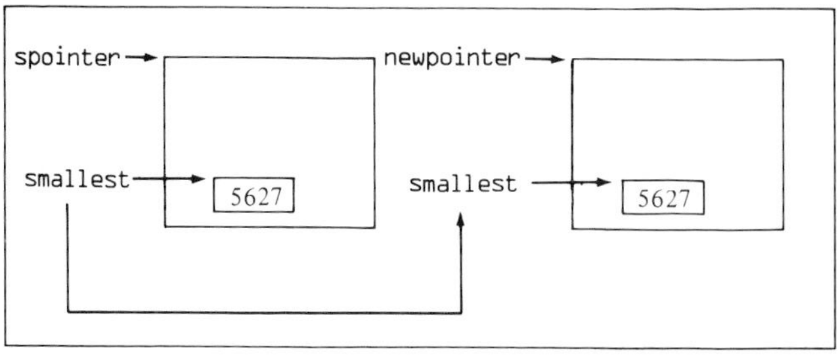

program: offset.c

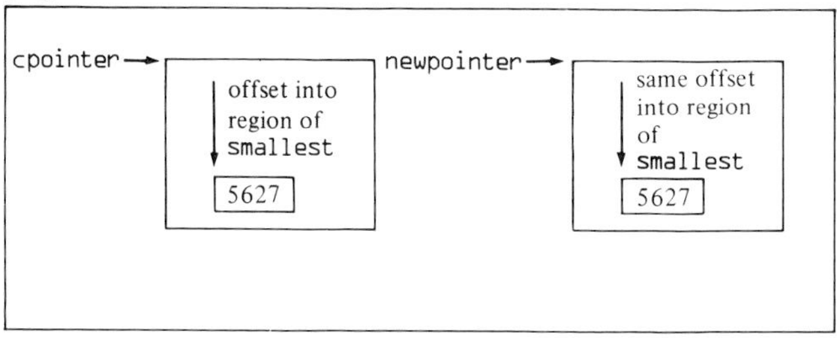

You should notice that the expressions used to reference the integers stored in this region of memory look very familiar (lines 35 and 41). As you will remember, the following expressions are equivalent:

```
*(newpointer + smallest)    and    newpointer[smallest]
```

If an expression of the second form is used in a program, it should be well documented. Although expressions of this form represent questionable programming practice, you will need to be familiar with them because they exist in a surprisingly large percentage of C language code.

POINTERS TO STRUCTURES

Pointers to structures may be declared similarly to pointers to simple variables and arrays. For example:

```
struct structure_name *pointer_name;
```

where

```
struct structure_name
```

replaces the variable type.

When a pointer to a structure is involved in an arithmetic expression, the arithmetic is scaled by the size of one of these structures (including any holes needed for alignment). This means that we can use one of these pointers to reference each element of an array of structures sequentially.

Referencing Members Using Pointers

If a pointer variable is declared as a pointer to a structure, we access one of the members of the structure using the arrow (–>) operator. This operator is used this way:

```
pointer_to_structure->member_name
```

where the expression to the left of the arrow is the address of a structure and the expression to the right is the name of one of its members. For example, if we have the following structure:

```
struct sample
{
        char first[20];
        char middle[20];
        char last[20];
} *ptr, name;
ptr = &name;
```

and a pointer to the structure ptr that points to name, then we can reference the middle name (middle) in two ways. We can use the dot (.) operator as shown in Chapter 11:

```
name.middle
```

or, we can use the pointer variable with the arrow operator:

```
ptr->middle
```

The arrow operator has been implemented for the programmers' convenience; the expression could also be formed using the dot operator as follows:

```
(*pointer_to_structure).member_name
```

The dot operator requires a structure to its left and the name of one of the members to the right. The arrow operator requires a pointer to a structure preceding it. The parentheses are needed in the previous expression because

the dot and arrow operators are applied before the pointer dereferencing operator. Similarly, the arrow operator can be used in conjunction with a member
name in the following manner:

```
(&structure_name)->member_name
```

Although the two previous techniques are legal, they are not generally
used. To access a structure member using the structure name, use the dot
operator; if you want to access a structure member using a pointer to the
structure, use the arrow operator.

The following program illustrates arrow operator use:

program: arrow.c

```
 1    #include "structdef.h"
 2
 3    main()
 4    {
 5        struct pqueue *q_pointer;
 6        char          *cpointer, *calloc(), *ctime(), *getenv();
 7        long          time();
 8        int           getpid();
 9
10        cpointer = calloc( 1, sizeof(struct pqueue) );
11        q_pointer = (struct pqueue *)cpointer;
12
13        /* getpid(): function that generates unique number */
14        q_pointer->control_id = getpid();
15
16        printf( "Enter filename: " );
17        gets( q_pointer->filename );
18
19        /* getenv: gets a variable from user's environment  */
20        strcpy( q_pointer->owner, getenv( "LOGNAME" ) );
21
22        /* time: returns time in seconds from a fixed point  */
23        q_pointer->q_time = time( (long *)0 );
24
25        printf( "\ncontrol id: %d\n", q_pointer->control_id );
26        printf( "file name: %s\n", q_pointer->filename );
27        printf( "owner: %s\n", q_pointer->owner );
28        /* ctime formats the time into character string */
29        printf( "time queued: %s\n",
30            ctime( &(q_pointer->q_time) ) );
31    }
```

program output:

```
Enter filename: /etc/passwd

control id: 625
file name: /etc/passwd
owner: hutch
time queued: Wed Jan 8 14:32:07 1986
```

The pqueue structure is defined as follows:

source file: queue.h

```
        .
        .
        .
10    struct pqueue
11    {
12          int     control_id;         /* spooler id              */
13          char    filename[FILE_NAME_SIZE];
14          char    owner[10];          /* login name of owner     */
15          short   priority;           /* 1: high, 10: low        */
16          long    file_length;        /* size in bytes           */
17          char    description[50];    /* user defined for
18                                         status reporting         */
19          short   n_copies;           /* number of copies        */
20          char    class[10];          /* defines pre and
21                                         postfix for printing */
22          long    q_time;             /* time queued      *
23          node    r_next;             /* record # of next        */
24    };
        .
        .
        .
```

POINTERS TO POINTERS

It is possible to declare a pointer variable that will contain another pointer variable's address. Variables of this type are declared this way:

```
char **name_of_pointer;
```

This declaration creates a variable named name_of_pointer that contains the address of a pointer to a character. If used in an arithmetic expression, the arithmetic is scaled by the size of a *pointer*. Pointers to pointers are sometimes referred to as *indirect pointers*.

Dereferencing Indirect Pointers

If we declare a pointer variable and set it equal to the value of a pointer to an integer as follows:

```
int *ipointer;
int **ppointer;
int i;

i = 15;
ipointer = &i;
ppointer = &ipointer;
```

we can obtain the value of the variable i through any of the following expressions:

```
i
*ipointer
**ppointer
```

The last expression in this list combines two expressions that can be made clearer by adding parentheses:

```
*(*ppointer)
```

The value of the expression:

```
*ppointer
```

is the *address* of an integer, the same value that is stored in the variable ipointer. When we apply the dereferencing operator to *ppointer we obtain the integer at that location. The following program illustrates this more fully:

program: doublep.c

```
1    main()
2    {
3         int i, *ipointer, **ppointer;
4
5         i = 01234; /* octal */
6         ipointer = &i;
7         ppointer = &ipointer;
```

```
 8
 9          printf( "i == %o\n\n", i );
10
11          printf( "&ipointer == %o\n", &ipointer );
12          printf( " ipointer == %o\n", ipointer );
13          printf( "*ipointer == o\n\n", *ipointer );
14
15          printf( " &ppointer == %o\n", &ppointer );
16          printf( "  ppointer == %o\n", ppointer );
17          printf( " *ppointer == %o\n", *ppointer );
18          printf( "**ppointer == %o\n", **ppointer );
19   }
```

program output:

```
i == 1234

&ipointer == 177502
 ipointer == 177504
*ipointer == 1234

  &ppointer == 177500
   ppointer == 177502
  *ppointer == 177504
**ppointer == 1234
```

Exhibit 13-5 shows a schematic diagram of the memory allocated by this program.

EXHIBIT 13-5

Values and addresses of i, *ipointer, and **ppointer

ppointer
```
┌──────────┐
│  177502  │
└──────────┘
   177500
```

ipointer
```
┌──────────┐
│  177504  │
└──────────┘
   177502
```

i
```
┌──────────┐
│   1234   │
└──────────┘
   177504
```

Tables of Pointers

Tables of pointers are a useful method for keeping track of several pointers to variables. An array of pointers is declared as follows:

```
variable_type *array_name[size];
```

where `variable_type` describes the type of variable pointed to by the elements of the array. For example, an array of pointers to characters is declared as:

```
char *array_name[20];
```

Arrays of this type can be used to keep track of several character strings, perhaps representing error messages. The following program sets up an error message table that may be used later to report errors based on the return values of other function calls:

program: errors.c

```
1    #include <stdio.h>
2
3    #define  MESSAGE_LENGTH 100
4    #define  N_ERRORS        50
5    #define  YES              1
6    #define  NO               0
7
8    main()
9    {
10        char e_array[ MESSAGE_LENGTH ];
11        char *cptr, *errors[ N_ERRORS ];
12        char *getenv(), *calloc(), *strcpy();
13        int end_of_file, msg_number, sub;
14        FILE *errfile;
15
16        errfile = fopen( getenv("ERRORFILE"), "r" );
17        if ( errfile == NULL )
18        {
19            fprintf( stderr, "Cannot open error file\n" );
20            exit(1);
21        }
22
23        msg_number = 0;
24        end_of_file = NO;
25
```

```
26          while( end_of_file == NO )
27          {
28              if ( fgets( e_array, MESSAGE_LENGTH,
29                          errfile ) == NULL ||
30                      msg_number >= N_ERRORS )
31              {
32                  end_of_file = YES;
33              }
34              else
35              {
36                  cptr = calloc( (unsigned)strlen(e_array) + 1,
37                          sizeof(char) );
38                  strcpy( cptr, e_array );
39                  errors[msg_number] = cptr;
40              }
41              msg_number++;
42          }
43
44          for ( sub = 0; sub < msg_number; sub++ )
45          {
46              fputs( errors[sub], stdout );
47          }
48      }
```

program output:

```
cannot open input file
too many arguments specified
cannot fork: try spoon
invalid magic number in file
cannot open output file
```

We could have achieved the same result by declaring a two-dimensional array of characters with 100 characters reserved for *each* of the character strings. Our solution is preferable because memory is only allocated where needed to store the error messages. In memory, this pointer array appears as shown in Exhibit 13-6.

EXHIBIT 13-6

A table of pointers to error messages

errors		
[0]		→ "cannot open input file \n"
[1]		→ "too many arguments specified \n"
[2]		→ "cannot fork: try spoon \n"
[3]		→ "invalid magic number in file \n"
[4]		→ "cannot open output file \n"

Passing Arguments to main( )

It is often desirable to pass information to the program from the invoking command line. These arguments could be file names on which the program is to act or options that influence the logic of the program. Command-line arguments and options are passed to the main( ) function as follows:

```
main( argc, argv )
int argc;
char *argv[];
{
        variable declarations;

        executable statements;
}
```

where the value stored in argc is the number of words on the command line including the command name itself. The value stored in the second argument, here named argv, is the starting address of a table of pointers to character strings that represent the arguments to the program. For example, if a program is executed as follows:

```
program filename1 filename2
```

then the table pointed to by the second argument to main( ) appears as shown in Exhibit 13-7.

The following program prints its arguments:

program: printargs.c

```
 1    #include <stdio.h>
 2
 3    main( argc, argv )
 4    int     argc;
 5    char    *argv[];
 6    {
 7         int sub;
 8
 9         for ( sub = 0; sub < argc; sub++ )
10         {
11              puts( *(argv + sub) );
12         }
13    }
```

command line:

```
printargs file.c printer.c /etc/passwd
```

program output:

```
printargs
file.c
printer.c
/etc/passwd
```

EXHIBIT 13-7

A table of program arguments

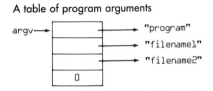

Although the value passed to the main function as the second argument is a pointer to a table, it is often used as if it were the name of the table, changing line 11 of the previous program to:

```
puts( argv[sub] );
```

As we have seen, the two representations are equivalent. How can we refer to a particular character in one of these strings? For example, to access the second character of the command name, we use the name of the command pointed to by the first element in the argv table. The character string can be represented by either of the following two expressions:

```
*(argv + 0)      or      argv[0]
```

Both of these expressions yield the address of the command name's first character. The second character's address can be represented by either of the following expressions:

```
*(argv + 0) + 1      or      argv[0] + 1
```

To access the character itself, we can use either of the following expressions:

```
*( *(argv + 0) + 1)      or      *( argv[0] + 1 )
```

In fact, the compiler would even treat the following expression as equivalent to the preceding two:

argv[0][1]

Although argv is not a two-dimensional array, it can be accessed as if it were.

Accessing the Environment

In previous programs, we saw the getenv() function used to access an environment variable's value. Environment variables are set by the program that is the normal interface to the system. In the UNIX operating system this interface is the shell; in MS-DOS it is the command interpreter. The system can pass the environment to a program in several different ways. One method is by creating a table of pointers that is passed to the program as the third argument to main(). The table can be accessed as follows:

program: showenv.c

```
 1    #include <stdio.h>
 2
 3    main( argc, argv, envp  )
 4    int     argc;
 5    char    *argv[], *envp[];
 6    {
 7         int sub;
 8
 9         for ( sub = 0; envp[sub] != 0; sub++ )
10         {
11              puts( envp[sub] );
12         }
13    }
```

program output:

```
ERRORFILE=errorfile
HOME=/usr/hutch
LOGNAME=hutch
MORE=-c -s
PATH=/bin:/usr/bin:/usr/hutch/bin:.:..:../..
TERM=ansi
TZ=EST5EDT
```

Since we do not have a count of the number of environment variables, we assume the table ends with a null pointer.

Although it is possible to access the table in this manner, it is preferable to use the getenv() library function which has the effect of enhancing the program's portability.

SUMMARY

In this chapter we have covered pointers in some detail. As we have seen, pointers are one of the most powerful C language features. Through pointer arithmetic we can manipulate simple variables, arrays, and structures. Pointer arithmetic is conveniently scaled by the type of object pointed to. In Chapters 16, 17 and 18 we will use pointers to develop more complex data structures such as linked lists and binary trees.

In Chapter 14 we will see how pointers play an important role in passing arguments to functions and how they are used to bypass the "call by value" nature of C functions.

EXERCISES

1. Rewrite the program in Chapter 10, Exercise 1 to multiply two arrays using pointer arithmetic.

2. As we discussed in Chapter 8, Exercise 5, the Fibonacci series is created by summing the two previous numbers in the series:

1, 1, 2, 3, 5, 8, 13, 21, . . .

Write a program that prints out all numbers between one and 100 that are not part of the Fibonacci series.

3. The period of repetition for a random-number generator can be defined as the number of unique numbers generated before any number is generated a second time. Write a program to generate random numbers between one and 1000 and determine how many are generated before any number is repeated.

4. Read in two strings of characters. Read in a word that appears in character string 1. Replace all occurences of this word in character string 1 with character string 2.

5. Given an 80-character Boolean string, write a program to search the string for an arbitrary sequence of 0s and 1s from one to 30 characters long and print out either success or failure. If the search is successful print out the position at which the sequence begins.

6. Write a program to print out any number (up to three digits) in words. For example, 297 is written as:

two hundred ninety seven

7. Write a program that reads a number n from the invoking command line. The program should then open a file and print the first n records. If n is greater than the number of records in the file, print the first n records followed by a warning message.

8. Write a program that accepts one to three filenames from the invoking command line and prints the files in order at the terminal.

9. Modify the above program to interlace the output from the files, alternately printing a line from each file. If the files are of unequal length, continue printing the larger file(s) until all lines are printed.

CHAPTER 14

FUNCTIONS II

OVERVIEW

In this chapter we continue our discussion of functions. In Chapter 8 we looked at the basics of C language functions including the structure of a function and return values. Now, we combine the pointer, structure, and array topics to discuss passing pointers, structures, and arrays to functions, some searching and sorting techniques, and recursive functions.

PASSING POINTERS TO FUNCTIONS

For a *called* function to change the value of a variable in the *calling* function, we must supply the function with the address of the variable to be changed rather than the value of the variable. For example, assume that we have a structure defined as follows:

```
struct pqueue
{
        int    control_id;        /* lp queue job #       */
        char   filename[FILE_NAME_SIZE];
        char   owner[10];         /* login name of owner */
        short  priority;          /* 1: high, 10:low      */
        long   file_length;       /* size in bytes        */
        char   description[50];   /* user defined for
                                     page header          */
        short  n_copies;          /* number of copies     */
        long   q_time;            /* time queued          */
};
```

This structure is part of a line printer queuing system; it defines a file to be printed. In the main() procedure we declare one of these structures; other functions will fill values into the structure. We do this as follows:

1. Put the structure definition in a file named queue.h.

2. Create a main() procedure that calls a function to clear the structure, and then call "get" functions to fill in the structure values.

3. Create another file with the "get" functions in it. These functions prompt the user for some information and also fetch some data by executing system utilities.

The following are excerpts from the main() function and the function called to clear the structure:

program: main.c

```
1    #include "queue.h"
2    #define END 4
3    main()
4    {
5         short command, menu();
6         struct pqueue temp;
7
```

```
 8          while ( (command = menu()) != END )
 9          {
10              switch( command )
11              {
12
13              case 1:     /* queue a file */
14
15                  clear( &temp );
16                  getcontrol( &temp );
     .
     .
     .
25                  break;
26
27              case 2:   /* remove a file from the queue */
28
29                  removeq( askcontrol() );
30                  break;
31
32              case 3:     /* print queue */
33
34                  printq( 0 );
35                  break;
36
37              }
38          }
39      }
```

In line 8, the program calls a function that displays a menu on the user's terminal, prompts for a selection, and verifies that the user has chosen a valid option. The menu() function is part of the queueing system and is omitted here; it is not a standard library function. The menu() function returns a command number which is then interpreted by the main() function. If the command number is 1, the user wants to print a file. The information about the file to be printed is collected in several routines, but before the information is collected, the structure holding the information about the file is cleared by the clear() function. This function clears each field of the structure individually. The function is kept in a separate source file and is written as follows:

source file: clear.c

```
1    #include "queue.h"
2
3    clear( temp )
4    struct pqueue *temp;
```

(*program continues*)

```
 5    {
 6         strcpy( temp->filename, "" );
 7         strcpy( temp->owner, "" );
 9         temp->priority = 0;
10         temp->file_length = 0;
11         temp->control_id = 0;
12         temp->n_copies = 0;
13         temp->q_time = 0;
14    }
```

Passing Structures

In more recent implementations of the C compiler, it is possible to pass entire structures to functions as well as supply them as return values. It is also possible to make structure assignments. Therefore, the previous program could be rewritten without using pointers:

program: main.c

```
          .
          .
          .
 8         while( (command = menu()) != END )
 9         {
10             switch( command )
11             {
12
13             case 1:      /* queue a file */
14
15                 temp = clear( temp );
16                 getcontrol( &temp );
          .
          .
          .
```

source file: clear.c

```
 1    #include "queue.h"
 2
 3    struct pqueue clear( temp )
 4    struct pqueue temp;
 5    {
 6         strcpy( temp.filename, "" );
 7         strcpy( temp.owner, "" );
 9         temp.priority = 0;
10         temp.file_length = 0;
```

```
11          temp.control_id = 0;
12          temp.n_copies = 0;
13          temp.q_time = 0;
14          temp.r_next = 0;
15          return( temp );
16    }
```

This method produces the same results as the first program but the first is preferred because it requires less processing at run time. In the first example, the only information passed is a pointer to the structure; in the second, the entire contents of the structure is passed.

In the first example, the arrow operator is used to reference structure members while in the second example the dot operator is used. This is necessary because the first example is using the structure's address while the second is using the structure name.

Passing Arrays

As we discussed earlier, it is possible to have functions operate on an array. Unlike structures, in which the entire structure is passed, when an array's name is given as an argument to a function, the value passed is the array's starting address and not the array itself. The function then operates on the actual array.

When an array is passed as an argument to a function, the array's size is unknown to the function unless it is explicitly passed as an argument. Arrays are included as members of function argument lists as follows:

```
main()
{
        void func();
        int array[40];

        func( array );
}

void func( i_array )
int i_array[];              /*size must be left out */
{
        local variables;

        executable statements;
}
```

In the `main()` function, the size of `array` is supplied and storage is allocated for the array. When the `func()` function is called, the array's starting address (the value of the expression `array`) is passed to the function.

Inside the function, the argument received is the starting address of an array of integers. The size may not be specified in the function. If the function needs the size, it should be passed as a separate argument.

When defining an array as a function argument, the following two defini- tions are equivalent:

```
int i_array[];          and          int *i_array;
```

Both definitions inform the compiler to expect the starting address of an integer array. Unlike the expression supplied in the calling function (the name of the array), this is a variable and can appear on the left side of an assignment operator. The following program illustrates passing arrays to functions:

program: pass.args.c

```
 1   #define ARRAY_SIZE 5
 2
 3   main()
 4   {
 5        int  array[ ARRAY_SIZE ];
 6        void randomize(), a_print();
 7
 8        randomize( array, ARRAY_SIZE );
 9        a_print( array, ARRAY_SIZE );
10   }
11
12   void randomize( i_array, i_size )
13   int  i_array[], i_size;
14   {
15        int indx;
16
17        for( indx = 0; indx < i_size; indx++ )
18        {
19             i_array[indx] = rand();
20        }
21   }
22
23   void a_print( p_array, p_size )
24   int  *p_array,          /* address of array to print   */
25         p_size;           /* size of array               */
26   {
27        int *current, *end;
28
29        end = p_array + p_size;
30        current = p_array;
31
```

```
32        while( current < end )
33        {
34            printf( "%d ", *current );
35            current++;   /* look at next element */
36        }
37        printf( "\n" );
38   }
```

program output:

16838 5658 10113 17515 31051

You should note that even though the two functions do not return values, they are declared in the `main()` function. This is done for readability. You should also note that although the same values are passed, they are treated differently in the two functions. The `randomize()` function uses the first argument as it would the name of an array and subscripts it. (Actually, the pointer variable `i_array` is being used as an array name.)

The second function treats the first argument as a pointer to an integer and assumes that an array of integers begins there. It sets one of its own local variables to the value of the address and then uses it to reference the elements in the array. The argument itself could have been modified because it has all the properties of a variable. If it were modified, none of the information in the calling function would be disturbed except the elements of the array.

It is interesting that although C language is a call-by-value language, it is common to have functions modify the contents of variables declared in the calling function. As we have seen, this is done by passing an address to the function, informing the function *where* the variable is, not just its value. The function is then able (using the dereferencing operator) to access the variable indirectly through its address.

Passing Multidimensional Arrays

Different rules exist for defining a multidimensional array in a function's argument list. The size of all but the first dimension must be specified. For example, suppose we have an array declared in our `main()` function as follows:

```
char array[20][30];
```

This would be defined in the function as:

```
function_name( temp )
char array[][30];
{
    . . .
}
```

The argument defines a pointer to an array of arrays of 30 characters each. When the value of the argument is used in an arithmetic expression, the arithmetic is scaled by the size of one of the arrays, or the size of 30 integers. The argument could be replaced with the following pointer notation:

```
function_name( temp )
char (*array)[30];   /* parentheses needed to
                        force operator precedence
                     */
{
    .
    .
    .
}
```

If the size of the second dimension were left out, then the compiler would assume that an array of pointers to characters was passed and not a two-dimensional array of characters.

Arrays with more dimensions are treated similarly; the sizes of all the dimensions except the first must be specified. The compiler requires this so that it can distinguish a multidimensional array from an array of pointers. It is not a syntax error to supply the first dimension, but even if supplied, the compiler will not perform bounds checking.

The Binary Search

The following program is another example of how functions can break a complex problem into a series of manageable ones.

This example is part of a larger system that maintains a customer account file for a business. This file contains information about each of the company's vendors. The file is kept sorted by account number and is searched to see if a person placing an order owes any money to the company. The program searches the database for the appropriate record and displays its information.

To do this we use a binary search, inspecting the record in the middle of the file first. If the desired number is less than (or greater than) that number, we divide the file in two and repeat the process with either the first or second half until we either find the record we are looking for or the region diminishes to zero. Exhibit 14-1 illustrates this.

The Account Record

All the source files in this program include the file named acct.h where the account record is defined. This file contains the following:

header file: acct.h

```
1    #include <stdio.h>
2
```

```
 3   #define N_ACCOUNTS 10
 4
 5   struct account
 6   {
 7       int acct_no;     /* customer id # */
 8       long balance;    /* past due balance */
 9       int flag;
10       char name[2][30];
11       char address[2][30];
12   };
```

For the purposes of this example, the maximum size to which the database can grow is limited to 10, the value defined by N_ACCOUNTS. The field that holds the past due balance is kept in pennies and is converted to dollars and cents when printed. The flag field is currently unused, but could be used to further describe the past due balance (e.g., whether it is 30, 60, or 90 days past due).

EXHIBIT 14-1

Binary search for index number 516 which is found on the fourth attempt

Attempt	Index Number
	100
	107
	128
	153
	211
	217
	300
	412
1 →	414
	501
3 →	507
4 →	516
2 →	603
	611
	616
	700
	800

The main() Procedure   This function contains the program's broad logic:

```
main( argument_count, argument_table )
{
        check to see that arguments were properly
            specified;

        open account file and read it into the
            array named "accts[]";
```

(pseudocode continues)

> search the array for the desired record;
>
> print contents of desired record;

}

As we have done here, it is always best to limit the number of tasks any single function performs. Do not try to put all the program's logic in the main() function. It should simply define the tasks performed and their order. The details should be relegated to other functions. Exhibit 14-2 shows the function hierarchy for this program.

EXHIBIT 14-2

Function hierarchy for the binary search program

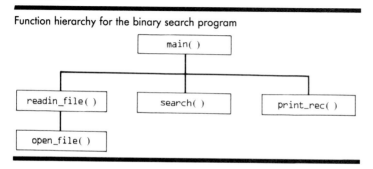

The main() function is written this way:

program: main.c

```
 1    #include "acct.h"
 2
 3    main( argc, argv )
 4    int argc;
 5    char *argv[];
 6    {
 7        struct account accts[ N_ACCOUNTS ], *search(), *ret;
 8        int recs;   /* number of records on file */
 9
10        if ( argc >= 3)   /* specified argument */
11        {
12            recs = readin_file( argv[1], accts ); ·
13        }
14        else
15        {
```

```
16              fprintf( stderr,
17                  "Improper number of arguments supplied\n" );
18              exit(3);
19          }
20
21          ret = search( accts, recs, atoi(argv[2]) );
22
23          if ( ret != (struct account *)NULL )
24          {
25              print_rec( ret );
26          }
27      }
```

This function declares an array of structures of type account that will eventually hold the data structures stored in the file. The file name is supplied to the function as the first argument and the record number to be printed is supplied as the second. If three words do not appear on the command line executing the program (the name of the program and the two other arguments), an error message prints and the program exits. In line 16, stderr is referred to, but the file stdio.h, where stderr is defined, is not explicitly included. If you remember, it is in the other included file acct.h.

If the arguments are properly specified, the readin_file() function is called with two arguments: the name of the file where the information is stored and the name of the array where the information will be stored. Next, the search() function finds a record in the array and the print_rec() function prints this record's contents. The program's output looks like this:

command line:

search accounts 104

program output:

Account number: 104
Name 1: Quality Computers, Inc.
Name 2: Hammond Aigs, pres.
Address 1: 123 Disk Drive
Address 2: Sunnyside, NJ 05555
Balance: 995.00

The readin_file() Function This function actually performs two tasks: it opens the file and populates the structure whose starting address is supplied as an argument. The file it opens is supplied as the first argument. The readin_file() function is defined in the file fileio.c as follows:

source file: fileio.c

```
1    #include "acct.h"
2
3    readin_file( filename, s_array )
4    char *filename;
5    struct account s_array[];
6    {
7        /* reads in entire array into the specified table.
8            assumes that the array is at least N_ACCOUNTS
9            long */
10
11       FILE *iptr, *openfile();
12       int  indx;
13
14       iptr = openfile( filename, "r" );
15
16       indx = 0;
17       while( indx < N_ACCOUNTS &&
18              fread( (char *)(&s_array[indx]),
19                 sizeof(struct account), 1, iptr ) != 0 )
20       {
21           indx++;
22       }
23
24       /* return the number of records actually read in */
25       return( indx - 1 );
26   }
```

The readin_file() function calls the openfile() function to open the file in which the account records are kept. It then reads the records into the structure pointed to by s_array. Assumably, s_array points to a place in memory large enough to hold at least N_ACCOUNTS records. Other designs would eliminate the need for these limits. For example:

- dynamically allocate memory
  This alternative would replace the table declared in main() with a table of pointers to account structures. The actual memory used to hold these structures would be allocated in the while loop in the previous routine using the calloc() routine. This design is left as an exercise for the student.

- only read in needed records
  This alternative would put reading the records in the search routine and would cause it to read only those records needed. It would be a better strategy if only one search were being done each time this program was

invoked. If many inquiries are performed in the same program, it would be preferable to have them all in memory before the search begins.

The openfile( ) Function   The openfile() function has been generalized so that it can be used in other parts of the system and is defined in the last part of the same file as readin_file():

```
        .
        .
        .
27
28    FILE *openfile( filename, mode )
29    char *filename;
30    char *mode;
31    {
32        /* open the specified file, check for validity,
33           and return pointer to FILE */
34
35        FILE *f_pointer, *fopen();
36
37        f_pointer = fopen( filename, mode );
38        if ( f_pointer == NULL )
39        {
40            fprintf( stderr, "Cannot open: %s\n", filename );
41            exit(1);
42        }
43
44        return( f_pointer );
45    }
```

The search( ) Function   This function, called by main(), is the heart of the program. It accepts three arguments: the starting address of the table to be searched, the size of the table, and the account number of the record to be found. The table size is supplied as the readin_file() function's return value and is less than the array size if there are only a few records in the file.

The search() function uses the following logic to locate the record in question:

while (record still not found)
{
*   if (the range of uncertainty is empty)*
*   {*
*   return(It's not there);*
*   }*

(pseudocode continues)

*middle of range = midpoint between lower and upper
        bounds;*

*if (account # of account in middle > desired
                account number)*
{
        *reshape range of uncertainty so that
                the lower limit = midpoint + 1;*
}
*else if (account # of account in middle < desired
                account number)*
{
        *reshape range of uncertainty so that
                the upper limit = midpoint − 1;*
}
else
{
        found it;
}
}

The search() function, found in the search. c file implements this algorithm:

program: search.c

```
 1   #include "acct. h"
 2
 3   struct account *search( table, recs, find_rec )
 4   struct account *table;
 5   int recs, find_rec;
 6   {
 7       struct account *start, *middle, *end;
 8
 9       start = table;
10       end = table + recs;
11       middle = start;   /* it better be something */
12
13       while ( middle->acct_no != find_rec )
14       {
15           /* not found */
16           if ( start > end )
17           {
18               return( (struct account *)NULL );
19           }
```

```
20
21              /* slightly clumsy because two pointers
22                  cannot be added together */
23              middle = ((end - start) / 2) + start;
24
25              if( middle->acct_no < find_rec )
26              {
27                  start = middle + 1;
28              }
29              else if ( middle->acct_no > find_rec )
30              {
31                  end = middle - 1;
32              }
33          }
34
35          return( middle );
36      }
```

On line 23, we want to compute the value

```
(start + end) / 2
```

but cannot because adding two pointers is not allowed in the C language.

To demonstrate the search() function's inner logic, we have written a slightly more verbose version, compiled it with the rest of the functions, and executed it with account numbers 108 and 104. The output below shows the account numbers at the lower end, the upper end, and the midpoint records:

command line:

```
search accounts 108
```

program output:

```
middle = 105
start  = 101
end    = 110
changing lower limit: 106

middle = 108
start  = 106
end    = 110


Account number: 108
Name 1: Lester's Fish Market
Name 2: Lester Haddocks
```

```
Address 1: 123 Sammone Blvd.
Address 2: Perch, NJ 05555
Balance: 110.23
```

command line:

```
search accounts 104
```

program output:

```
middle = 105
start  = 101
end    = 110
changing upper limit: 104

middle = 102
start  = 101
end    = 104
changing lower limit: 103
```

EXHIBIT 14-3

Binary search for account numbers 108 and 104

Search for account number 108:

First Attempt:		Second Attempt:	
start →	101		101
	102		102
	103		103
	104		104
middle →	105		105
	106	start →	106
	107		107
	108	middle →	108
	109		109
end →	110	end →	110

Search for account number 104:

First Attempt:		Second Attempt:		Third Attempt:		Fourth Attempt.	
start →	101	start →	101		101		101
	102	middle →	102		102		102
	103		103	start, middle →	103		103
	104	end →	104	end →	104	start, middle, end →	104
middle →	105		105		105		105
	106		106		106		106
	107		107		107		107
	108		108		108		108
	109		109		109		109
end →	110		110		110		110

```
middle = 103
start  = 103
end    = 104
changing lower limit: 104

middle = 104
start  = 104
end    = 104


Account number: 104
Name 1: Quality Computers, Inc.
Name 2: Hammond Aigs, pres.
Address 1: 123 Disk Drive
Address 2: Sunnyside, NJ 05555
Balance: 995.00
```

Exhibit 14-3 shows the search procedure pictorially.

The print_rec() Function   When the record is found, the print_rec() function prints it. This function requires only one argument, the address of the structure to be printed. It prints each of the fields, converting the balance into a more readable format:

program: print.c

```
 1     #include "acct.h"
 2
 3     print_rec( s_ptr )
 4     struct account *s_ptr;
 5     {
 6          printf( "Account number: %d\n", s_ptr->acct_no );
 7          printf( "Name 1: %s\n", s_ptr->name[1] );
 8          printf( "Name 2: %s\n", s_ptr->name[2] );
 9          printf( "Address 1: %s\n", s_ptr->address[1] );
10          printf( "Address 2: %s\n", s_ptr->address[2] );
11          /* assume in dollars and cents */
12          printf( "Balance: %ld.%02ld\n", s_ptr->balance/100,
13                              s_ptr->balance%100 );
14     }
```

Recursively Called Functions

Sometimes, it is simpler to define a concept recursively—in terms of itself. For example, an integer's definition is, in general terms, a digit followed by another digit and so on. A more precise definition would be a digit followed by another integer. With this precise definition, we could prove that the number 448 is an integer. We begin by looking at the first character, check that it is a digit and then treat the two remaining characters as another integer. We check these two characters, applying the same definition, continuing until the string of characters is exhausted. In any recursive definition, it is necessary to get closer to the desired answer through each step in the recursion and to reduce the known problem into a simpler one. If we don't, this can lead to a circular or infinitely recursive definition.

The C language is a recursive language; that is, a function is permitted to call itself (be defined in terms of itself) or call a parent (or calling) function. It is necessary that the conditions under which the function is called are different from one invocation to the next (e.g., the arguments to the function call are different). The ability to call functions recursively permits the programmer to formulate more elegant solutions to certain problems.

In mathematics, some problems are more easily defined recursively. For example, the definition of factorial is defined recursively as follows:

$$n! = n * (n-1)!$$

The definition of the factorial function is defined in terms of itself; hence, it is recursive. In programming, a recursive function is one that calls itself or its parent function. The following example illustrates the factorial function's recursive nature:

program: factorial.c

```
 1    main()
 2    {
 3         long factorial();
 4
 5         printf( "10! == %d\n", factorial( 10L ) );
 6    }
 7
 8    long factorial( number )
 9    long number;
10    {
11         if ( number > 1 )
12              return( factorial( number - 1L ) * number );
13         else
14              return( 1 );
15    }
```

program output:
```
10! == 3628800
```

The function is called recursively in line 12. The argument to the function is one less than the value supplied. The value returned to the calling function is the value it returns, multiplied by the number it was supplied. This function, like the mathematical definition, halts its recursion when it receives the number 1 as its input.

This example could have been written in a variety of other ways including using iteration instead of recursion. Using iteration we write the function this way:

program: factorial.c

```
         .
         .
         .
8    long factorial( number )
9    long number;
10   {
11       long answer, sub;
12
13       answer = number;
14       for ( sub = number - 1; sub > 1; sub-- )
15       {
16           answer *= sub;
17       }
18   }
```

program output:

```
10! == 3628800
```

Most problems with a recursive solution also have equivalent iterative solutions. Recursion usually makes the program's logic simpler, facilitating proofs of correctness. In the examples shown above, the iterative solution is the more efficient of the two. If many local variables are declared within a function, recursive functions can be fairly expensive; these variables are declared and have to be allocated each time the function is called. In the iterative version, the variables are allocated only once. The recursive solution is also space-inefficient because it declares a set of local variables for each instance of the function.

The following program uses a recursive function to print its input backwards:

program: backprint.c

```
1    #include <stdio.h>
2
3    main( argc, argv )
4    int argc;
5    char *argv[];
6    {
7        char string[256], *strcpy();
8
9        if ( argc < 2 )
10       {
11           prompt( "Enter strings: ", string );
12       }
13       else
14       {
15           strcpy( string, argv[1] );
16       }
17
18       print_back( string );
19       putchar( '\n' );
20   }
21
22   print_back( cptr )
23   char *cptr;'
24   {
25       if ( *cptr != '\0' )
26           print_back( cptr + 1 );
27       else
28           return;
29
30       putchar( *cptr );
31   }
32
33   prompt( message, array )
34   char *message, *array;
35   {
36       char *strcpy();
37
38       strcpy( array, "" );
39
40       while ( strcmp( array, "" ) == 0 )
41       {
42           printf( "%s", message );
43           gets( array );
44       }
45   }
```

command line:

```
backprint hello
```

program output:

```
olleh
```

There is one call to the function named `print_back()` for each character in the character string. Exhibit 14-4 shows the backwards printing process.

The character's value is only printed after the recursive call has been made. Also, if the end of the string has been reached, the function is not called recursively. It is very important to have the function only called conditionally within the function. If not, something similar to an infinite loop occurs—infinite recursion. Infinite recursion is worse than an infinite loop because memory is allocated for local variables each time a function call is made, so a program in infinite recursion is not only ''hogging'' the processor, it is also allocating all available memory.

EXHIBIT 14-4

Recursive function to print its input backwards

h	e	l	l	o	\n	\0

address   2001 2002 2003 2004 2005 2006 2007

value of `cptr` for 1st invocation of `print_back()` == 2001
value of `cptr` for 2nd invocation of `print_back()` == 2002

⋮

value of `cptr` for 7th invocation of `print_back()` == 2007

Recursive Binary Search

Previously, we saw how the binary search technique efficiently found its way to a given record in a file or array. This routine can be simplified somewhat by defining the search function recursively:

```
search( lower limit, upper limit, desired record )
{
            if ( lower limit > upper limit )
                   return ( record not found )
            if ( middle record = desired record )
                   return middle record
            else if ( middle record < desired record )
                   return ( search ( second half of file ) )
            else
                   return ( search ( first half of file ) )
}
```

The following function implements this algorithm:

program: rsearch.c

```
1    #include "acct.h"
2
3    struct account *rsearch( first, recs, find_rec )
4    struct account *first;
5    int recs, find_rec;
6    {
7        struct account *start, *middle, *end;
8
9        start = first;
10       end = first + recs;
11       if ( start > end )
12       {
13           return( (struct account *)NULL );
14       }
15
16       middle = ((end - start) / 2) + start;
17
18       if ( middle->acct_no == find_rec )
19       {
20           return( middle );
21       }
22
23       if( middle->acct_no < find_rec )
24       {
25           return ( rsearch( middle + 1, end - (middle + 1),
26               find_rec ) );
27       }
28       else if ( middle->acct_no > find_rec )
29       {
30           return ( rsearch( start, end - (middle + 1),
31               find_rec ) );
32       }
33   }
```

program output:

```
Account number: 109
Name 1: Ace Tree Surgery, Inc.
Name 2: Bill Botany, owner
Address 1: 123 Muscular Arms Dr.
Address 2: Long Branch, NJ 55555
Balance: 1025.00
```

The Quick Sort

The quick-sort algorithm lends itself to recursive programming techniques. It solves the problem of sorting numbers in an array by continually reducing the problem to another instance of a solved problem.

For example, consider the following situation: one thousand pieces of paper are sitting on a desk in front of you; each paper has a number on it. Your job is to sort these into numerical order. One way to solve this problem is to take a piece of paper from the top of the stack and note its number. You then form two stacks of paper from the rest of the pile, placing numbers smaller than the first number to the left and numbers larger than the first number to the right, with the piece of paper you first selected in the middle. Next, you hire two other people to do the same thing to each of the smaller stacks of paper, explaining your procedure, including instructions to hire two other paper sorters, and so on. This continues until there is only one piece of paper in each of the paper sorter's stacks. At this point the lowest level paper sorters will do nothing except tell their bosses that the work is done. Their bosses will then pass the message on to their bosses, and so forth. When you, as the president of this newly formed hierarchy, hear from the two you hired that all the work has been done, you go and pick up all the pieces of paper and they will be in order. We can implement this technique through the following program:

program: qsort.c

```
1    #define ARRAY_SIZE 20
2
3    main()
4    {
5         int i, array[ARRAY_SIZE];
6
7         randomize( array );
8         print_array( "BEFORE", array );
9         quicksort( &array[0], &array[ ARRAY_SIZE - 1 ] );
10        print_array( "AFTER", array );
11   }
12
13   quicksort( lower, upper )
14   int *lower, *upper;
15   {
16        int partition;
17        int *iptr, *previous_low;
18
19        if( lower < upper )
20        {
21             partition = *lower;
22             previous_low = lower;
```

(*program continues*)

```
23
24          for ( iptr = lower + 1; iptr <= upper; iptr++ )
25          {
26              if ( *iptr < partition )
27              {
28                  previous_low++;
29                  swap( previous_low, iptr );
30              }
31          }
32          swap( lower, previous_low );
33
34          quicksort( lower, previous_low - 1 );
35          quicksort( previous_low + 1, upper );
36
37      }
38  }
```

program output:

BEFORE
16838 5758 10113 17515 31051 5627 23010 7419 16212 4086
2749 12767 9084 12060 32225 17543 25089 21183 25137 25566

AFTER
2749 4086 5627 5758 7419 9084 10113 12060 12767 16212
16838 17515 17543 21183 23010 25089 25137 25566 31051 32225

Exhibit 14-5 shows a simple quick sort procedure.

EXHIBIT 14-5

Sorting using the quick sort procedure. Bracketed items are in the same "pile"

Initial Order	After First Iteration	After Second Iteration	After Third Iteration
37	21	19	18}
21	19	18	19}
38	22	21}	21}
19	18	22}	22}
22	37}	37}	37}
18	38	38}	38}
44	44	44	42}
42	42	42	44}

SUMMARY

In this chapter, we have seen how arrays, pointers, and structures can be used in conjunction with function calls to permit the function to change values of variables from the calling function. We have also given examples of somewhat larger programs that justify the use of functions to modularize the program logic. In these programs we have shown how arguments may be passed from the command line to the C program.

Using these features we implemented a binary search program and then, after introducing recursive functions, we implemented a quick-sort procedure. Recursive functions can always be written using iterative rather than recursive techniques. Recursion is usually preferable stylistically, but iteration often consumes fewer resources.

EXERCISES

1. Write a function to read in a sentence and break the sentence into words, then sort and print the words in alphabetical order.

2. A palindrome is a string of characters that is the same forwards and backwards (ignoring blanks). Write a function that reads in a string and writes it out as a palindrome. For example, given:

mirror image

write:

mirror imageegami rorrim

3. Write a program to test if a string is a palindrome. Try these:

not so boston
step on no pets
yale relay
emordnilap is not a palindrome
one zoo zeno
sun on us

4. Write a function using the rand() function with two arguments (low and high) that represent the range of the random number to be generated.

5. Write a function that reads in a positive number containing a decimal point and prints out the number of digits to the left of the decimal point.

6. As defined in Chapter 10, the C language contains a library function strcpy(s1, s2) that copies string s2 into s1, stopping after the null character has been copied. Write your own version of this function.

7. Write a function called message() that accepts an integer as an argument. The message() function should print one of the following, depending on the value of its argument:

Argument Value	Message
0	file not opened
1	file full
2	file not found
3	not enough memory
4	illegal data

8. To convert a decimal number to base 2, we can continually divide the quotient by two until it is zero. The remainders give the binary number. For example to convert decimal 6 to base 2:

	Quotient	Remainder
6/2	3	0
3/2	1	1
1/2	0	1

And decimal 6 is 110 in binary.

Write a recursive function to convert a decimal number to binary.

9. Write a recursive function that raises any number x to an arbitrary power n. Do not use the pow() function.

Remember that $x^0 = 1$.

10. Revise program backprint.c to use iterative rather than recursive techniques.

CHAPTER 15

STORAGE CLASSES AND CONVERSIONS

OVERVIEW

This chapter describes local, global, and private variable types as they are implemented in the C language. We will discuss allocating automatic variables and their effect on a C language program's execution, and how register variables may be used to increase program efficiency. In Chapters 8 and 14 we noted the merits of dividing a program into several source files. In this chapter we will show how variables may be shared across source files using the external storage class. We will also cover the two types of static variables and discuss how they are different from external variables.

Other topics in this chapter include: increasing the space efficiency of programs by declaring units of storage as constants, initializing variables when they are declared, and the conversions that occur when operands of two different types are used in assignment and arithmetic operations.

AUTOMATIC VARIABLES

Automatic variables are declared within a set of braces and are only valid within that block. Automatic variables can be declared within any set of braces immediately following the opening brace. In the following example the variables x and y are valid only within the braces in which they are declared:

program: automatic.c

```
 1     main()
 2     {
 3          int a, b, c;
 4
 5          /* useful part of program goes here */
 6          /* somewhere the value of a is set */
 7
 8          if ( a < 20 )
 9          {
10              int x, y;
11              /* more useful parts using x
12                  and y as temporary variables */
13
14          }
15
16          /* x and y not valid here */
17     }
```

The variables a, b, and c may be used anywhere in the function, but the variables x and y may only be used within the inner braces.

EXHIBIT 15-1

The process stack for program automatic.c *during* execution of the innermost block

y
x
c
b
a

Initial Values

Because they are allocated through storage on the process stack, automatic variables initially have unpredictable values and should always be explicitly initialized before they are used. The process stack is created when the program begins its execution and is updated each time a new function or block starts its execution. Storage for all automatic variables is allocated on this last-in-first-out data structure and is deallocated from the stack when the block or function is finished. Exhibit 15-1 shows a conceptual view of the process stack while the statements inside the innermost braces of the previous program are executing. The values of a, b, and c are known and accessible, as are the values of x and y. When the innermost block is finished, the memory used to store the values of x and y is deallocated and is reallocated when the next block or function in the program is encountered. Exhibit 15-2 shows the process stack after the innermost block is completed.

Within the innermost block, program automatic.c is able to access all declared variables. After the block is completed (after line 14), the values of the variables declared inside the innermost braces are not available. Likewise, variables declared in one block may not necessarily be available in another, even if they are at the same calling depth. For example:

program: twoblocks.c

```
1       #define MAX 100
2       main()
3       {
4            int always_available;
5
6            /* part of program omitted */
7
8            if ( always_available < MAX )
9            {
10                int inside_first;
11
12                /* part of program omitted
```
(program continues)

EXHIBIT 15-2

The process stack for program automatic.c *after* execution of the innermost block

```
13                  using always_available and
14                  inside_first */
15          }
16
17          /* part of program omitted */
18
19          if ( always_available  > MAX )
20          {
21               int inside_second;
22
23               /* part of program omitted
24               using always_available and
25               inside_second */
26          }
27      }
```

The variable inside_second is only available to the statements executed if the second if condition is true (inside the second block.) The variable
named always_available is available anywhere inside the routine main().

EXHIBIT 15-3

The process stack for program twoblocks.c

```
┌──────────┐  after
│          │  line 4
├──────────┤
│          │
├──────────┤
│          │  always_available
└──────────┘
```

```
┌──────────┐  after
│          │  line 10
├──────────┤
│          │
├──────────┤
│          │  inside_first
├──────────┤
│          │  always_available
└──────────┘
```

```
┌──────────┐  after
│          │  line 15
├──────────┤
│          │
├──────────┤
│          │  always_available
└──────────┘
```

```
┌──────────┐  after
│          │  line 21
├──────────┤
│          │
├──────────┤
│          │  inside_second
├──────────┤
│          │  always_available
└──────────┘
```

Exhibit 15–3 shows the process stack's condition at various points in the program's execution.

Looking at Exhibit 15–3, it is possible to assume that the value of inside_second is initially equal to the previous value of inside_first, after the program finishes executing the first block. This may be the case, but probably it is not. Never assume that an automatic variable's initial value is useful.

Automatic Variables and Functions

Beginning C programmers sometimes attempt to return a pointer to an automatic variable declared in a function. For example:

program: wrong.c

```
1    main()    /* THIS PROGRAM DOES NOT WORK */
2    {
3        char array1[50], array2[50], *ret_val;
4        char *strcpy(), *str_combine();
5
6        strcpy( array1, "Hello " );
7        strcpy( array2, "there" );
8
9        ret_val = str_combine( array1, array2 );
10       printf( "%s\n", ret_val );
11   }
12
13   char *str_combine( ptr1, ptr2 )
14   char *ptr1, *ptr2;
15   {
16       char temp[100], *source, *dest;
17
18       source = ptr1;
19       dest = temp;
20       while ( *source != '\0' )
21       {
22               *dest = *source;
23               dest++;
24               source++;
25       }
26
```

(*program continues*)

```
27          source = ptr2;
28          while ( *source != '\0' )
29          {
30                    *dest = *source;
31                    dest++;
32                    source++;
33          }
34
35          return ( temp );
36     }
```

program output:
~H *; [

It seems that the str_combine() function should be copying the strings correctly into the array temp[]. But when the temp[] address is returned and the string at that address is printed, garbage results. This occurs because the storage for the array temp[] is allocated on the stack and then is deallocated when the function str_combine() returns. When printf() is called, it overwrites that memory with its own local variables, destroying the array temp[]. The correct solution is to declare the destination array in the main() function and pass its address to the str_combine() function as a third argument. The str_combine() function should then return the destination array's address as a verification, or a value of NULL (as defined in the file stdio.h) if there is a problem.

REGISTER VARIABLES

On most machines, a subset of the registers are reserved for register variables. These variables are more easily accessed when the program is executing and therefore are faster than automatic variables. They can hold any variable type that can be stored in a machine register. They are declared this way:

```
register int loop_control;
register char input_char;
```

where the word register acts as an adjective preceding an otherwise ordinary variable declaration. The number of registers reserved for register variables differs from machine to machine, from none to as many as six. If more register variables are requested than there are machine registers available to hold them, then the variables are treated as automatic variables. Some compilers completely ignore requests for register variables and assign variables to registers based on their usage in the program.

The following compares register variable use with automatic variables:

program: register.c

```
1     main()
2     {
3          register unsigned int fast;
4          unsigned int slow;
5          long start_loop, end_loop;
6          long timer();
7
8          fast = 1;
9          start_loop = timer();
10         while( fast < 65535 )
11         {
12              fast = fast + 1;
13         }
14         end_loop = timer();
15         printf(  "First executed in %d clock ticks\n",
16              end_loop - start_loop );
17
18         slow = 1;
19         start_loop = timer();
20         while( slow < 65535 )
21         {
22              slow = slow + 1;
23         }
24         end_loop = timer();
25         printf( "Second executed in %d clock ticks\n",
26              end_loop - start_loop );
27    }
```

program output:

```
First executed in 33 clock ticks
Second executed in 58 clock ticks
```

The calls made to timer() collect the current time (in machine clock ticks) and are used in this program to time the loops. The return value from the call is the number of machine clock ticks from a fixed point. You will notice that the time it took to execute the first loop was significantly less than the time it took to execute the second.

Assume that the timer() function is defined elsewhere; it is not part of the standard library.

Using register variables does not always guarantee that the program will run faster. In fact, sometimes it can actually slow a program down. When compiling a program, the compiler will often use unused register variables to evaluate large, complex expressions. If many register variables are used in the same block, then the compiler will have to evaluate the complex expressions using memory on the program stack instead of using registers. For example, consider the following two examples:

program: inefficient.c

```
1     main()
2     {
3          register int a, b;
4          int x, y;
5
6          /* many complex expressions; assume that x and
7             y are set                                    */
8
9          while ( x < y )
10         {
11             /* simple operations involving a and b
12                as temporary but  often  referenced
13                variables                            */
14             x++;
15         }
16    }
```

program: efficient.c

```
1     main()
2     {
3          int x, y;
4
5          /* many complex expressions here; assume that x
6             and y are set                                 */
7
8          while ( x < y )
9          {
10             register int a, b;
11
12             /* simple operations involving a and b
13                as temporary but  often  referenced
14                variables                            */
15             x++;
16         }
17    }
```

The second example is more efficient because it leaves the registers otherwise used to hold the values of a and b for the compiler. The compiler will use these registers to speed up the evaluation of the complex expressions in lines 5 and 6. Notice also that the two register variables in the second example will have useless values each time the loop body is exited. In the first example, the variables retain their values for the duration of the `main()` function's execution.

Initial Values

Register variables, like automatic variables, contain no useful or preinitialized values. Register variables should always be initialized before using.

Restrictions

For the most part, register variables may be used interchangeably with the same type of automatic variables except that the address of a register variable cannot be referenced. On most machines, applying the ampersand operator to a register variable will generate an error at compile time.

EXTERNAL VARIABLES

The external storage class is used when a program is split into several functions that appear in separate source files. External variables function as global variables and may be referenced from one file to the next as well as from multiple functions within the same source file. Unlike other variable type declarations, a variable is not declared external by preceding it with a modifying word. Rather, a variable is declared external by its placement within the source file. For example, the variable named `global_var` in the following program is assumed to be of the external storage class:

program: external.c

```
 1      int global_var;
 2
 3      main()
 4      {
 5          int auto_var;
 6
 7          /* program contents go
 8             here and may reference
 9             global_var or auto_var */
10      }
```

If there were other functions defined in this source file, they could also reference the value of the variable `global_var`; these functions would be accessing the same variable as the `main()` function. The variable named `auto_var`, by contrast, can only be referenced from the function `main()`.

The following program illustrates external variable declaration and use:

program: external.c

```
1       int global_var;  /* external variable */
2
3       main()
4       {
5           int auto_var;
6
7           global_var = 345;
8           auto_var = function( global_var );
9           printf( "%d %d\n", auto_var, global_var );
10      }
11
12      function( argument )
13      int argument;
14      {
15          int private_var;
16
17          /* in this function we can reference either
18              the variable global_var or private_var
19              but not auto_var (from main())          */
20
21          global_var = 876;
22          private_var = argument;
23          return( private_var );
24      }
```

program output:

345 876

The variable global_var may be referenced anywhere in this source file, either in main() or in function(). In addition, each of these two functions has its own automatic variables that are private to the function in which they are declared.

Often, when a program contains many functions, these functions are stored in multiple source files and are compiled separately; then, at a later point, the functions are linked to form an executable program. External variables can be referenced by functions that are defined in different source files. This is done by declaring the variable as in the previous example and then explicitly defining it in the second source file. For example:

source file: main.c

```
1
2      int global_var;   /* external variable */
3
4      main()
5      {
6          int auto_var;
7
8          global_var = 345;
9          auto_var = function( global_var );
10         printf( "%d %d\n", auto_var, global_var );
11     }
```

source file: function.c

```
1
2      extern int global_var;   /* external variable
3                                   declared elsewhere */
4
5      function( argument )
6      int argument;
7      {
8          int private_var;
9
10         /* in this function we can reference either
11             the variable global_var or private_var
12             but not auto_var (from main())        */
13
14         global_var = 876;
15         private_var = argument;
16         return( private_var );
17     }
```

program output:

345 876

This example is identical to the previous program except that the two functions forming the program have been placed in separate source files. In the second source file, we need to reference a variable declared in the first, so we *define* the variable in the second file in line 2. This statement is a directive to the compiler to leave a hook at this point in the program, assuming that the variable will be declared elsewhere. It is then the link editor's responsibility to *resolve* this reference—to find the variable declaration in the other file and to link the two. Many beginning programmers mistakenly precede all references to the variable name with the modifier extern. The modifier should not be used where storage is actually allocated for the variable, only where secondary references are made in other source files.

The placement of the statement:

```
extern int global_var;
```

is important even in the secondary source file because its placement indicates where the variable may be accessed. For example, if the function named function() were written as follows:

source file: function.c

```
1      function( argument )
2      int argument;
3      {
4           int private_var;
5           extern int global_var;   /* external variable
6                                       declared elsewhere */
7
8           global_var = 678;
9           private_var = argument;
10          return( private_var );
11     }
```

then the variable global_var could only be referenced inside that function and not in any other functions appearing in the same source file. In the original function definition the variable may be accessed anywhere in the source file. In the following program, assume that main.c and aux.c are placed in two separate files:

source file: main.c

```
1      int global_var;
2
3      main()
4      {
5           int local_var;
6
7           local_var = 1;
8           global_var = 2;
9           printf( "%d "%d\n", local_var, global_var );
10          test1( local_var );
```

```
11          printf( "%d %d\n", local_var, global_var );
12          test2( local_var );
13          printf( "%d %d\n", local_var, global_var );
14          test3( local_var );
15          printf( "%d %d\n", local_var, global_var );
16      }
17
18      test1( arg )
19      int arg;
20      {
21          int local_to_test1;
22
23          local_to_test1 = 3;
24          global_var = 4;
25          arg = 5;
26      }
```

source file: aux.c

```
1       test2( arg )
2       int arg;
3       {
4           extern int global_var;
5           int local_to_test2;
6
7           local_to_test2 = 6;
8           global_var = 7;
9       }
10
11      test3( arg )
12      int arg;
13      {
14          int local_to_test3;
15
16          local_to_test3 = 8;
17          global_var = 9;
18      }
```

compiler diagnostics:

```
aux.c:17: global_v undefined; func. test3
```

To reference the variable global_var in the test3() function, line 4 would have to be placed before line 1 in the file or repeated after line 13 inside the test3() function.

Internal Storage

Unlike automatic variables, external variables are not stored on the system stack. Instead, they are stored in a static section of memory called the *heap*. It does not disappear when a function exits and is therefore always available. In previous examples, we saw that an automatic variable declared in one block is not available to the next block, because the storage for these variables is allocated on the program stack. The storage area is reused for another block after the current block is finished. If we could see an image of a program while it is running, it would appear as shown in Exhibit 15-4.

EXHIBIT 15-4

Memory image during execution of a program

```
+---------------------------+
|                           |
|       instructions        |
|                           |
+---------------------------+
|                           |
|                           |
|      fixed data (heap)     |
|                           |
|                           |
|                           |
+---------------------------+
|/////////////////////////// |
|//// unallocated memory ////|
|/////////////////////////// |
+---------------------------+
|                           |
|                           |
|           stack           |
|    (extends from bottom)   |
|                           |
|                           |
+---------------------------+
```

The first section in memory contains the instructions that constitute the program, followed by external variables, and then a large pool of memory holding the process stack. Space is allocated in this stack while the program is running and is deallocated when a block or function is finished.

Initial Values

Unlike automatic variables, external variables are initially set to null. At compile time, space is allocated for these variables and they are initialized to null values.

Writing Large Programs

In a large programming project, it is good practice to split up the program's functions into several files. After a function is tested and considered stable, it is placed in a source file, compiled, and then linked with all the other program modules. In these systems, external variables are often declared in a separate source file of their own:

source file: externs.c

```
1     int x, y, z;
2     char c;
3     float fpoint;
4     double dfpoint;
```

This file is then compiled with the other source files that collectively make up the program. However, each of the other source files needs to reference the variables declared in externs.c, defining them in the individual source files. Instead of preceding each source file with the following:

```
extern int x, y, z;
extern char c;
extern float fpoint;
extern double dfpoint;
```

these definitions are held together in a file called a *header file* whose name traditionally ends with the suffix .h. It is included into (or added to) the contents of a source file using the #include preprocessor statement. For example:

source file: includer.c

```
1     #include "externs.h"
2
3     main()
```

(*program continues*)

```
 4     {
 5           x = 15;
 6           fpoint = 123.45;
 7
 8           /* useful program here that
 9               may use x, y, z, c, fpoint and
10               dfpoint
11           */
12     }
```

When this program is compiled along with the program externs.c, the compiler assumes that the file externs.h is in the current directory (on operating systems with directory structures) because its name is enclosed in quotes. If the header file name were enclosed with angle brackets, the preprocessor would look for the header files in a standard location. After the C preprocessor finds and includes the file externs.h, the program will look like:

preprocessed file: includer.i

```
 1    extern int x, y, z;
 2    extern char c;
 3    extern float fpoint;
 4    extern double dfpoint;
 5
 6    main()
 7    {
 8           x = 15;
 9           fpoint = 123.45;
10
11           /* useful program here that
12               may use x, y, z, c, fpoint and
13               dfpoint
14           */
15    }
```

This will then be delivered to the C compiler. It assumes that the external variables are declared elsewhere and the link editor will resolve the references.

An external variable may be defined (i.e., included in a header file) but never referenced in any routine.

STATIC VARIABLES

Static variables are similar to external variables. Storage is allocated at compile time rather than at run time. The variable remains for the duration of the program execution and can be accessed by more than one function. Unlike external variables, static variables are private to the source file in which they are declared.

Declaration

A static variable is declared by preceding the variable type with the modifier static, as follows:

```
static int always_there;
```

There are two types of static variables—static local and static global. A static variable's type depends on where it is declared. For example, in the following program,

program: static.c

```
1     static int stat_ext;
2     int global_variable;
3
4     main()
5     {
6         int local_var;
7         static int stat_local;
8
9         /* useful program statements go here and
10            can use stat_ext, global_variable,
11            local_var, and stat_local */
12
13        local_var = func( stat_local );
14     }
15
16     func( argument )
17     int argument;
18     {
19         int func_local;
20
21         /* this function can use stat_ext,
22            global_variable, argument (passed
23            argument) or func_local */
24
25         return( func_local );
26     }
```

five variables are declared. The variable stat_ext is an integer of type static global. The value of this variable can be referenced from anywhere in the source file. Since it is static, it cannot be linked to a variable definition in another source file. The variable named stat_local is a local static variable and may only be referenced within the main() function; it cannot be referenced in the function named func(). If static local variables can only be referenced within the function in which they are defined, then how do they differ from automatic variables? Internally, if a variable type is static, then its storage is allocated at compile time rather than at execution time. In the previous program, the variable stat_local could have been declared as "automatic" with little consequence. However, if a local static variable is declared inside a function,

program: static2.c

```
1     static int state_ext;
2     int global_variable;
3
4     main()
5     {
6         int sample, local_var;
7
8         local_var = func( sample );
9         local_var = func( sample );
10    }
11
12    func( argument )
13    int argument;
14    {
15        static int stat_local;
16
17        /* change value of stat_local */
18    }
```

and if the function is called more than once, then the value of the static local variable will be retained from one function call to the next. Furthermore, since stat_local is a static variable, we can assume that its value is initially null.

In the previous example, the variable named global_variable is an external variable and can, unlike the static variables, be referenced from another source file. The variables sample and local_var are automatic variables and may only be referenced within the block or function in which they are declared.

VARIABLE INITIALIZATION

Variables may be initialized when they are declared. For example:

```
static int prime = 11;
```

initializes the variable prime to the value 11. More than one variable of the same type can be declared and initialized on one line:

```
int a = 5, prime = 11, lending = 19;
```

where the names and values are separated by an equal sign and name/value pairs are separated by commas. If the variable is of type external or static, then the value is assigned when the program is compiled, otherwise the assignment is made when the program is executed. If the variable is of the automatic storage class, then it can be initialized to the value of an arithmetic expression:

```
int a = 5;
int b = 6;
int c = 20 * a;
```

For obvious reasons, any variable used in an initialization arithmetic expression must have been previously initialized itself. Static and external variables can only be initialized to constant values.

INITIALIZING ARRAYS

An array can be initialized when declared by specifying the values of some or all of its elements. For example:

```
static int xyz[10] = { 78, 23, 67, 56, 87, 76 };
```

Although the array has 10 elements, we have only defined values for the first six. When initializing static or external arrays, if fewer than all members have values specified, then the rest will be assigned a null value by default. (Many compilers allow the initialization of static or external, but not automatic arrays.)

Two-dimensional arrays can be initialized similarly. The following example illustrates this:

```
static int iarray[3][4] = { { 123, 234, 345, 543 },
                            { 456, 567, 678, 876 },
                            { 789, 987, 765, 542 }  };
```

Note the placement of the commas and the relative positions of the braces. The inner braces are not required, but are usually put in for clarity. If all the values for a row are not specified, then the braces are needed. For example:

```
static int iarray[3][4] = { { 123,  234 },
                            { 567,  678,  876 },
                            { 789,  987,  765,  542 }  };
```

Only two members in the first row of this two-dimensional array are specified, three are specified in the second row, and all four are specified in the last row. Arrays with more than two dimensions are initialized by using extra sets of nested braces to specify the dimensionality.

Character Arrays

We can initialize character arrays two different ways. We can initialize them in the same way we initialize numeric arrays:

```
static char carray[20] = { 'h', 'e', 'l', 'l', 'o', '\0' } ;
```

by specifying character constants for each of the values. Or, we can initialize them in this way:

```
static char carray[20] = "hello";
```

Although this looks like a pointer assignment (the character string address) into a character array, it is not. It is a notational convenience the compiler provides for character strings. This cannot be done in any place other than an initialization expression. If we want to put another character string into the array after it has been initialized, we must either place the characters there one at a time or use the strcpy() library function.

INITIALIZING STRUCTURES

Structures can be initialized similarly to arrays. When initializing structures, each member of the structure must be listed and enclosed by braces as follows:

```
struct sample
{
        int x;
        char y;
        float z;
};

static struct sample temp = { 123, 'a', 123.45 };
```

As with arrays, the structure initialization is limited to static and external declarations. If all the elements for a particular structure are not listed, the remaining members are initialized to null.

Arrays of Structures

Arrays of structures are initialized similarly to two-dimensional arrays—by using extra sets of braces. The following is an example of initializing an array of structures:

```
static struct sample sarray[3] = { { 123, 'a', 123.45 },
                                   { 234, 'b', 234.67 },
                                   { 345, 'c', 765.67 } };
```

INITIALIZING UNIONS

Unions can be initialized as if they were another scalar type (int, char, or float). The value initialized is the one that first appears in the union's definition. For example:

```
union sample2
{
        int i;
        char c;
        float f;
};

static union sample2 test = 1234;
```

initializes the value of i to 1234.

Like arrays and structures, the union initialization is limited to static and external variables. Many older compilers do not allow union initialization at all.

CONVERSIONS

We have seen that an expression's value can be represented in a different way than one of the parts of the expression. Consider the expression:

```
(float)x
```

where x is an integer variable. The value of the expression (float)x is the value of x, but the representation and characteristics of the value have changed. When (float)x is used in an arithmetic expression, the computation will treat it as a floating-point number. This ability is known as *type casting*.

EXHIBIT 15-5

Conversion of variable types by initial conversion

Variable Type	Converted To	Notes
short	int	depending on word size
unsigned short	unsigned int	
char	int	possible sign preservation
unsigned char	unsigned int	
float	double	

Initial Conversion

Whenever certain types of variables are used in an expression, their values are automatically converted to a different type so that computations and assignments can be more easily performed. For example, on a 32-bit machine, the size of a short integer is a half-word. If the hardware does not perform operations on half-words, the value will be converted to a full word (integer). Exhibit 15-5 shows those variable types converted when used in an expression.

Conversion by Assignment

Whenever the value of a variable of one type (int, float, etc.) is assigned to another variable of a different type, a conversion takes place. For example, when the value of an integer is assigned to a character variable, then the high-order bits are discarded and the resulting value in the character variable will

EXHIBIT 15-6

Conversion by assignment

Variable =	Expression	Notes
int	double	fraction part truncated double must be small enough
int	long	high-order bits dropped
unsigned	int	sign dropped
char	int	high-order bits dropped
char	double	fractional part truncated double must be small enough
unsigned char	int	sign, high-order bits dropped
unsigned char	char	sign dropped
float	int	OK
float	char	OK
double	int	OK
double	char	OK

EXHIBIT 15-7

Arithmetic conversions

Operand 1	Operand 2	Operation & Result
int	long	long
int	double	double
int	unsigned	unsigned
long	double	double

only be equal to the value of the integer if the integer value is less than 128 (256 if characters are stored unsigned).

Exhibit 15-6 summarizes the conversions that occur when an expression of one type is assigned to a variable of another type.

Arithmetic Conversions

Whenever two variables of different types are used together in an expression, the representation of one will be converted to match the other. Exhibit 15-7 shows the rules for these conversions.

The C language standard does not define other possible conversions and results will vary by compiler. When combining two different types of variables in an expression, never assume rules of conversion. It is always safer, and more portable, to explicitly force the conversion. For example, the following two expressions are equivalent:

assume:

```
int i = 3;
double x = 123.45, y;
```

statement 1:

```
y = x * i;
```

statement 2:

```
y = x * (double)i;
```

The second statement is preferable to the first for two reasons: it will work the same way on all machines and it is more readable.

SUMMARY

In this chapter we discussed variable scoping rules. While largely unimportant for small programs developed by a single programmer, storage classes assume great importance for large-scale programming projects with many program-mers. External variables permit multiple source files to share common data while local scoping of automatic variables protects variables from inadvertant naming collisions across separate source files.

It is not uncommon to create mixed-type expressions and/or assign the value contained within a variable of one type to a variable of a different type. When this is done it is important to be aware of the C language conversion rules.

EXERCISES

1. In the same source file as the main() function, declare an external variable named ex_int of type int. In the main() function set its value to 15. Create a new function p_external() in another source file. Have p_external() print the value of ex_int; do not pass the variable as an argument.

2. Rewrite program wrong.c so that it works properly.

3. Write a program that declares a static, three-dimensional integer array:

```
threedim [2][3][2]
```

and initializes all values of the array at declaration. Print out the values of the array with their array position as a check that you have declared the array correctly.

4. Type in and run the following program:

```
#include <stdio.h>

main()
{
        char a[50], b[50];
        char *concat();

        fgets( a, 50, stdin );
        fgets( b, 50, stdin );
        printf( "Both strings are: <%s>\n", concat( a, b ) );
}

char *concat( x, y )
char x[], y[];
        char total[100];
```

```
        strcpy( total, x );
        strcpy( total + strlen( total ), y );
        return( total );
}
```

Now run the following variation:

```
#include <stdio.h>

main()
{
        char a[50], b[50];
        char *concat();
        char *ret_val;

        fgets( a, 50, stdin );
        fgets( b, 50, stdin );
        ret_val = concat( a, b );
        f();
        printf( "Both strings are: <%s> n", ret_val );
}

char *concat( x, y )
char x[], y[];
{
        char total[100];

        strcpy( total, x );
        strcpy( total + strlen( total ), y );
        return( total );
}

f()
{
        char x[1000];
        int i;

        for ( i = 0; i < 1000; i++ )
        {
                x[i] = 'A';
        }
}
```

What is wrong? Correct the program by changing the variable storage classes or by declaring the array differently.

PART

COMPLEX
DATA TYPES

CHAPTER 16

ARRAYS, LINKED LISTS, AND STACKS

OVERVIEW

This chapter discusses two simple stack implementations, their layout in memory, and the operations needed to maintain them. A stack is a method for organizing data that can be implemented using arrays, linked structures, or other complex data types. Stacks organize and deliver data in a last-in-first-out (LIFO) manner. Operations on stacks include putting (pushing) messages onto the stack, retrieving (popping) messages from the stack, and looking at the first message on the stack without removing it from the stack. To introduce you to these operations, we include two programs in this chapter that use different methods for implementing a stack. In the first example, we allocate an array of one hundred pointers to character strings and use this for the stack. As messages are entered, we dynamically allocate memory to store the messages. In the second example, we implement the same LIFO access method using a linked list.

THE STACK

In general, a stack is a collection of objects (pointers to character strings in our first example) and a set of functions that add objects and remove objects. Exhibit 16-1 shows a picture of a typical stack.

A stack must have a pointer to the next available slot in the array. In our first example, we use an integer named s_pointer for this purpose, since this pointer is typically referred to as the *stack pointer*. This field, although often implemented using a pointer variable, could also be an index into an array. Exhibit 16-2 shows the stack with the stack pointer.

Stack Operations

Typical stack operations include initialize, push, pop, and look.

The initialize operation may be used at any time. It clears the stack, deallocates any dynamically allocated memory, and resets the stack pointer.

The push operation uses the stack pointer to find the next available slot in the array, puts the message in this slot, and then increments the stack pointer. Exhibit 16-3 shows the push operation on the stack.

The stack pointer may also be used to retrieve (pop) messages from the stack. Since the stack pointer points to the next available slot in the table, its value must be decremented before retrieving the message. After the message is retrieved, the stack pointer remains pointing to this slot in the table, which can then be reused for the next message. Exhibit 16-4 shows the pop operation.

The look operation is similar to the pop operation, but it returns the top element in the stack without decrementing the stack pointer.

Implementing a Stack Using an Array

Our first stack implementation uses an array and has six major functions:

EXHIBIT 16-1

A typical stack structure

element 6
element 5
element 4
element 3
element 2
element 1

EXHIBIT 16-2

A stack with a stack pointer

element 3
element 2
element 1

← s_pointer

main()	This function controls the program's execution by calling functions based on input the user enters.
getcommand()	This function prints a menu of choices. The menu is printed only on every fifth user interaction. The prompt to the user, however, is printed each time.
init_stack()	This function is implemented as a convenience to the user. Any time during the program's execution, the user may elect to clear the stack and start over. Any memory dynamically allocated for the character strings is deallocated and the stack pointer is reset.
push_stack()	This function adds a text message to the stack. The message is stored in dynamically allocated memory and only the pointer to the memory is stored on the stack.

EXHIBIT 16-3

The push operation

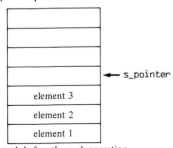

The stack *before* the push operation

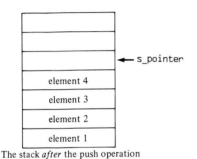

The stack *after* the push operation

EXHIBIT 16-4

The pop operation

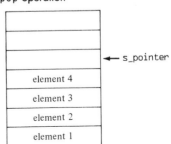

The stack *before* the pop operation

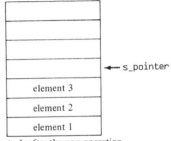

The stack *after* the pop operation

pop_stack()	This function copies the text of the last message on the stack into the character array whose address is passed to it as an argument. In addition, the message is removed from the stack.
look_stack()	This function is similar to pop_stack() but does not remove the message from the stack and does not adjust the stack pointer.

Controlling the Program Flow

The main() function calls the getcommand() function. It prints a menu of stack manipulation options and prompts for and accepts user input. The getcommand() function returns the entered command number and the main() function branches to the appropriate function. The main() function is defined as follows:

source file: stack.c

```
 1   #include <stdio.h>
 2
 3   #define INIT 1
 4   #define PUSH 2
 5   #define POP 3
 6   #define LOOK 4
 7   #define END 5
 8
 9   #define FAILURE 0
10   #define SUCCESS 1
11
12   #define MESSAGE_SIZE 256
13
14   main()
15   {
16       int command;
17       char msg_buf[MESSAGE_SIZE];
18
19       while ( (command = getcommand( "Enter command: " )) != END )
20       {
21
22           switch ( command )
23           {
24           case INIT:
25               init_stack();
26               break;
```

```
27
28          case PUSH:
29              if ( push_stack() == SUCCESS )
30              {
31                  if ( look_stack( msg_buf ) == SUCCESS )
32                  {
33                      char *cpointer;
34
35                      cpointer = strchr( msg_buf, '\n' );
36                      *cpointer = '\0';
37
38                      fprintf( stdout,
39                          "<%s> added to stack\n",
40                          msg_buf );
41                  }
42              }
43              break;
44
45          case POP:
46              if ( pop_stack( msg_buf ) == SUCCESS )
47              {
48                  fputs( msg_buf, stdout );
49              }
50              break;
51
52          case LOOK:
53              if ( look_stack( msg_buf ) == SUCCESS )
54              {
55                  fputs( msg_buf, stdout );
56              }
57              break;
58
59          default:
60              fprintf( stderr, "Invalid command\n" );
61
62          }
63      }
64  }
```

To improve readability, in lines 3 through 7 we define symbolic names for the command options to the program. The two symbolic names defined in lines 9 and 10 describe the return status of the functions that add messages to and read messages from the stack.

The character array msg_buf[] is used to pass character strings from called functions to the main() function. The character array cannot be declared as an automatic array in the called functions because memory used to hold it is released when the function completes. Therefore, it is declared in main() and its address is passed to the called functions.

The main program loop is in lines 19 through 63. It specifically directs the getcommand() function to retrieve input from the terminal in the form of a command number. If the returned number is equal to the symbolic constant END, we terminate the loop and drop out of the main() function.

To initialize the stack, we call the init_stack() function in line 25. To add a message to the stack, we call push_stack() and then call look_stack() to print a verification to the user. In lines 35 and 36, we remove the newline character stored in the string. (The fgets() function places this character there.) If we are successful in reading a message from the stack, we print the message on the terminal (lines 45 through 50).

The look_stack() function reads a message but leaves it on the stack. If the called function is successful, then we print the message. At the end of the switch statement we have a default case because the getcommand() function performs no error checking. If erroneous input is supplied, we print an error message and reprompt.

Presenting a Menu To the User

The getcommand() function prints a menu and prompts the user for input. The function is defined as follows:

source file: stack.c

```
        .
        .
        .
66    #define COMMAND_LENGTH 10
67
68    getcommand( prompt )
69    char *prompt;
70    {
71        char ascii_command[COMMAND_LENGTH];
72        int command;
73        static int need_prompt;
74
```

```
75          if ( need_prompt == 0 )
76          {
77              need_prompt = 5;
78              printf( "Enter 1) Initialize stack\n" );
79              printf( "      2) Push message on stack\n" );
80              printf( "      3) Pop message from stack\n" );
81              printf( "      4) Look at top of stack\n" );
82              printf( "      5) End\n\n" );
83          }
84      else
85          {
86              need_prompt--;
87          }
88
89      printf( prompt );
90      fgets( ascii_command, COMMAND_LENGTH - 1, stdin );
91      command = atoi( ascii_command );
92      return( command );
93  }
        .
        .
        .
```

We do not want to show the menu each time input is requested. Therefore, we keep a counter and display the menu only once for each five input requests. This function accepts ASCII input from the terminal; we convert it to an integer using the atoi() library function.

The variable need_prompt declared in line 73 is of the static storage class. This is necessary because we want the variable's value to be retained across calls to this function. Alternatively, we could have declared it external.

Declaring Stack Variables

The following variables and symbolic constants are needed for manipulating the stack data structure:

source file: stack.c
```
        .
        .
        .
95  #define STACKSIZE 100
96
97  char *stack[STACKSIZE];
98  int s_pointer; /* always contains the index of the
99                    next element not being used */
        .
        .
        .
```

In lines 95 and 97, we declare stack[] to be an array of one hundred (represented by the symbolic name STACKSIZE) pointers to character strings. Thus, the stack will be able to contain pointers to at most one hundred character strings. Later, we will see how to remove this restriction.

In line 98, we declare the stack pointer. The variable name implies that it is a pointer variable, but we have chosen to implement it as an index into the array.

Implementing the push Operation

The push_stack() function adds a message to the stack. It prompts for and accepts the message to be placed on the stack. It allocates just enough memory to store the character string (the size of the string as well as an extra byte needed for the string termination character), then places the character string address on the stack where the s_pointer variable indicates. The function is defined this way:

source file: stack.c

```
            .
            .
            .
115    push_stack()
116    {
117         char message[MESSAGE_SIZE];
118         char *malloc(), *strcpy();
119
120         if ( s_pointer >= STACKSIZE )
121         {
122              printf( "Stack is full\n" );
123              return( FAILURE );
124         }
125         else
126         {
127              printf( "Enter message: " );
128              fgets( message, MESSAGE_SIZE, stdin );
129
130              stack[s_pointer] =
131                   malloc( (unsigned)(strlen( message ) + 1));
132              strcpy( stack[s_pointer], message );
133
134              s_pointer++;
135              return( SUCCESS );
136         }
137    }
```

The character array message[] is used to hold the character string temporarily until we can allocate permanent memory for it. This array's size (256) defines the character string's maximum length. Since it is only needed temporarily, we can declare it as an automatic array. The section of the function in lines 120 through 124 checks for stack overflow. If there are already a hundred messages on the stack (the value of s_pointer is one hundred, we cannot add any more), we generate an error message and return the defined value of FAILURE.

If there is still room left in the stack, we prompt for the message, read the message into the temporary array, dynamically allocate memory for the message, and copy the contents of the temporary array into the newly allocated memory. Before returning, we increment s_pointer so that it still refers to the next unused slot in the stack[] array.

Implementing the pop Operation

The pop_stack() function takes a message off the stack and makes a copy of the message for the calling function. This is implemented as follows:

source file: stack.c

```
          .
          .
          .
139    pop_stack( ret_array )
140    char ret_array[];
141    {
142          void free();
143          char *strcpy();
144
145          if ( s_pointer <= 0 )
146          {
147               printf( "Stack is empty\n" );
148               strcpy( ret_array, "" );
149               return( FAILURE );
150          }
151          else
152          {
153               strcpy( ret_array, stack[--s_pointer] );
154               free( stack[s_pointer] );
155               return( SUCCESS );
156          }
157    }
          .
          .
          .
```

The only argument to this function is the address of the array of characters. This will be used to pass the message removed from the stack back to the
calling function. If no messages are on the stack, print an error message and
return the defined value of FAILURE. Before returning, copy an empty string
into the array.

If there is a message on the stack (lines 151 through 156), we decrement
s_pointer, use the decremented value to access the stack, and copy the
string pointed to by the array element. After the copy is made, we free() the
memory used to hold the message. It is not necessary to clear the element of
the array since it cannot be accessed (s_pointer refers to it as an empty slot).
The defined value of SUCCESS is returned.

Implementing the look Operation

The look_stack() function is essentially the same as the pop_stack()
function except that this function does not remove the message from the stack.
It is defined as follows:

source file: stack.c

```
              .
              .
              .
159   look_stack( ret_array )
160   char ret_array[];
161   {
162         if ( s_pointer <= 0 )
163         {
164               printf( "Stack is empty\n" );
165               strcpy( ret_array,  "" );
166               return( FAILURE );
167         }
168         else
169         {
170               strcpy( ret_array, stack[s_pointer - 1] );
171               return( SUCCESS );
172         }
173   }
```

Unlike the pop_stack() function, the variable s_pointer is not decremented and the memory for the message is not deallocated. The function still
checks that there are elements on the stack.

Initializing the Stack

Depending on the application, you may want to enable the user to clear the
stack and begin over again. The init_stack() removes all messages from

the stack and deallocates any memory dynamically allocated to hold the messages. This function is defined as follows:

source file: stack.c

```
           .
           .
           .
101   init_stack()
102   {
103        void free();
104
105        /* deallocate memory for individual
106          elements on stack */
107
108        for ( ; s_pointer > 0 ; s_pointer-- )
109        {
110             free( stack[s_pointer] );
111        }
112        printf( "Stack initialized\n" );
113   }
```

If we are not concerned about freeing the memory we dynamically allocated to hold the character strings, we could simply set s_pointer to zero. However, we have chosen to deallocate all memory allocated by the character strings. When the loop finishes, the value of s_pointer will be equal to zero and a message will be printed.

The free() library function frees memory dynamically allocated by the malloc() library function call.

THE LINKED LIST

An access method (e.g., a stack) can frequently be implemented using one of several alternate data structures. In this chapter's second example, we illustrate how a stack can be implemented using a linked list. Linked lists have certain advantages over arrays because it is not necessary to impose *a priori* restrictions on the stack's size (other than those the machine's available memory imposes).

A linked list is a collection of structures ordered not by their physical placement in memory (like an array), but by logical links that are stored as part of the data in the structure itself. In this example, the link is in the form of a pointer to another structure of the same type. However, it could be any information that would locate the next logical structure. If the linked list was stored in a file, the link could be the offset in the file where the next structure begins. Exhibit 16-5 shows a schematic diagram of a linked list.

The way the two structures in Exhibit 16-5 are ordered is not dictated by their physical placement but rather by the links that connect them. The start of the list is in a constant location; it contains the address of the first structure in the list. That structure contains the address of the next structure, which contains the address of the next structure, and so on. The last structure in the list contains a NULL address indicating that no more structures are in the list. Sometimes, for convenience, the end of the list points to (or contains the address of) the first member of the list. This is known as a *circular list* and is shown in Exhibit 16-6. Another common variation on linked lists is to have each structure also point to its predecessor in the list. This is known as a two-way or doubly linked list and is shown in Exhibit 16-7.

EXHIBIT 16-5

Schematic diagram of a linked list

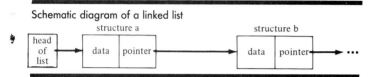

EXHIBIT 16-6

A circular list

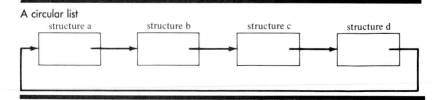

Implementing a Stack Using a Linked List

In this example, we reimplement the previous example's initialization, push, pop and look procedures using a linked list. Instead of using an array and a variable named s_pointer, we use the following:

source file: lstack.c

```
            .
            .
            .
95    struct node
96    {
97          char *message;
98          struct node *next;
99    };
100
101   struct node *head;       /* head of the linked list */
            .
            .
            .
```

The structure defined here contains a pointer to a message and a pointer to the structure that contains the next logical message.

The pointer declared in line 101 contains either a NULL value if the list is empty, or the address of the structure logically placed on the top of the stack. That structure points to the next structure, and so on.

The push Operation

The push_stack() function does the same thing as the previous program's push_stack() function, but uses a linked list:

source file: lstack.c

```
         .
         .
         .
124   push_stack()
125   {
126       char temp_message[MESSAGE_SIZE];
127       char *malloc(), *calloc(), *strcpy();
128       struct node *n_pointer;
129
130       /* allocate node structure */
131       n_pointer = (struct node *)calloc( 1,
132               (unsigned)sizeof(struct node) );
133
134       if ( n_pointer == (struct node *)NULL )
135       {
136           printf( "Memory is full\n" );
137           return( FAILURE );
138       }
139       else
140       {
141           printf( "Enter message: " );
142           fgets( temp_message, MESSAGE_SIZE, stdin );
143
144           n_pointer->message =
145               malloc( (unsigned)(strlen( temp_message ) + 1));
146
147           if ( n_pointer->message != (char *)NULL )
148           {
149               strcpy( n_pointer->message, temp_message );
150               n_pointer->next = head;
151               head = n_pointer;
152               return( SUCCESS );
153           }
154           else
155           {
156               printf( "Memory is full\n" );
157               return( FAILURE );
158           }
159       }
160   }
         .
         .
         .
```

EXHIBIT 16-7

A two-way linked list

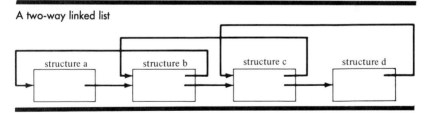

Unlike the array version, this version has no program-imposed maximum stack size. Nodes for each message are allocated dynamically as needed. The return value of the call to calloc() is typecast to make the return type (normally, char *) the same type as the pointer variable. We use calloc() instead of malloc() because we want the memory's initial contents to be zeroed. If the call to calloc() fails (lines 134 through 138), we must be at a system-imposed restriction.

As before, we prompt for the message and store it in a temporary array. We then allocate permanent memory to store the string using the malloc() library function. If the call to malloc() fails, we return the defined value of FAILURE in line 157.

If the memory allocation is successful, we logically add this structure onto the stack. Using the head variable, we locate the first structure on the stack and insert the new structure between these two. Since head points to the "old" first structure, we store this pointer in the new structure and set head to point to the "new" structure. Exhibit 16-8 illustrates this.

EXHIBIT 16-8

The push operation on a linked list

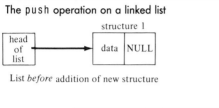

List *before* addition of new structure

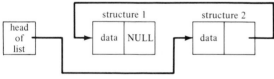

List *after* addition of new structure

The pop Operation

To remove a node from a singly linked list, we must access the structure logically preceding the structure to be removed. We copy the "next" field from the structure we are removing to its predecessor. This logically removes the structure. Exhibit 16-9 (page 295) illustrates this process. The function that implements this for a linked list is defined as follows:

source file: lstack.c

```
162    pop_stack( ret_array )
163    char ret_array[];
164    {
165         char *strcpy();
166
167         if ( head == (struct node *)NULL )
168         {
169              printf( "Stack is empty\n" );
170              strcpy( ret_array, "" );
171              return( FAILURE );
172         }
173         else
174         {
175              struct node *temp_pointer;
176
177              strcpy( ret_array, head->message );
178              temp_pointer = head->next;
179              free( head->message );
180              free( (char *)(head) );
181              head = temp_pointer;
182              return( SUCCESS );
183         }
184    }
           .
           .
           .
```

In line 167 we check if the head variable has a NULL value. If so, then the list is empty and we copy an empty string to the array and return the defined value of FAILURE.

Since the variable head contains the address of the first structure in the list, the expression:

```
head->message
```

EXHIBIT 16-9

The pop operation on a linked list

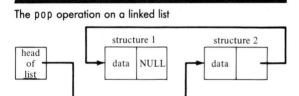

List *before* removal of top structure from stack

List *after* removal of top structure from stack

refers to that structure's message field. The expression:

head->next

therefore refers to the address of the second structure in the list. In line 177, we copy the contents of the first message to the array whose address is passed as an argument.

In line 178, we save the next pointer of the structure we are removing from the list. It will later be put in the head field. In line 179, we use head as a pointer to the first structure and free the memory allocated for the message. Line 180 frees the memory allocated for the node structure. More memory will be allocated if we want to add another message to the list later. Finally, in line 181 we logically remove the node from the list by placing in head the address of the structure that was previously the second structure in the list.

The look Operation

The look_stack() function is similar to the pop_stack() function except that the message (structure) is not removed from the stack. This function is defined as follows:

source file: lstack.c

```
        .
        .
        .
186     look_stack( ret_array )
187     char ret_array[];
188     {
```

(*program continues*)

```
189          if ( head == (struct node *)NULL )
190          {
191              printf( "Stack is empty\n" );
192              strcpy( ret_array, "" );
193              return( FAILURE );
194          }
195          else
196          {
197              strcpy( ret_array, head->message );
198              return( SUCCESS );
199          }
200      }
```

The Initialization Operation

The init_stack() function traverses the list, deallocating the memory for each node and the memory used to store the message. Finally, it sets the pointer head to NULL. It is implemented as follows:

source file: lstack.c

```
103  init_stack()
104  {
105      struct node *n_pointer;
106
107      /* deallocate memory for individual elements on stack */
108
109      for ( n_pointer = head ; n_pointer != (struct node *)NULL ; )
110      {
111          struct node *temp_pointer;
112
113          free( n_pointer->message );
114          temp_pointer = n_pointer->next;
115
116          free( n_pointer );
117          n_pointer = temp_pointer;
118      }
119      head = (struct node *)NULL;
120
121      printf( "Stack initialized\n" );
122  }
```

In line 114, we save the pointer to the next member of the list so it can be referenced after the structure containing it is deallocated. When all the memory for the messages and the node structures has been deallocated we set the variable `head` to `NULL`.

SUMMARY

In this chapter we have discussed stack creation and management. We have shown two distinct methods for implementing a stack—arrays and linked lists. Using these two techniques we implemented and described push, pop, initialize, and look, the most common stack operations.

If we use an array to implement the stack, we create a stack pointer to keep track of the top of the stack. When the stack pointer refers to the beginning of the array, we have an empty stack; when it refers to the end of the array, we have a full stack.

If we use a linked list to implement the stack, we add to and remove from the list at the beginning of the list because of the stack's nature. When using a linked list we do not have to know the stack's size beforehand; the program dynamically allocates memory as it is needed. However, we need to keep track of the structure that is logically next on the stack; this requires additional memory to store the pointers.

EXERCISES

1. Rewrite the `getcommand()` function so that it checks for valid user input (1–5). If the input is out of range, print an appropriate message and reprompt.

2. In the `push_stack()` function (array implementation) we should really make sure the `malloc()` function (line 131) does not fail. Add this check to the function and return `FAILURE` if it does.

3. Rewrite `pop_stack()` (both implementations) so that more than one message can be retrieved. Rewrite `getcommand()` to prompt for the number of messages to be popped and pass this as a parameter to `pop_stack()`.

4. Write a function that traverses the linked list implementation of the stack and prints out the messages in alphabetical order.

5. A sparse matrix is defined as a large matrix in which many of the elements have a zero value. A two-dimensional sparse matrix can be conveniently represented as a linked list where each element contains five values:

- the element's row designation
- the element's column designation

- the element's value
- a pointer to the next, nonzero-row element
- a pointer to the next, nonzero-column element

Write a program to reduce a large sparse matrix to a linked list.

6.   Write a program containing functions to total the columns, rows, and diagonals of a sparse matrix.

7.   Write a program to add two sparse matrices.

8.   Write a program to multiply two sparse matrices.

CHAPTER 17

ARRAYS, LINKED LISTS, AND QUEUES

OVERVIEW

In this chapter we discuss two queue implementations using techniques similar to those used in Chapter 16. Our first example uses an array to implement a queue, the second uses a linked list. We will discuss queue management and the operations necessary to maintain a queue.

QUEUES

Like the stack, the queue is an access method. It may be implemented using an array, a linked list, or some other data structure. However, queue management is different from stack management. The elements placed on the queue (messages, in our examples), are returned in the same order in which they were put onto the queue (as opposed to a stack where elements are delivered in reverse order of storage).

Implementing a Queue Using an Array

The first example uses an array to store the queue. The array is defined this way:

source file: squeue.c

```
          .
          .
          .
70    #define QUEUESIZE 100
71
72    char *queue[QUEUESIZE];
73    int read_end, write_end;
          .
          .
          .
```

We will need two indexes into the array: one that refers to the first valid message on the queue (read_end) and the other that refers to the next available slot in the array (write_end). Exhibit 17-1 illustrates this.

EXHIBIT 17-1

Implementation of a queue using an array with two indexes

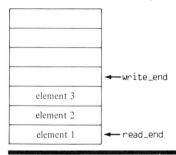

EXHIBIT 17-2

EXHIBIT 17-2

An empty queue

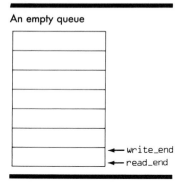

If read_end is equal to write_end, there are no outstanding messages on the queue. If either of the two indexes is incremented past the end of the array, it is reset back to the beginning and we attempt to reuse slots in the array that once had messages, but whose messages have since been read and removed from the queue. If, when incremented, write_end becomes equal to read_end, we have used all slots in the array and the queue is full. Exhibit 17-2 shows an empty queue. Exhibit 17-3 shows a partially full queue where write_end has wrapped around. Exhibit 17-4 shows a full queue.

Thus, the array functions as a circular-data structure because it wraps around when all the slots in the array have been used.

Presenting the Queue-Management Choice Menu

This main() function is similar to the main() function in Chapter 16. A similar getcommand() function displays a prompt on the user's terminal and waits for input. The input is converted from ASCII to an integer and the integer

EXHIBIT 17-3

A partially full queue in which write_end has wrapped around

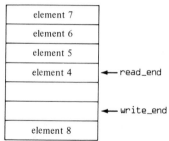

EXHIBIT 17-4

A full queue

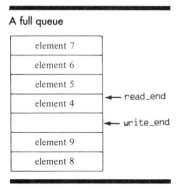

value is returned. For queues, only two operations are allowed: putting (writing) a message and getting (reading) a message. Here is the main() function:

source file: squeue.c

```
1    #include <stdio.h>
2
3    #define PUT 1
4    #define GET 2
5    #define END 3
6
7    #define SUCCESS 1
8    #define FAILURE 0
9    #define MESSAGE_SIZE 256
10
11   main()
12   {
13       int command;
14       char ret_val[MESSAGE_SIZE];
15
16       while ( (command = getcommand( "Enter command: " )) != END )
17       {
18
19           switch ( command )
20           {
21           case PUT:
22               if ( put_message() == FAILURE )
23               {
24                   fprintf( stderr,
25                   "Try reading messages\n" );
26               }
27               break;
```

```
28
29                   case GET:
30                       if ( get_message( ret_val ) == SUCCESS )
31                       {
32                           fputs( ret_val, stdout );
33                       }
34                       break;
35
36                   default:
37                       fprintf( stderr, "Invalid command\n" );
38
39                   }
40       }
41   }
          .
          .
          .
```

Array Manipulation

As we discussed earlier, we maintain two indexes into the array: one used for adding messages (write pointer) and the other for retrieving messages (read pointer). The write pointer must always refer to an unused entry in the array, so that we do not attempt to add a message over an existing message.

Adding a Message

The put_message() function adds messages to the queue:

source file: squeue.c

```
     .
     .
     .
 7    #define SUCCESS 1
 8    #define FAILURE 0
 9    #define MESSAGE_SIZE 256
     .
     .
     .
75    put_message()
76    {
77        char *gather_input();
78
```

(*program continues*)

```
79          /* wrap around */
80          if ( write_end >= QUEUESIZE - 1 )
81          {
82              if( read_end != 0 )
83              {
84                  queue[write_end] = gather_input();
85                  write_end = 0;
86                  return( SUCCESS );
87              }
88              else
89              {
90                  printf( "Queue is full\n" );
91                  return( FAILURE );
92              }
93          }
94          else if ( (write_end + 1) == read_end )
95          {
96              printf( "Queue is full\n" );
97              return( FAILURE );
98          }
99          else
100         {
101             queue[write_end] = gather_input();
102             write_end++;
103             return( SUCCESS );
104         }
105     }
```

This function expects no argument. It can access the array named queue because it is declared as an external array.

In lines 80 through 93, we manage the write pointer wraparound, if necessary. Some messages in the queue may have already been read, others not. Since we do not want the write pointer to refer to an unread message, we have to take special care. In lines 82 through 87, we handle the case in which the read pointer does not refer to the first element in the array (the message stored there has been read). We call the gather_input() function to prompt for the message and store the pointer to the message in the array's last element. We then set the write pointer to refer to the first element of the array. What if the write pointer points to the array's last element and read pointer points to the first? This special case is handled in lines 88 through 92 of the function. Although the last entry in the array is not being used, we cannot store a message there because the write pointer cannot be changed to refer to an unused element. (Remember, the first message has not been read yet.) The "Queue is full" message is printed and the defined value of FAILURE is returned to the calling function.

Lines 94 through 98 are executed if the write pointer refers to an element that is not at the end of the array and the queue is full. We can determine this because no unused elements are between the write pointer and the read pointer.

Lines 99 through 104 of the if-else-if statement are executed when a message is to be stored in the middle of the array. The gather_input() function is called and the pointer to the message is stored in the array. The write pointer is incremented and the defined value of SUCCESS is returned.

Reading the Message from the Terminal

The overhead function gather_input() is defined below:

source file: squeue.c

```
          .
          .
          .
107  char *gather_input()
108  {
109       char *malloc(), *strcpy();
110       char message[MESSAGE_SIZE], *mptr;
111
112       printf( "Enter message: " );
113       fgets( message, MESSAGE_SIZE, stdin );
114
115       mptr = malloc( (unsigned)(strlen( message ) + 1));
116       strcpy( mptr, message );
117
118       return( mptr );
119  }
```

This function returns a noninteger value. Consequently, the return type must be defined (line 107). In line 115, memory is allocated for the string, the string is copied, and the address of the memory is returned to the calling function. The calling function then places this value in the queue[] array.

Reading Messages from the Queue

The get_message() function reads messages as follows:

source file: squeue.c

```
          .
          .
          .
121  get_message( ret_array )
122  char ret_array[];
```

(program continues)

```
123   {
124        void free();
125        char *strcpy();
126
127        if ( read_end == write_end )
128        {
129            printf( "Queue is empty\n" );
130            strcpy( ret_array, "" );
131            return( FAILURE );
132        }
133        else
134        {
135            strcpy( ret_array, queue[read_end] );
136            free( queue[read_end] );
137
138            read_end++;
139            /* wrap around if necessary */
140            if( read_end >= QUEUESIZE )
141            {
142                read_end = 0;
143            }
144            return( SUCCESS );
145        }
146   }
```

The function requires one argument—the address of an array of characters where the message will be copied.

If it is the case that the read pointer points to the next empty element in the array (write_end), then the queue is empty. We print an appropriate message and return the defined value of FAILURE.

If the read pointer is not equal to the write pointer, we copy the string referred to by read_end into the character array whose address is supplied to the function.

In line 136, we free the memory used to hold the message contents. (This memory was allocated in the gather_input() function, line 115.)

Finally, we advance the read pointer to the next message. If advancing the pointer causes it to refer to an element beyond the end of the queue[] array, we reset the pointer to 0, wrapping the read pointer around to the front of the array.

QUEUES USING LINKED LISTS

The following example shows how a queue can be implemented using a linked list instead of an array. The linked list has some distinct advantages over the array, mostly in terms of space needed to store the messages. The linked list seldom encounters the "queue full" error condition (only after all of memory has been used) and it only uses the memory it needs.

This program has two functions not implemented in the previous example. These functions are init_queue() and look(). The init_queue() function deallocates all messages on the queue and frees the memory reserved for the text. The look() function prints the message at the beginning of the queue without removing it from the queue. The main() function for this program is shown below:

source file: queue.c

```
1     #include <stdio.h>
2
3     #define INIT 1
4     #define PUT 2
5     #define GET 3
6     #define LOOK 4
7     #define END 5
8
9     #define SUCCESS 1
10    #define FAILURE 0
11
12    #define MESSAGE_SIZE 256
13
14    main()
15    {
16        int command;
17        char returned_message[MESSAGE_SIZE];
18
19        while ( (command = getcommand( "Enter command: " )) != END )
20        {
21
22            switch ( command )
23            {
24            case INIT:
25                init_queue();
26                break;
27
28            case PUT:
29                if ( put() == FAILURE )
30                {
31                    fprintf( stderr,
32                    "Memory is full, Try reading messages\n");
33
34                }
35                break;
```

(program continues)

```
36
37              case GET:
38                  if ( get( returned_message ) == SUCCESS )
39                  {
40                      fputs( returned_message, stdout );
41                  }
42                  break;
43
44              case LOOK:
45                  if ( look( returned_message ) == SUCCESS )
46                  {
47                      fputs( returned_message, stdout );
48                  }
49                  break;
50
51              default:
52                  fprintf( stderr, "Invalid command\n" );
53
54          }
55      }
56  }
    .
    .
    .
```

The put(), get(), and look() functions all return the defined value of either SUCCESS or FAILURE. Each branch of the switch statement calls the function, checks the return value and prints either an error message or the string from the array returned_message[].

The queue Structure

The structure used in this example is identical to that used for the stack implementation:

source file: queue.c

```
    .
    .
    .
87  struct queue
88  {
89      char *message;
90      struct queue *next;
91  };
```

As in the previous example, space will be allocated for the message through the `malloc()` library function and this memory's address will be stored in the queue. The field `next` links the structures in the queue.

To implement a queue using a linked list, we need to keep track of both ends of the list. We use one end to add to the list and the other to remove nodes from the list. Therefore, the head of the linked list is defined like this:

source file: queue.c

```
        .
        .
        .
 93     struct q_head
 94     {
 95          struct queue *first;
 96          struct queue *last;
 97     };
 98
 99     static struct q_head head;
        .
        .
        .
```

This structure is declared as `static` external. It can be referenced by name in any function that follows line 99, but not by functions before line 99 or in other source files.

Writing to the Queue

The `put()` function writes to the queue as follows:

source file: queue.c

```
        .
        .
        .
122     put()
123     {
124          char temp_message[MESSAGE_SIZE];   /* holds typed in message */
125          struct queue *temp_structure;      /* points to memory allocated
126                                                 for queue structure */
127          char *malloc(), *strcpy();
128
```

(*program continues*)

```
129            printf( "Enter message: " );
130            fgets( temp_message, MESSAGE_SIZE, stdin );
131
132            temp_structure =
133                (struct queue *)malloc( (unsigned)(sizeof(struct queue)) );
134            if ( temp_structure == (char *)NULL )
135            {
136                return( FAILURE );
137            }
138
139            temp_structure->message =
140                malloc( (unsigned)(strlen( temp_message ) + 1));
141            if ( temp_structure->message == (char *)NULL )
142            {
143                free( (char *)temp_structure );
144                return( FAILURE );
145            }
146
147            strcpy( temp_structure->message, temp_message );
148
149            temp_structure->next = (struct queue *)0;
150
151            if ( head.first == (struct queue *)0 )
152            {
153                /* empty queue */
154                head.first = temp_structure;
155                head.last = temp_structure;
156            }
157            else
158            {
159                /* put at end */
160                head.last->next = temp_structure;
161                head.last = temp_structure;
162            }
163            return( SUCCESS );
164     }
         .
         .
         .
```

No arguments are given to this function. It can access the queue structure through the static variable head.

The temp_message[] array will be used to store the message entered in line 130. It is declared as an automatic variable and must be copied to permanent memory before the function finishes.

In lines 132 through 137, we allocate a block of memory large enough to store a struct queue. If this request fails (out-of-memory condition), we return the defined value of FAILURE to the calling function. The calling function will print an error message and allow for retry. In line 133, the return value of malloc() is cast to (struct queue *) to ensure that the type of expression to the right of the assignment operator is the same as the variable to its left.

In lines 139 through 145, we allocate a block of memory large enough to store the previously entered character string as well as one extra character for the string termination character. If this fails, we cannot add this message to the queue. We free the memory allocated in lines 132 and 133 and return the defined value of FAILURE to the calling function.

Note that in line 149 the malloc() function allocates memory but does not clear it. We cannot assume that malloc() will give us "clean" memory, so we have to initialize it ourselves. The structure is put logically at the end of the list. Since no other nodes follow it, its next field is given a zero value.

In the special case of an empty list (lines 151 through 156), we add the node and have both pointers point to it. Exhibit 17-5 shows this.

To add a node to a nonempty list (lines 157 through 162), we use the next field of the last structure on the list, add the new mode after it, and set head.last to point to the new structure. Exhibit 17-6 illustrates this process.

EXHIBIT 17-5

Adding the first node

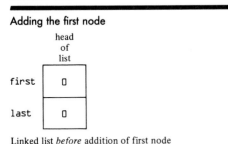

Linked list *before* addition of first node

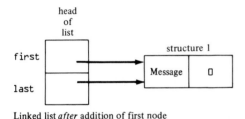

Linked list *after* addition of first node

EXHIBIT 17-6

Adding the second node

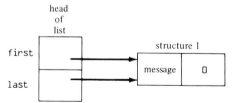

Linked list *before* adding second node

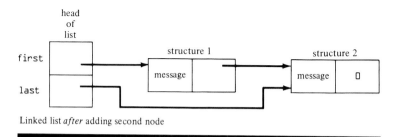

Linked list *after* adding second node

Reading from the Queue

The get() function reads a message from the queue. Using a pointer to the beginning of the list it references the first structure, copies the message into the array whose address it was given, and removes the structure from the linked list. The get() function is listed below:

source file: queue.c

```
        .
        .
        .
166     get( ret_array )
167     char ret_array[];
168     {
169          char *strcpy();
170          struct queue *temp;
171
172          if ( head.first != (struct queue *)0 )
173          {
174
175              strcpy( ret_array, head.first->message );
176              free( head.first->message );
```

```
177                  temp = head.first;
178                  head.first = temp->next;
179                  free( (char *)temp );
180                  return( SUCCESS );
181             }
182        else
183             {
184                  printf( "Empty queue\n" );
185                  strcpy( ret_array, "" );
186                  return( FAILURE );
187             }
188     }
```

If there are any unread messages on the queue, the first message will be copied; otherwise the character array will have an empty string (" ") copied into it.

Assuming there is an unread message, we copy the first message's contents into the array whose address is supplied and deallocate the memory used to store the character string while it was part of the queue. We remove the structure from the queue by setting head.first equal to the structure pointed to by the first structure, and free the memory used to store the logically removed structure.

If there are no messages on the queue, we print an error message, copy an empty string into the destination array, and return the defined value of FAILURE.

Looking at Messages

Using the function look(), it is possible to just look at the first message without removing it from the queue. The look() function is a slightly modified version of the get() function:

source file: queue.c

```
       .
       .
       .
190    look( ret_array )
191    char ret_array[];
192    {
193         char *strcpy();
194
195         if ( head.first != (struct queue *)0 )
196         {
197              strcpy( ret_array, head.first->message );
198              return( SUCCESS );
199         }
```
(program continues)

```
200          else
201          {
202              printf( "Empty queue\n" );
203              strcpy( ret_array, "" );
204              return( FAILURE );
205          }
206      }
```

Initializing the Queue

It is sometimes necessary to traverse a linked list. This is often done when searching for a particular element. The function named init_queue() frees all members of the queue by traversing the linked list and removing each member.

source file: queue.c

.
.
.

```
101    init_queue()
102    {
103        struct queue *q_pointer, *next_structure;
104
105        /* traverse the list, removing each member
106           and deallocating the memory used for each */
107        for ( q_pointer = head.first;
108              q_pointer != (struct queue *)0;
109              q_pointer = next_structure )
110        {
111            next_structure = q_pointer->next;
112            free( q_pointer->message );
113            free( (char *)q_pointer );
114        }
115
116        head.first = (struct queue *)0;
117        head.last = (struct queue *)0;
118
119        printf( "Queue initialized\n" );
120    }
```

.
.
.

The traversal starts at the first message in the queue, to which the variable head.first points.

If the list is empty, head. first has a zero value and the loop is termi-nated immediately. Otherwise, we look at each structure on the list until the next field of one of the structures has a zero value, which indicates the end of the list. As an alternative, we could have compared the address of the structure we deallocated last against the variable head. last.

We move from structure to structure by saving the address of the next structure in the linked list before freeing the current structure.

In lines 112 and 113 we deallocate the memory used to store the message and the structure that held it in the linked list. When we deallocate the structure we need to cast the structure's address to (char *) so that the type of the argument expression will match that expected by the free() function.

SUMMARY

In this chapter we have discussed two methods for implementing queues. The first used an array as the data structure; the second used a linked list. Unlike the stack, we had to keep two pointers (or indexes) into the queue: one for the read end and the other for the write end. As with the stack program, the size of the array limits the number of messages on the queue, but when using linked lists, only available memory limits it.

EXERCISES

1. The getcommand() function is not listed for either the array or linked list implementation of the queue. It is a slightly modified version of the function from Chapter 16. Write it.

2. We have created two functions, init_queue() and look() for the linked list implementation, but not for the array implementation. Write both of these functions for the array implementation.

3. In the init_queue() function (linked list implementation) we traverse the list until we encounter a zero value for the next field. As an alternative, we could compare the address of each node against head. last to determine comple-tion. Implement list traversal using a comparison against head. last.

4. Write a function count_mess() (both implementations) that counts the number of messages currently on the queue.

5. Write a program that maintains a linked list in numerical order by inserting each new structure in its appropriate place in the list. The data the structure maintains are integer numbers between zero and 100 generated by the rand() function.

6. Write a function (both array and linked list implementations) that prints out the elements on the queue in reverse input order (i.e., as if the queue were a stack).

7. Given two queues maintained as linked lists, write a program that merges the two queues in alternating order. If one queue is longer, continue to put its elements on the end of the queue.

8. A *deque,* or double ended queue, is an access method in which insertions and deletions may be made at either end. Write a program that places numbers on a deque with all negative numbers placed on one end and all positive numbers on the other. "Seed" the deque with the number zero, which will always separate the positive and negative numbers.

9. Write a program that creates a circular list. Populate the list with alphabetic characters. Write a function that, when given a character on the list, prints all the characters from that point on the list, forward until the character just preceding it is printed.

CHAPTER 18

BINARY TREES

OVERVIEW

In this chapter we use structures, pointers, and recursive programming techniques to create and maintain an ordered binary tree. These data structures are conveniently used to maintain and access sorted data. The application program we develop in this chapter stores alphabetically sorted character strings, allows searching for a particular string, and permits ordered printing of the entire tree.

TREES

Trees, or rooted trees, are generally used by algorithms where linear searching and updating techniques are not efficient. Although other methods, such as hashing (see Case Study 3), also permit searching for a particular record (or structure) rapidly, binary trees allow collections of objects to be printed in order without sorting. Exhibit 18-1 illustrates a rooted tree. Each structure that is a tree member is called a *node*. Binary trees have the following properties:

- There is always exactly one root and all routines that access the tree know its location or name. This is usually done by making the root node an externally declared variable.

- In a binary tree, each node points to either zero, one, or two other nodes. These nodes are called *child* nodes.

- Each node, except the root node, is pointed to by exactly one other node. This node is referred to as the *parent* node.

- Each node in the tree is addressable by a unique *node pathname*.

- A node and its descendants are called a *subtree*. A node without children qualifies as a subtree, as does the root node.

The binary tree we will develop in this chapter is an example of an ordered tree. Each node has, at most, two children, known as the *left child* and the *right*

EXHIBIT 18-1

A rooted binary tree

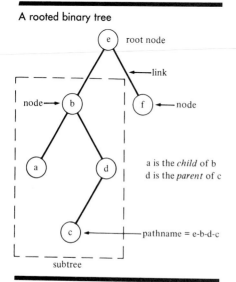

child. We will organize the tree so that, for each node, the value of its left child is less than the value of the node and the value of the right child is greater than the value of the node. In this way, the tree always maintains a perfectly sorted order of nodes. No duplicates are allowed.

Defining the Binary Tree Structure

This example is similar to the examples in Chapters 16 and 17. It accepts and stores character strings in the form of messages, organizes them using a data structure, and allows the user to read a message. However, in Chapters 16 and 17, when we read a message, we were given either the first or the last. In this example, we will be able to select the message to be read or we will be able to read all messages in alphabetical order.

The data structure used to store a tree node is defined as follows:

source file: btrees.c

```
        .
        .
        .
12      struct node
13      {
14            char *value;
15            struct node *left_child, *right_child;
16      };
17
18      struct node root;
```

Lines 12 through 16 define a `node` structure. In this program, one of these structures represents each of the circles in Exhibit 18-1. The structure consists of a field called `value` and two pointers to other structures of the same type. The `value` field points to a character string, the memory for which will be allocated as necessary. The two pointers will point to other nodes in the tree.

In line 18, the root node is declared. This variable is declared as external and is available by name to all other functions in the source file. The memory for all the other nodes in the tree will be allocated dynamically as necessary through the `calloc()` library function.

Presenting the User Option Menu

This function is similar to the `main()` function discussed in Chapters 16 and 17 except that additional options are available. The `main()` function is defined as follows:

source file: btrees.c

```
 1    #include <stdio.h>
 2
 3    #define INIT 1
 4    #define ADD_MESSAGE 2
 5    #define FIND_KEY 3
 6    #define PRINT_ALL 4
 7    #define END 5
 8
 9    #define MESSAGE_SIZE 256
 .
 .
 .
20    main()
21    {
22        int command;
23        char returned_message[MESSAGE_SIZE];
24
25        while ( (command = getcommand( "Enter command: " )) != END )
26        {
27
28            switch ( command )
29            {
30            case INIT:
31                init_tree();
32                break;
33
34            case ADD_MESSAGE:
35                add_message();
36                break;
37
38            case FIND_KEY:
39                find_key();
40                break;
41
42            case PRINT_ALL:
43                print_all();
44                break;
45
46            default:
47                fprintf( stderr, "Invalid command\n" );
48
49            }
50        }
51    }
```

EXHIBIT 18-2

Menu of user options for binary tree example

```
Enter          1) Initialize queue
               2) Add message
               3) Search for message
               4) Print entire collection
               5) End

Enter command:
```

Adding Messages to the Tree

Exhibit 18-2 shows the menu presented to the user. Exhibit 18-3 shows a sample interaction for adding messages to the tree. Let's look at the development of the tree in response to the user interaction depicted in Exhibit 18-3:

1. After the first message is entered it is automatically placed in the root node. Exhibit 18-4 shows this.

2. Since we are sorting lexicographically, the second message "second message" is placed in the right child of the root node. (It sorts lexicographically greater than "first message".) Exhibit 18-5 shows this.

EXHIBIT 18-3

User interaction to add messages to the tree

```
Enter command: 2
Enter message: first message
Enter command: 2
Enter message: second message
   Looking at message: first message
   Adding right child
Enter command: 2
Enter message: third message
   Looking at message: first message
   Looking at message: second message
   Adding right child
Enter command: 2
Enter message: fourth message
   Looking at message: first message
   Looking at message: second message
   Adding left child
Enter command: 2
Enter message: fifth message
   Looking at message: first message
   Adding left child
Enter command: 5
```

EXHIBIT 18-4

Adding the first message first message

EXHIBIT 18-5

Adding the second message

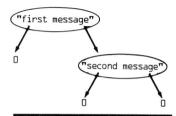

3. The third message is lexicographically greater than "first message" and therefore is placed at its right child. But there is already a message at its right child, so "third message" is compared to "second message", which it is lexicographically greater than, and placed in its right child. Exhibit 18-6 shows this.

4. The fourth message sorts greater than "first message", but less than

EXHIBIT 18-6

Adding the third message

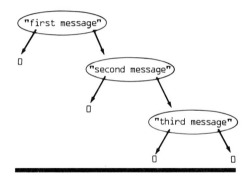

EXHIBIT 18-7

Adding the fourth message

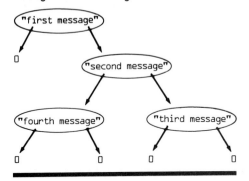

"second message", so it is placed in the left child of "second message". Exhibit 18-7 shows this.

5. Finally, the fifth message is added as the left child of "first message". Exhibit 18-8 shows this.

The add_message() function adds messages to the tree. This function allocates memory for the character string and the struct node that will maintain it. If no messages are in the tree, the message is placed in the root node. If there are messages in the tree, then the proper location is found and the added node becomes either a left or right child of an existing node. The add_message() function is defined as follows:

EXHIBIT 18-8

Adding the fifth message

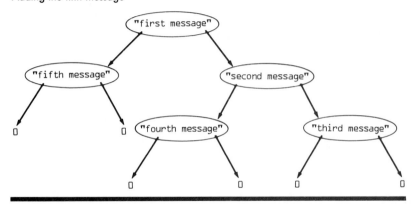

source file: btrees.c

.
.
.

```
90    #define SUCCESS 0
91    #define FAILURE 1
92    #define ALREADY_THERE 1
93
94    add_message()
95    {
96        char temp_message[MESSAGE_SIZE]; /* holds typed in message */
97        char *cpointer;
98
99        char *calloc(), *strcpy();
100
101       printf( "Enter message: " );
102       fgets( temp_message, MESSAGE_SIZE, stdin );
103
104       cpointer = calloc( 1, (unsigned)(strlen( temp_message ) + 1));
105       strcpy( cpointer, temp_message );
106
107       if ( root.value == (char *)0 )
108       {
109           /* empty tree */
110           root.value = cpointer;
111       }
112       else
113       {
114           /* find spot in tree; start looking at root */
115           if ( r_add( &root, cpointer ) == ALREADY_THERE )
116           {
117               fprintf( stderr, "   Is already there\n" );
118           }
119       }
120   }
```

First, we display a prompt on the terminal and accept a string of characters. Then, we place the string of characters in the temp_message array.

Line 104 allocates permanent memory for the character string dynamically. Note that the calloc() library function is used instead of malloc(). They essentially serve the same purpose except that calloc() clears the memory after allocating it and before delivering it to the program. The extra byte allocated is used to store the string termination character.

The program logic proceeds this way:

- If no messages are in the tree, we have the root node point to the message.

- If messages are already in the tree, we find the proper location for this message and add it to the tree. The r_add() function is responsible for finding the proper location in which to place the message.

The r_add() function is passed a pointer to a node—the beginning of a subtree. The function is recursive and is implemented in pseudocode as follows:

```
r-add( node, entered string )
{
        if ( two arguments are same )
        {
                duplicate record;
                return( FAILURE );
        }
        else if ( entered string comes before value
                        stored in current node )
        {
                if ( left child exists )
                {
                        /* find proper place in left child
                           subtree */
                        r_add( left child, entered string );
                }
                else
                {
                        /* there is no left subtree */
                        allocate new node and have left child
                                point to it;
                        return( SUCCESS );
                }
        }
        else if ( entered string comes after value
                        stored in current node )
        {
                if ( right child exists )
                {
                        /* find proper place in right child
                           subtree */
                        r_add( right child, entered string );
                }
```

(pseudocode continues)

```
                            else
                            {
                                    /* there is no right subtree */
                                    allocate new node and have right child
                                              point to it;
                                    return( SUCCESS );
                            }
                    }
            }
    }
```

The function continues recursively until either it finds a duplicate (no duplicate strings are allowed) or it hits a dead end. If it determines that the string belongs in the left-child subtree and there is no left-child node, it creates one. If a left-child node exists, then it begins its search with the subtree beginning at this node. If the function determines that the entered string belongs to the right of the current node, a similar process occurs. The r_add() function is defined as follows:

source file: btrees.c

```
        .
        .
        .
122   r_add( current_node, string )
123   struct node *current_node;
124   char *string;
125   {
126           struct node *alloc_node();
127
128           printf( "Looking at message: %s", current_node->value );
129
130           if ( strcmp( string, current_node->value ) == 0 )
131           {
132                   /* is already there */
133                   return( ALREADY_THERE );
134           }
135           else if ( strcmp( string, current_node->value ) < 0 )
136           {
137                   /* message to add is less than current node value */
138                   if ( current_node->left_child == (struct node *)0 )
139                   {
140                           /* no left child */
141                           printf( "Adding left child\n" );
142                           current_node->left_child = alloc_node( string );
143                   }
```

```
144              else
145              {
146                  /* recursively look at next node */
147                  if ( r_add( current_node->left_child,
148                      string ) == ALREADY_THERE )
149                  {
150                      return( ALREADY_THERE );
151                  }
152              }
153          }
154      else
155      {
156          /* message to add is greater than current node value */
157          if ( current_node->right_child == (struct node *)0 )
158          {
159              /* no right child */
160              printf( "Adding right child\n" );
161              current_node->right_child = alloc_node( string );
162          }
163          else
164          {
165              /* recursively look at next node */
166              if ( r_add( current_node->right_child,
167                  string ) == ALREADY_THERE )
168              {
169                  return( ALREADY_THERE );
170              }
171          }
172      }
173
174      return( SUCCESS );
175  }
```

If the entered string is the same as the one pointed to by an existing node, we return an error. Duplicates are not allowed in the binary tree. If the entered string is lexicographically less than the string pointed to by the node we are inspecting, the node we are adding should be in the left-child subtree (lines 135 through 153). If there is no left-child subtree, we make a new one by adding the new node as the left child of the node we are inspecting. If there is already a left child, we call r_add() recursively. If r_add() returns the defined value ALREADY_THERE, we return that same value to the calling function. If the entered string is lexicographically greater than the node we are examining, the new string should be part of the right-child subtree (lines 154 through 172). We then proceed the same way we did for the left subtree.

Searching for a Message

To search the binary tree for a particular node, we use procedures similar to those we used when adding to it. Beginning at the root node, the current node and the entered character string are compared. If the strings are equal, the string is printed. If the entered string is lexicographically less than the string in the node, then it must be in the left-child subtree. If there is no left-child subtree, the string is not in the tree. If there is a left-child subtree, then it is examined the same way. Similarly, if the entered string is greater than the string in the current node, the right child is searched. Exhibit 18-9 shows the path through the tree followed in the search for the message "third message".

The procedure to implement this consists of the find_key() and r_find() functions. The find_key() function is executed only once; it calls the routine r_find() which examines the appropriate nodes in the tree. The find_key() function is implemented as follows:

source file: btrees.c

```
  .
  .
  .
195    find_key()
196    {
197         char search_key[MESSAGE_SIZE];
198         char *strchr();    /* index() on some systems */
199         char *cptr;
```

EXHIBIT 18-9

Searching the tree for the message third message

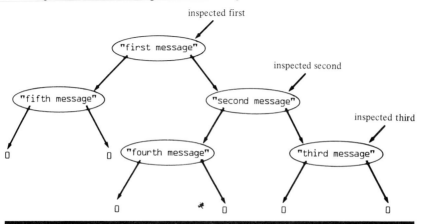

```
200
201         printf( "Enter message to find: " );
202         fgets( search_key, MESSAGE_SIZE, stdin );
203
204         if ( r_find( search_key, &root ) != SUCCESS )
205         {
206             /* get rid of newline character */
207             cptr = strchr( search_key, '\n' );
208             *cptr = '\0';
209             fprintf( stderr, "  Key <%s> not found\n", search_key );
210         }
211     }
```

This function requires no arguments; it prompts for a character string and calls r_find() to find the string in the tree. If the r_find() function does not find the string, then an error message is printed. The recursive function (r_find()) is called the first time with the root node address. The r_find() function is implemented in pseudocode as follows:

```
r_find( entered string, node )
{
        if ( two arguments are same )
        {
                print value stored in node;
                return( SUCCESS );
        }
        else if ( entered string comes before value
                        stored in current node )
        {
                if ( left child exists )
                {
                        examine_current_node( entered string,
                                left child );
                }
                else
                {
                        there is no left subtree;
                        return( string not found )
                }
        }
        else if ( entered string comes after value
                        stored in current node )
        {
                if ( right child exists )
```

(pseudocode continues)

```
                    {
                            examine_current_node( entered string,
                                        right child );

                    }
                else
                    {

                            there is no right subtree;
                            return( string not found )

                    }
              }
}
```

The function returns when any of the following conditions arise:

- The string is found. The string is printed and the function returns the defined value of SUCCESS.

- The string entered is less than the string in the current node and there is no left child. This means that the string is not in the binary tree and an error is returned.

- The string entered is greater than the string in the current node and there is no right child. This means that the string is not in the binary tree and an error is returned.

If none of these conditions are true, then the r_add( ) function continues by calling itself recursively to examine either the left-child or the right-child subtrees. Eventually, the function will return with one of the above conditions. Each time the function returns, the calling function also returns and passes back the return value it received.

The r_find( ) function is defined as follows:

source file: btrees.c

```
    .
    .
    .
213  r_find( message, current_node )
214  char message[];
215  struct node *current_node;
216  {
217      printf( " Looking at node: %s", current_node->value );
218
```

```
219          if ( strcmp( message, current_node->value ) == 0 )
220          {
221              printf( "  Found value: %s", current_node->value );
222              return( SUCCESS );
223          }
224          else if ( strcmp( message, current_node->value ) < 0 )
225          {
226              if ( current_node->left_child == (struct node *)0 ||
227                  r_find( message, current_node->left_child )
228                      == FAILURE )
229              {
230                  return( FAILURE );
231              }
232          }
233          else if ( strcmp( message, current_node->value ) > 0 )
234          {
235              if ( current_node->right_child == (struct node *)0 ||
236                  r_find( message, current_node->right_child )
237                      == FAILURE )
238              {
239                  return( FAILURE );
240              }
241          }
242      }
```

If the current node has the same value as the target string, we print the value of the node and return the defined value of SUCCESS to the calling function (lines 219 through 223).

If the entered string has a value less than the string pointed to by the current node (lines 224 through 232), the string is in the left-child subtree (if it is in the tree at all).

Note the if statement beginning in line 226. If there is no left child, the function fails and returns the defined value of FAILURE. If there is a left child, the r_find() function is called recursively. If you remember from Chapter 3, this is because of the logical or operator's nature; it only evaluates the second expression if the first fails.

If the entered string has a value greater than the string pointed to by the current node (lines 233 through 240), the string is in the right-child subtree (if it is in the tree at all). If there is no right child, the function fails and returns the defined value of FAILURE. If there is a right child, r_find() is called recursively.

Printing the Entire Tree

The print_all() function prints the values of the tree's elements in alphabetical order. They are printed in this order because this is the order in which they are stored in the tree. Exhibit 18-10 shows the path traversed while the entire tree is being printed. The print_all() function calls the recursive

EXHIBIT 18-10

Traversing the tree and printing all nodes

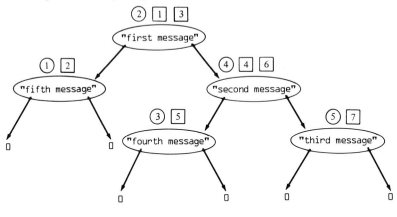

Key : (#)   print order

[#]   order inspected/visited

r_print() function and provides the starting point—the root node. The following pseudocode describes the recursive procedure:

```
r_print( current node )
{
        if ( there is left child )
        {
                r_print( left child )
        }
        print current node value;
        if ( there is right child )
        {
                r_print( right child )
        }
}
```

This method of traversing the tree is known as *inorder traversal* and is summarized this way:

visit the left subtree
visit the root
visit the right subtree

There are two other methods of traversing a binary tree: *preorder* and *postorder* traversals. The preorder traversal is defined this way:

visit the root
visit the left subtree
visit the right subtree

The postorder traversal is defined this way:

visit the left subtree
visit the right subtree
visit the root

In our example, we use inorder traversal to print the messages. The print_all() and r_print() functions are defined as follows:

source file: btrees.c

```
        .
        .
        .
244    print_all()
245    {
246        void r_print();
247
248        if ( root.value != (char *)0 )
249        {
250            r_print( &root );
251        }
252    }
253
254    void r_print( current )
255    struct node *current;
256    {
257        if ( current->left_child != (struct node *)0 )
258        {
259            r_print( current->left_child );
260        }
261
262        printf( "  %s", current->value );
263
264        if ( current->right_child != (struct node *)0 )
265        {
266            r_print( current->right_child );
267        }
268    }
```

If there are any messages in the tree, print_all() calls the r_print() function. Lines 257 through 260 process the left subtree, line 262 prints the current node's value, and lines 264 through 267 process the right subtree.

SUMMARY

In this chapter, we combined several C language programming techniques—structures, lists, and recursion—to create a binary tree. The binary tree is an effective way to maintain data in a sorted order. In our example, we sorted the incoming data lexicographically, although the tree could also have been used to maintain the data in the order in which it was originally received.

There are, of course, other algorithms for maintaining sorted data using a linked list. The binary tree is simple because, when adding data, we never have to break chains in the structure to insert a new node—we can always just add the new node to the end of a path in the tree.

EXERCISES

1. Using the algorithms from this chapter, populate an inorder binary tree with 20 random numbers ranging from 1 to 100. Do not permit duplicate values in the tree.

2. Write a function to find the lowest value in the tree from Exercise 1.

3. Write a function to find the highest value in the tree from Exercise 1.

4. Using the tree from Exercise 1, write a function to list all numbers in a given range where the lower and upper bounds are passed as parameters.

5. Write a program that maintains an inorder binary tree in the order in which the messages arrive. Write a function to print the messages in their order of arrival.

6. Populate a sorted binary tree with the letters of the alphabet generated randomly. Write a function that, when given a letter, prints the full pathname of the node containing the letter.

7. A binary tree is useful for maintaining a concordance (i.e., a frequency count for the occurrence of each word in a text). Each structure stores a word and a frequency of occurrence of the word. As each new word is read, we search for it in the tree. If it is not in the tree we add it and set the counter to one. If it is already in the tree we increment the counter. Write this program.

PART 7

CASE STUDIES

CASE STUDY

1

USING A STACK
TO INDENT
A SOURCE FILE

OVERVIEW

In this case study we apply stacks to the problem of
indenting a nonindented source file. Although the example
is purely illustrative and does not directly address the
indentation of C language source programs, it could be
extended to do so.

THE indent PROGRAM

The indentation program operates on nonindented files with lines containing the keywords START and END. It uses these keywords to start and end new levels of indentation in its output. With a little more work the program could be used to indent a program source file based on the control structures within a C language program.

Let's assume that the input file is:

input file: sample

```
 1    preceding text
 2    preceding text
 3    START *** LEVEL 1 START ***
 4    111 line of text
 5    111 line of text
 6    111 line of text
 7    START *** LEVEL 2 START ***
 8    222 line of text
 9    222 line of text
10    222 line of text
11    START *** LEVEL 3 START ***
12    333 line of text
13    333 line of text
14    333 line of text
15    END *** LEVEL 3 END***
16    222 line of text
17    222 line of text
18    222 line of text
19    START *** LEVEL 3 START ***
20    333 line of text
21    333 line of text
22    333 line of text
23    END *** LEVEL 3 END ***
24    222 line of text
25    222 line of text
26    222 line of text
27    END *** LEVEL 2 END ***
28    111 line of text
29    111 line of text
30    111 line of text
31    END *** LEVEL 1 END ***
32    ending text
33    ending text
```

and the output will look like:

command line:

```
stack sample
```

program output:

```
preceding text
preceding text
*** LEVEL 1 START ***
    111 line of text
    111 line of text
    111 line of text
    *** LEVEL 2 START ***
        222 line of text
        222 line of text
        222 line of text
        *** LEVEL 3 START ***
            333 line of text
            333 line of text
            333 line of text
        *** LEVEL 3 END ***
        222 line of text
        222 line of text
        222 line of text
        *** LEVEL 3 START ***
            333 line of text
            333 line of text
            333 line of text
        *** LEVEL 3 END ***
        222 line of text
        222 line of text
        222 line of text
    *** LEVEL 2 END ***
    111 line of text
    111 line of text
    111 line of text
*** LEVEL 1 END ***
ending text
ending text
```

To do this, we will use a stack to:

- keep track of the headers for each of the levels of indentation;

- keep track of the level of indentation itself, by determining the size of the stack (how many section titles are stored within it.)

Since we need to store character strings on our stack, as in Chapter 16, we have two alternatives: we can either declare a two-dimensional array of characters as follows:

```
char stack[STACK_SIZE][LINE_SIZE];
```

or we can declare the stack array as an array of pointers as follows:

```
char (*stack)[STACK_SIZE];
```

and dynamically allocate room for the character strings as needed. When we are finished with an element, we can use the `free()` library function to deallocate the memory. We will take the latter approach in this example.

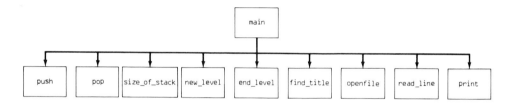

The Structure of the indent Program

The figure above contains a diagram showing the user-defined functions' hierarchical structure within the `indent` program.

The Header File: stack.h

This file defines some of the symbolic constants used in the rest of the program source files. Its contents are:

header file: stack.h

```
1   #define TRUE 1
2   #define FALSE 0
3   #define BAD -1     /* return value */
4   #define GOOD 1
5   #define WHITE_SPACE "\t ,\n"
6   char *getenv();
7   #define START getenv("START")!=NULL ? getenv("START") : "START"
8   #define END getenv("END")!=NULL ? getenv("END") : "END"
9
```

```
10    #define STACK_SIZE 100
11    #define LINE_SIZE   80
```

Line	Comments
1–4	These statements define variables used as truth values in expressions.
5–8	The WHITE_SPACE, START, and END constants are used to inspect a line of text and determine if it begins or ends a level of indentation, or if it is a line of text to be printed. The values substituted for START and END are conditional expressions that yield either the value of a pointer to a character string representing the environment variables, or, if getenv() fails, a pointer to a substitute character string. The function call is repeated to avoid allocating a temporary pointer variable to save the getenv() return value.
10–11	The remaining constants define the line of input size and the stack size. The stack size limits the indentation levels to one hundred.

The main( ) Function

The main() function controls the action of the program at the highest level. Below, we represent its actions in pseudocode:

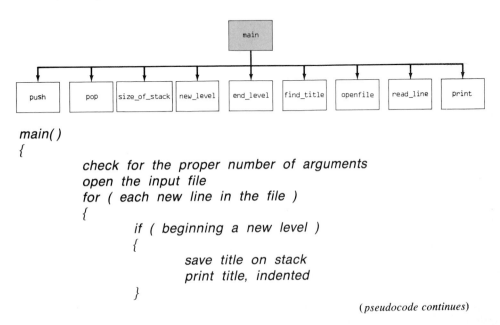

main( )
{

    check for the proper number of arguments
    open the input file
    for (each new line in the file)
    {

        if (beginning a new level)
        {

            save title on stack
            print title, indented

        }

(pseudocode continues)

```
            else if ( ending a new level )
            {
                    get title from stack
                    print title, indented
            }
            else /* line of text */
                    print input line, indented
        }
}
```

Translating the pseudocode into C language statements, we have:

program: smain.c

```
 1    #include <stdio.h>
 2    #include "stack.h"
 3
 4    main( argc, argv )
 5    int argc;
 6    char *argv[];
 7    {
 8        char input[LINE_SIZE], *title, *onstack;
 9        char *read_line(), *find_title(), *pop();
10        int indent;
11
12        if ( argc < 2 )
13        {
14            fprintf( stderr, "Usage: %s filename\n", argv[0] );
15            exit( 1 );
16        }
17        else
18        {
19            openfile( argv[1] );
20        }
                    .
                    .
                    .
57        }
```

Line	Comments
8	Allocate a temporary buffer to hold the contents of a line from the input file.
12–16	Check for the correct number of arguments. If the proper number is not supplied, print a message and end the program.
17–20	Call a function to open the input file, passing the first command line argument to it. The

openfile() function is in another source file named fileio.c and will be discussed later in this case study.

program: smain.c (continued)

```
     .
     .
     .
21
22      while( read_line( input ) != (char *)0 )
23      {
24          if ( new_level( input ) )
25          {
26              title = find_title( input );
27              indent = size_of_stack();
28              print( indent, title );
29              if ( push( title ) == BAD )
30              {
31                  fprintf( stderr, "stack overflow\n" );
32                  exit( 2 );
33              }
34          }
     .
     .
     .
57      }
```

Line	Comments
22	Continually call the read_line() function until it returns a NULL value. This statement reads a line from the input file and stores its contents in the array whose address is supplied as its argument.
24–34	Check to see if the line just read begins a new level. Look at the first few characters on the line to see if they match the START character string as defined in the header file.
26	Extract the title from the line of input using the find_title() function. This function returns a pointer to the beginning of the title somewhere in the array input[].
27	To print the title properly indented, we check the current indentation level by determining the number of titles currently stored on the stack. The size_of_stack() function returns the number of items stored on the stack.

| 28 | Finally, the title is printed. The print() function expects two arguments, the level of indentation and the character string to print. It calculates the appropriate number of spaces to insert in the line, prints them, and then prints the character string. |
| 29–33 | The new function title is added to the stack and the indentation level is increased. If the return value from push() is the defined value of BAD, this is an indication that the title cannot be put on the stack because one hundred titles are already on the stack. In this case, an error message is printed and the program exit()s. |

program: smain.c (continued)

```
                .
                .
                .
35              else if ( end_level( input ) )
36              {
37                  title = find_title( input );
38                  onstack = pop();
39                  if ( onstack == (char *)NULL )
40                  {
41                      fprintf( stderr, "stack underflow\n" );
42                      exit( 3 );
43                  }
44                  else if ( strcmp( title, onstack ) != 0 )
45                  {
46                      fprintf( stderr, "Warning: mismatch\n" );
47                  }
48                  indent = size_of_stack();
49                  print( indent, title );
50              }
                .
                .
                .
57     }
```

Line	Comments
35	Check to see if the input line begins with the characters defined by the END character string in the header file stack.h. If so, end an indentation level and reprint the title at the previous indentation level.

37	Extract the title from the input line.
38	Extract the top character string from the stack. This function will decrease the stack size by one and return a pointer to the character string on the top. If the stack is empty and this request is made, then it returns a NULL value. The NULL value is returned rather than -1 because, as a pointer, onstack cannot have a negative value. A negative number constitutes an error.
39–43	If the return value from pop() indicates that the request was invalid, then print an error message and end the program. This error would indicate there were more ENDs than STARTs in the file.
44–47	If the title popped from the stack does not match the title that follows the END character string, then generate a warning message. This might indicate that the input file is organized incorrectly.
48–49	Find the proper indentation level after pop()ing the top element from the stack and print the title.

program: smain.c (continued)

```
             .
             .
             .
51               else
52               {
53                     indent = size_of_stack();
54                     print( indent, input );
55               }
56         }
57   }
```

Line	**Comments**
51–55	The current line of text is neither a starting line nor an ending line. It should be printed as it was read from the file and indented the proper amount.

THE STACK FUNCTIONS

The main() function calls several other functions we have not yet seen. We have separated these functions into two files, the first containing the functions that manipulate the stack itself and the second containing the functions that interface to the "outside world," via files and the terminal. The second file also contains the functions that examine text strings to determine if they start or end a level.

The first part of the file declares variables used by all of the functions in the file. Both variables are of the external type, but could have been static external.

program: stack.c

```
1    #include "stack.h"
2
3    char *stack[ STACK_SIZE ];    /* array of pointers */
4    int s_index = 0;              /* top of stack + 1 */
5
     .
     .
     .
```

Line	Comments
3	This is the stack itself. It is an array of pointers to character strings, chosen over the alternate method of declaring a two-dimensional array for space efficiency. The array size is STACK_SIZE; memory for the character strings is allocated as needed.
4	This is the *stack pointer*. When referred to as an index, it references the next unused slot in the stack array. It can also be used as a counter for the number of items on the stack.

The push() Function

The following function adds a character string to the stack. It first checks to see if there is any room left on the stack and, if there is, allocates memory to store the character string, copies the contents of the array title[] into the memory, and then increments the stack pointer.

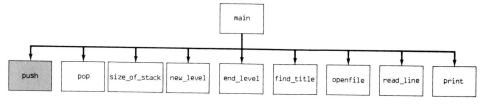

program: stack.c (continued)

```
     .
     .
     .
6    push( title )
```

```
 7      char *title;
 8      {
 9          char *malloc(), *strcpy();
10
11          if ( s_index < STACK_SIZE )
12          {
13              stack[s_index] = malloc(
14                  (unsigned)(strlen(title) + 1) );
15              strcpy( stack[s_index], title );
16              s_index++;
17              return( GOOD );
18          }
19          else
20              return( BAD );
21      }
22
```

.
.
.

Line	Comments
11	Check to see if the stack array is full. If it is, the defined value of BAD is returned in line 20.
13–14	Allocate enough memory to store the character string that starts at title and the following NULL character. The strlen() function will only return the number of nonnull characters in the string. We need to allocate one more character to store the trailing end-of-string character. The malloc() function is used here instead of the calloc() function because the program logic guarantees that the memory allocated will be populated. The only difference between these two functions, except for formatting the arguments, is that malloc() will not clear the allocated memory, while calloc() will. The return value from malloc() is a pointer to the beginning of the allocated memory. This address is stored in the next available slot in the stack array.
15	The temporary copy of the title (passed to this function) is copied into the memory just allocated. We do not store the address that is passed because it refers to the temporary (reusable)

buffer named input, defined in line 8 of the main() function.

16   Increment the stack pointer. This must always point to the next available entry in the stack array.

17   Return the successful completion of this function.

The pop() Function

This function returns the value of the entry on the top of the stack to the calling function. It checks for underflow—a request to pop() a record when the stack is empty. A pointer to the character string is returned, not the character string itself.

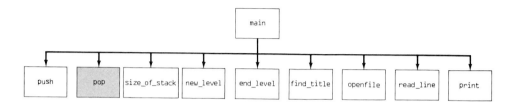

program: stack.c (continued)

```
          .
          .
          .
23   char *pop()
24   {
25        /* must be static */
26        static char return_title[ LINE_SIZE ];
27        char *strcpy();
28
29        if ( --s_index < 0 )
30             return( (char *)NULL );
31        else
32        {
33             strcpy( return_title, stack[s_index] );
34             free( stack[s_index] );
35             return( return_title );
36        }
37   }
38
          .
          .
          .
```

Line	Comments
26	This array holds the title of the line passed back to the calling function. We use a separate array so that we can deallocate the memory the push() routine allocated.
29	Since the stack pointer points to the next available slot in the table, we need to decrement it before accessing an element in the table. If the value was previously 0 (empty stack), we have more ENDs than STARTs; this results in a stack underflow condition.
30	Return a NULL pointer to the calling function indicating that the function was unsuccessful.
33	Copy the string referenced by the pointer on the stack into the temporary character array declared in line 26. This array is defined as static because we want it to remain after the function call is finished. If it were automatic, its memory would be deallocated when the function execution was completed.
34	Deallocate the memory that used to hold the character string now in the return_title array.
35	Return the starting address of the array return_title to the calling function.

The size_of_stack() Function

This function returns the number of elements on the stack. This value can be derived from the stack pointer.

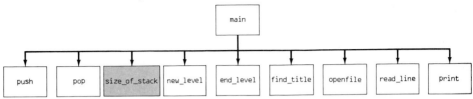

program: stack.c (continued)

```
        .
        .
        .
39   size_of_stack()
40   {
41        return( s_index );
42   }
```

Line	Comments
41	The variable s_index is used as a stack pointer to index the stack array. When used as an index, it points to the next available entry, but since array indexing starts at zero in the C language, it also contains exactly the number of entries in the array. This number is returned to the calling function.

THE STRING FUNCTIONS

The following functions determine whether a character string introduces a new indentation level or ends a previous one. This file also contains a function that extracts a title from the string it is passed.

The new_level() Function

This function compares the characters at the beginning of the line against the START value as defined in the stack.h header file.

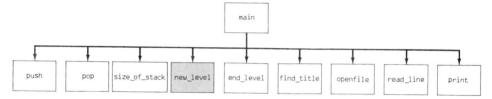

program file: string.c

```
1    #include "stack.h"
2
3    new_level( input )
4    char *input;
5    {
6        if( strncmp( input, START, strlen( START ) ) == 0 )
7            return( TRUE );
8        else
9            return( FALSE );
10   }
11
```

Line	Comments
6	A simple character comparison is performed to see if the line begins with the characters defined by START.

The end_level() Function

This function compares its input character string with the character string END as defined in the stack.h header file.

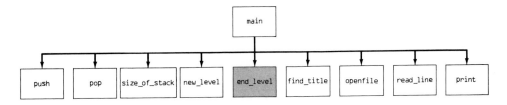

program file: string.c

```
         .
         .
         .
12    end_level( input )
13    char *input;
14    {
15         if( strncmp( input, END, strlen( END ) ) == 0 )
16              return( TRUE );
17         else
18              return( FALSE );
19    }
20
         .
         .
         .
```

The find_title() Function

This function extracts a title from lines identified as controlling lines (i.e., starting or ending a new level). This function's return value is the starting address of the title character string within the originally supplied string. The contents of the string must not be altered.

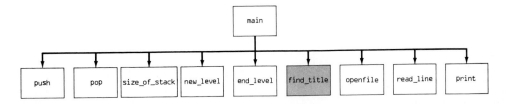

program file: string.c

```
        .
        .
        .
21   char *find_title( input )
22   char *input;
23   {
24        char *strpbrk(), *cpointer;
25
26        cpointer = strpbrk( input, WHITE_SPACE );
27        return( cpointer + 1 );
28   }
```

Line	Comments
26	The strpbrk() function, which is a C library function, returns the address of the first character in its first argument that matches a character defined by the second argument. Problems may arise if there is leading white space before the keywords START or END. This function would return this value, which would then be returned to the calling function.
27	This function's return value is the address of the character that immediately follows the first white space character. Problems occur if there are multiple spaces between the keyword START or END and the title. Only the first white space character will be discarded.

SUPPORT FUNCTIONS

The program needs the following functions to open files, read from files, and print indented lines.

The openfile() Function

This function opens the file whose name is supplied as an argument. It assumes that the filename is valid and that all necessary checking was done in the calling function.

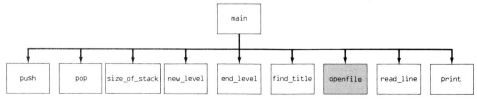

program: fileio.c

```
 1    #include <stdio.h>
 2    #include "stack.h"
 3
 4    FILE *iptr;
 5
 6    openfile( filename )
 7    char *filename;
 8    {
 9        if ( (iptr = fopen( filename, "r" )) == (FILE *)NULL )
10        {
11            fprintf( stderr, "Cannot open: %s\n", filename );
12            exit( 1 );
13        }
14    }
15
```

Line	Comments
4	This pointer to a FILE structure is declared as external so that all functions in this file can reference it. Since only functions defined in this file reference this variable, it could have also been defined as static external.
9	The return value of fopen() is stored in iptr to be used by other functions in this file. Its value is compared against the defined constant NULL.
11–12	If the fopen() fails, an error message is printed on the terminal and the program exit()s.

The read_line() Function

This function simply calls fgets() and returns the return value from the function call.

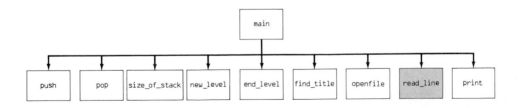

program: fileio.c (continued)

```
16    char *read_line( destination )
17    char *destination;
18    {
19         return( fgets( destination, LINE_SIZE, iptr ) );
20
21    }
22
```

The print() Function

This function prints a character string indented a specific amount. The function is defined as follows:

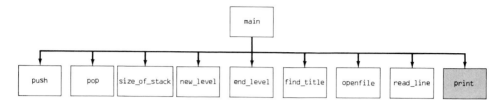

program: fileio.c (continued)

```
23    print( indent, input )
24    int indent;
25    char *input;
26    {
27         printf( "%*s%s", indent * 4, "", input );
28    }
```

Line	Comments
27	The * modifier is used in the control string to allow the function to define the field width dynamically. Normally, if a width is desired, it appears between the % symbol and the character that defines the output format, providing a fixed width. In this case the width does not appear as a constant value inside the control string, but is passed to the function as an argument. If a * appears in the control string, the width is to be supplied as a separate argument in the argument list to printf(). Here we multiply the passed argument by four to calculate the field width. The field contents are null, and the appropriate number of spaces are printed.

SUMMARY

In this case study, we used the stack access method, previously discussed in Chapter 16, to indent a nonindented source file. Since this application always looks at the *most recent* indentation keyword, it requires a last-in, first-out access method. We chose to implement the stack using an array, although, as we saw in Chapter 16, we could also have used a linked list.

It would be instructive to consider what changes to this program would be required to permit it to indent C language source programs.

CASE STUDY 2

IMPLEMENTING A LINE PRINTER SPOOLING SYSTEM USING A PRIORITIZED QUEUE

OVERVIEW

In this case study we will examine a fairly large program that uses a variety of data structures. The program implements a line printer spooling system, although it is designed so that it could also be used as a batch processing program for an interactive system. We have chosen this example because it uses several different types of data structures and also because it illustrates the development of a large program in the C language.

PROGRAM DESCRIPTION—LINE PRINTER SPOOLER

On most multiuser systems there are fewer printers than requests to print files. Therefore, these requests must be scheduled so that only one file is printing on a printer at any given time. As a simple solution, we could place a software lock on the line printer. If this lock is set, users are prevented from accessing the device and advised to try again later. After a file is finished printing, the lock is released, allowing another file to print. This solution has obvious problems. Files are not printed on a first-come, first-served basis; whoever happens to make the request to print a file soon after the lock is removed is granted permission to do so.

We will implement a more sophisticated system consisting of two programs. The system maintains a list of requests and prints files in an orderly way.

Design Considerations

The system needs to keep track of the names of the files to be printed. There will be no restriction on how many files can be on the queue except that imposed by the operating system under which the program will be run (file sizes, etc.). Furthermore, each print job will have an associated priority ranging from 1 to 10, inclusive, with a priority of one being the highest. We will keep status information about the print request initiator and be able to print the job queue's current status.

EXHIBIT CS2-1

Overview of the line printer spooler system

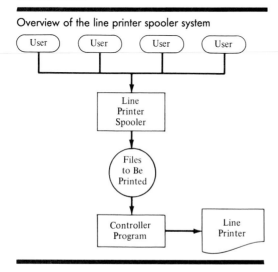

Program Structure

Schematically, the system will look as shown in Exhibit CS2-1. All users may execute a common program that adds the name of their file to the list of files to be printed, along with other control and status information relating to the file.

Another program directly associated with a printing device reads the names of files to be printed from this list and arranges for them to be printed, one at a time.

This program assumes a multiprogramming environment (i.e., two or more programs are allowed to run simultaneously). On some systems this program's usefulness is limited because we cannot have a separate controller program running unattended in the background. On a single-user system (i.e., many personal computers) this system could be used to queue the printing of several files and then print them sequentially in the foreground.

Information Maintained

The following header file defines a structure of type pqueue that describes the information kept for each request to print a file:

header file: queue.h

```
       .
       .
       .
 8   typedef int node;
 9
10   struct pqueue
11   {
12       int   control_id;         /* spooler id           */
13       char  filename[ FILE_NAME_SIZE ];
14       char  owner[10];          /* login name of owner */
15       short priority;           /* 1: high, 10:low      */
16       long  file_length;        /* size in bytes        */
17       char  description[50];    /* user defined for
18                                    status reporting     */
19       short n_copies;           /* number of copies     */
20       char  class[10];          /* defines pre and
21                                    postfix for printing*/
22       long  q_time;             /* time queued          */
23       node  r_next;             /* record # of next     */
24   };
       .
       .
       .
```

Line   **Comments**

8   A synonym named `node` is assigned to the vari-
              able type `int`. The synonym is used in place of
              `int` to define the variable type containing the
              record number within the file (`r_next`.)

12   The control number is assigned as a job number
              and must be unique for all queued requests. Re-
              quests to the queue to print or remove a job are
              made via this number. (Why isn't the name of the
              file sufficient?)

13   The file name format differs among systems.
              The controller program passes the file name to
              the operating system and assumes that the oper-
              ating system is able to interpret it. In the exam-
              ples that follow, we will use UNIX-style path-
              names.

14   The owner's name is kept in an array of 10 char-
              acters. The definition of this information is sys-
              tem dependent; in the UNIX system, we can use
              the user's login name.

15   Job priorities range from 1 to 10 with 1 being the
              highest priority and 10 the lowest. Since the pri-
              ority is stored in a short integer, priorities could
              theoretically range between 1 and 64K.

17   The description identifies the print job and prints
              out on the banner page that precedes the printing
              of the file itself. This description is also printed
              when the print queue is interrogated.

19   This is the number of copies to be printed. The
              printer controller program uses this information
              to reprint the file as necessary.

20   This identifies any of the print job's pre- or post-
              processing requirements. For example, the file
              may be in packed form and must be unpacked as
              it is printed, or the file may need to be stripped of
              control characters as it is printed. This class is
              cross-referenced with a file that might look as
              follows:

file: classfile

```
text    cat     >/dev/lp
pack    pcat    >/dev/lp
```

The first field on each line identifies the class type. The next field (fields are separated by tabs) identifies the name of the system command that will be used to print the file. The final field identifies the name of the system command that will direct the output to the proper printing device. The controller program supplies the file name and combines it with the appropriate pre- and postprocessors. For example, if the file name is frog and the class type is text, the controller program issues the following command to the system:

```
cat frog >/dev/lp
```

If the same file is to be printed with class type pack, then the following command will be issued:

```
pcat frog >/dev/lp
```

The pre- and postprocessors are machine dependent and are therefore isolated from the machine-independent parts. In fact, these parameters are not even compiled into the program; they reside in an external file and can be changed as needed without the program having to be recompiled. Thus, the controller program is *table driven.*

22   This is the time at which the file was queued for printing, expressed in numbers of seconds from a given point in time. (In the UNIX system, the reference date is January 1, 1970.) From this we can calculate the date, time, day of the week, and year that the file was queued.

23   This field logically links this record to the next record of the same type, forming a linked list.

THE PRINTER QUEUE PROGRAM

The system we are building consists of two programs: one that controls the physical line printer and a second that permits users to queue files. We will describe the second program first. This program permits three actions—add a file to the print queue, remove a file from the queue, and print status informa-

tion about all jobs on the queue. To add a file to the queue, the user will interact
with the program as follows:

```
1) Add file to queue
2) Remove file from queue
3) Print contents of queue

Enter selection: 1
Enter file name: /etc/passwd
Enter priority (1...10): 5
Enter number of copies (1...10): 1
Enter class: text
Enter description: the password file
```

Several pieces of information are requested and typed in from the terminal.
This information is stored in a structure that is then added to the queue. To
print the status of jobs on the queue the user types the following:

```
1) Add file to queue
2) Remove file from queue
3) Print contents of queue

Enter selection: 3

ID/    FILENAME/                   PRI/     SIZE DESCRIPTION
OWNER TIME QUEUED                  COPY          CLASS

211    /etc/passwd                   5      308 the password file
hutch Wed Feb 26 10:35:23 1986      1           text
```

All the information the user enters is printed, as is some information that
the queuing program takes directly from the system, such as the time the file
was queued.

When we remove a file from the queue, the interaction looks like this:

```
1) Add file to queue
2) Remove file from queue
3) Print contents of queue

Enter selection: 2
Enter control # of file to remove: 211
```

The Queue Program Structure

The queuing program's overall structure is shown in the diagram (facing page):

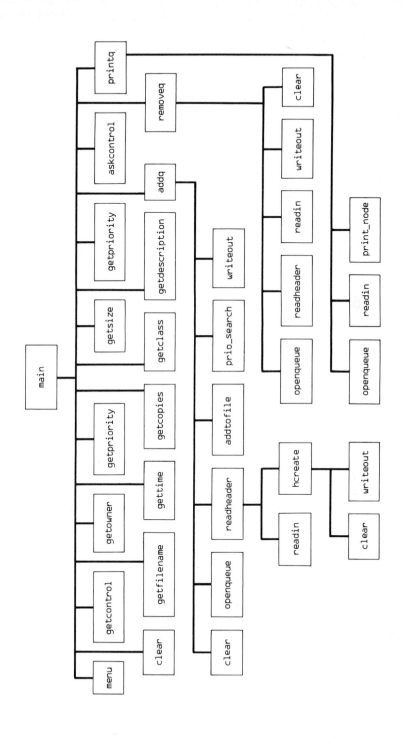

The main( ) Function

The main( ) function first calls a menu function from which the user selects an option—add a file to the queue, remove a file from the queue, or print descriptions of all the jobs on the queue. The menu( ) function returns a value of 1, 2, or 3 indicating which selection was made. Since the numbers 1, 2, and 3 can be considered "magic" numbers, they are given symbolic names using the #define preprocessor directive in the file queue.h:

header file: queue.h

```
 1    #include <stdio.h>
 2
 .
 .
 .
29    #define ADD       1
30    #define REMOVE    2
31    #define PRINTQ    3
32
33    #define START_OF_QUEUE 0
```

The main( ) function takes the return value from menu( ) and branches to the appropriate routine to implement the selection. The code for the main( ) function is as follows:

source file: main.c

```
 1    #include "queue.h"
 2
 3    main()
 4    {
 5         short command, menu();
 6         struct pqueue temp;
 7
 8         command = menu();
 9         switch( command )
10         {
11
12         case ADD:       /* queue a file */
13
14              clear( &temp );
15              getcontrol( &temp );
16              getfilename( &temp );
17              getowner( &temp );
18              getpriority( &temp );
```

```
19              getcopies( &temp );
20              getclass( &temp );
21              gettime( &temp );
22              getdescription( &temp );
23              getsize( &temp );
24              addq( &temp );
25              break;
26
27      case REMOVE:    /* remove a file from the queue */
28
29              removeq( askcontrol() );
30              break;
31
32      case PRINTQ:       /* print queue */
33
34              printq( START_OF_QUEUE );
35              break;
36
37      }
```

Line	Comments
5	Since the `menu()` function returns a value other than an integer, its return value must be defined. The return value of `menu()` will be placed in the variable named `command`.
6	Several of the routines called by the `main()` function need a structure of type `pqueue`. The structure is defined here; the adding, removing, and printing routines will use it as a temporary structure variable.
8	This is the call to the function `menu()`. The function will prompt the user for a selection and return a value between 1 and 3, inclusively. The return value from this function is stored in the variable named `command`.
9	Depending on the value returned by `menu()`, the `switch` statement will cause one of three groups of statements to be executed—those between lines 12 and 25, 27 and 30, or 32 and 35.
12–25	If the user elects to add a file to the print queue, then the functions in lines 14 through 23 prompt for information about the file. Several of these functions will be looked at later in this case study. The function named `addq()` (line 24)

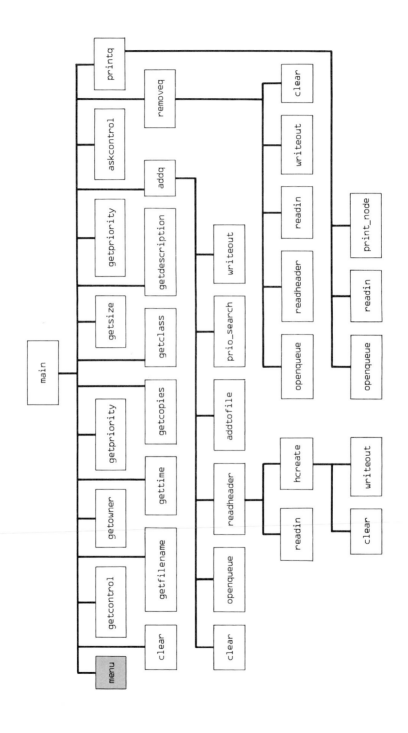

finds the appropriate place on the queue and inserts the record accordingly. The break on line
25 ensures that the statements for the other
branches of the switch statement are not executed and that control flows to the end of the
switch and hence, to the end of the program.

27–30   If a file is to be removed from the queue, the user
is requested, through the askcontrol() func-
tion, to enter the associated job number. The file
name is not enough because the same file could
have been queued twice. The removeq() function then removes the print request from the
print queue. In our initial program implementation, the record will be logically removed from
the queue but the space it used in the queue will
not be reused. In Case Study 4, we will see how
deleted records can be reused.

32–35   This option causes information about each file in
the queue to be printed. We will look at the printing routines later in this case study.

The menu( ) Function

On the terminal, the menu() function displays a menu from which the user
selects one of the available options. If an invalid selection is made, then the
user is prompted again. When the selection is in the proper range, the function
returns the selection's value. The menu() function is defined as follows:

source file: get.c

```
1    #include "queue.h"
2
3    short menu()
4    {
5        short answer = 0;
6
7        while ( answer < ADD || answer > PRINTQ )
8        {
9            printf( "%d) Add file to queue\n", ADD );
10           printf( "%d) Remove file from queue\n", REMOVE );
11           printf( "%d) Print contents of queue\n", PRINTQ);
12           printf( "\nEnter selection: " );
13           scanf( "%d", &answer );
14           getchar(); /* get rid of excess newline
15                           character */
```

(program continues)

```
16        }
17        return( answer );
18    }
```

In line 14, the function reads a character from the standard input and discards it. This is necessary because the scanf() function reads only the decimal digits from the standard input and leaves the newline character unread. This will not create a problem here but will cause a problem when the next function reads from the standard input; it will read the newline character.

In the following sections we describe the routines for adding a file to the queue, removing a file from the queue, and printing information about queued files in detail. First we will discuss the machine-specific functions and then proceed to the machine-independent routines.

ADDING A PRINT REQUEST

The following routines are called from the main() function to add a print request to the print queue.

The clear( ) Function

The first routine clears the temporary structure we will use to hold the information about the file to be printed. This function is written as follows:

source file: clear.c

```
1    #include "queue.h"
2
3    clear( temp )
4    struct pqueue *temp;
5    {
6        char *strcpy();
7
8        strcpy( temp->filename,    "" );
9        strcpy( temp->owner,    "" );
10       strcpy( temp->description,    "" );
11       strcpy( temp->class,    "" );
12
13       temp->priority = 0;
14       temp->file_length = 0;
15       temp->control_id = 0;
16       temp->n_copies = 0;
17       temp->q_time = 0;
18       temp->r_next = 0;
```

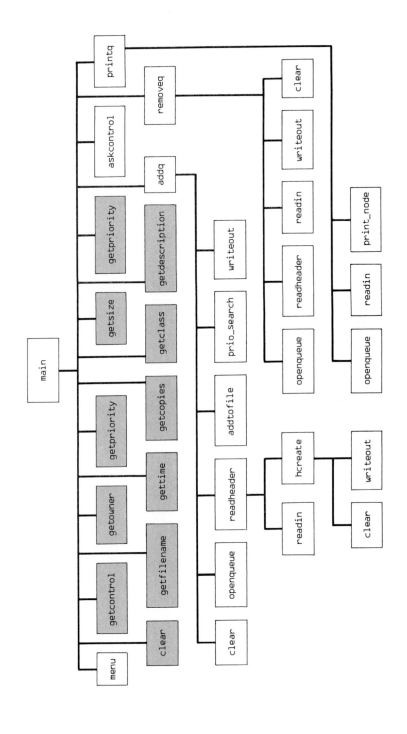

The argument passed to this function is a pointer to a structure of type pqueue. It is therefore necessary to use the arrow (–>) operator to access any of the structure members.

All the character arrays are cleared using the strcpy() function to copy a null string into the array. The same result could have been achieved by setting the first character in each array to null:

```
temp->filename[0] = '\0';
```

This is more efficient, but perhaps less readable. Although we are not inspecting or using the return value of strcpy(), we declare its return value type for consistency.

All integer-type fields are cleared by simply assigning a zero value to them.

The getcontrol( ) Function

This function returns a unique number, which is assigned as a job number to each queued request. Generating this number is system dependent. Therefore, because of portability concerns, we isolate this function in a separate source file. The getcontrol() function is placed in the source file machdep.c and is defined as follows:

source file: machdep.c

```
1      #include "queue.h"
2
3      getcontrol( temp )
4      struct pqueue *temp;
5      {
6            temp->control_id = getpid();
7      }
.
.
.
```

Like the other "get" functions in this program, the getcontrol() function is supplied with the starting address of a temporary structure in which the print request information is to be held temporarily.

In line 6, a function unique to the UNIX system is called. This function returns a unique identification number. It is guaranteed that no other invocation of this program will be returned the same value.

The getfilename( ) Function

The getfilename() function requests the name of the file to be printed. This function is also machine dependent and hence, is placed in the same source file as the previous function. The machine dependency arises because we may want to do some processing to the file name before we put the record in the queue. UNIX system file pathnames illustrate this. In the UNIX system, there are two types of pathnames: absolute (those that start at some fixed reference point) and relative (those described by their positioning to a local directory). In our system, we will have users entering file names from several different directories. However, the printer-controller program, which has to find the file in order to print it, does not know the user's position in the file hierarchy, so it cannot resolve relative file pathnames. The getfilename() function solves this problem; it converts all relative pathnames to absolute pathnames. After conversion, the file name shows the file's absolute location instead of its position relative to the user who queued it. For example, assume that the name of the file we are printing is:

```
frog
```

and it is in a directory whose pathname is:

```
/usr/hutch
```

then the absolute pathname to frog is:

```
/usr/hutch/frog
```

If the user printing the file has the directory /usr/hutch as his or her "working directory," then the file is referenced simply by its name. Unfortunately, the controller program does not have knowledge of the user's working directory. So the queueing program converts the following information:

Working Directory:	/usr/hutch
Filename:	frog

into an absolute pathname looking like:

```
/usr/hutch/frog
```

The getfilename() function is defined as follows:

source file: machdep.c

```
 1    #include "queue.h"
      .
      .
      .
33    getfilename( temp )
34    struct pqueue *temp;
```

(program continues)

```
35   {
36        char *strcpy(), *strcat(), *strchr();
37        char temp_array[ FILE_NAME_SIZE ];
38        FILE *cdir;
39
40        /* while no valid file name identification */
41        while ( strcmp( temp->filename, "" ) == 0 )
42        {
43             char *cpointer;
44
45             printf( "Enter file name: " );
46             fgets( temp_array, FILE_NAME_SIZE, stdin );
47
48             /* get rid of newline that fgets() puts in there */
49             cpointer = strchr( temp_array, '\n' );
50             *cpointer = '\0';
51
52             if( temp_array[0] != '/' )
53             {
54                  /* relative pathname */
55                  cdir = popen( "pwd", "r" );
56                  fgets( temp->filename, FILE_NAME_SIZE, cdir );
57                  pclose( cdir );
58                  cpointer = strchr( temp->filename, '\n' );
59                  *cpointer = '\0';
60                  strcat( temp->filename, "/" );
61                  strcat( temp->filename, temp_array );
62             }
63   }
```

Line	Comments
34	Like the other "get" functions, this function is also given the address of a structure of type pqueue in which it places the requested information. Because we have only the structure address and not the structure name itself, we use the arrow operator to access elements within the structure.
36	In this function, three library functions are called, each of which returns a pointer to a character. Although the return values may not be checked, for consistency we declare them anyway.
37	We declare an array of 80 characters (defined in queue. h) in which we will place a character

string corresponding to the current directory's pathname. The pathname is used when we convert the relative pathname into an absolute pathname.

41   Since the `getfilename()` function is called only after a call to `clear()`, we can safely assume that the structure's filename element is clear. We continue to loop as long as the field is empty. This prevents the user from skipping over the response to this question.

43   A pointer to a character named `cpointer` is declared. Although `cpointer` could have been declared outside this loop, it is declared here to show you that this is possible. If this function had other sections after the `while` loop, then they would not have been able to access `cpointer`; it is private to the body of the loop.

45   Issue a prompt to the terminal.

46   Use the `fgets()` library function to retrieve a line of characters from the terminal (`FILE_NAME_SIZE` maximum) and store them in the array named `filename` within the structure whose address was passed as an argument.

49–50   Since the `fgets()` function stores the terminating newline character in the array, we need to dispose of it. The controller program will eventually try to open the file whose name is in this array; it must not contain a newline character.

The `gets()` function does not store the newline character. However, we have chosen to use the `fgets()` function because it allows us to specify the size of the destination. It is important to limit the user input size because if it exceeded the array size some part of memory not part of the array would be overwritten with possibly disastrous consequences.

52–63   This is the machine-specific portion of this function. It converts a relative pathname to an absolute file pathname.

52   Look to see if the first character of the file name is a '/'. This would indicate that an absolute pathname was entered. If not, we have to make adjustments to the file pathname.

55   A call is made to the `popen()` function. This is similar to opening a file, but instead of reading

information from a file, we take it from the output of another command. The first argument to popen() is the name of the command we would like to have executed; the second indicates whether we are reading from or writing to the command. In this case, we are reading from the command pwd which normally prints the working directory's pathname. This call does not read the command's output; it just prepares the program to receive the output. The program could then read the command output a character at a time:

```
while ( ( c = fgetc( cdir ) ) != EOF )
{
          . . .
}
```

Rather, we have chosen to read the information a line at a time. The return type of the popen() function is a pointer to a FILE structure, which is the same as the return value of the fopen() library function.

56   Get a line of information from the pwd command output and store it in the array that is named filename[] within the structure whose address is supplied to this function. At the very most, FILE_NAME_SIZE characters will be read into the array.

57   We have now finished using the information from the pwd command, so we close the input stream associated with it. The pclose() function is similar to the fclose() function except that it causes the program to wait until the pwd command finishes and returns a value indicating successful execution. We assume that the command was successful; in general it would be best to check this value.

58–59   Once again, we remove the newline character fgets() put in the array. Since we perform this function often, it would probably be profitable to create a new function that combines the call to fgets() with the lines of code to erase the newline character at the end of the line. This could also be done using gets() after the destination size has been checked.

60   Since we want the '/' character to separate the name of the current working directory from the file name, we append it to the end of the current working directory pathname using the strcat() function. This function appends the second character string it receives to the end of the first.

61   Append the entered file name to the end of the string composed of the current working directory and the added '/' character. This forms a complete, absolute pathname from an entered relative pathname.

This function could be rewritten, placing all the machine-independent parts in one function and machine-dependent parts in another. The machine-independent function would be stored in the same file as the other machine-independent routines, such as getpriority(). The machine-dependent routine would be placed in the machdep.c file. The machine-independent function would request the filename and call the machine-dependent function to manipulate the file pathname. If the machine environment is such that the file pathname needs no alterations, then the machine-dependent routine would be empty.

The getowner( ) Function

This function obtains the owner identification from the process environment using the library function getenv(). It, too, is likely to be machine dependent. If this or a similar function is not available, getowner() could be rewritten to prompt for the user's initials and/or additional owner information (maximum ten characters—the width of the owner field in the pqueue structure).

The getowner() function is defined as follows:

source file: machdep.c

```
1    #include "queue.h"
     .
     .
     .
9    getowner( temp )
10   struct pqueue *temp;
11   {
12        char *getenv(), *strcpy();
13
```

(program continues)

```
14          /* if no valid owner identification */
15          if( getenv( "LOGNAME" ) == (char *)NULL )
16          {
17               strcpy( temp->owner, "UNKNOWN" );
18          }
19          else
20          {
21               strcpy( temp->owner, getenv( "LOGNAME" ) );
22          }
23      }
```

The getenv() function returns a NULL pointer if the environment parameter does not exist. Before using it as an argument to the strcpy() function, we must first be certain it has a value. Then we can successfully copy the desired string into our temporary structure. If the return value from getenv() is NULL, we copy the character string "UNKNOWN" to the field in the temporary structure.

The gettime( ) Function

This function samples the time from the system's clock. The time is stored in the form of a long integer and converted to a human-readable form through the ctime() library function when it is to be printed. We will discuss this function in more detail when we look at the print_node() function later in this case study. It is used to print information about pending printer jobs.

The gettime() function is defined as follows:

source file: machdep.c

```
1    #include "queue.h"
     .
     .
     .
25   gettime( temp )
26   struct pqueue *temp;
27   {
28        long time();
29
30        temp->q_time = time( (long *)0 );
31   }
```

As with the getcontrol() function, the function that returns the time is system dependent. Therefore, we place this function in the machine-dependent source file.

This is the last of the system-dependent functions.

The getpriority( ) Function

This function prompts the user to enter a priority and then stores it in the structure whose address is supplied as its argument.

source file: get.c

```
1    #include "queue.h"
     .
     .
     .
20   getpriority( temp )
21   struct pqueue *temp;
22   {
23        temp->priority = 0;
24        while ( temp->priority < 1 || temp->priority > 10 )
25        {
26             printf( "Enter priority (1...10): " );
27             scanf( "%d", &temp->priority );
28             getchar(); /* excess newline */
29        }
30   }
     .
     .
     .
```

As in the menu( ) function, the newline character must be discarded.

This function can be modified in a number of interesting ways. For example, a default priority of 5 could be assigned. To lower the priority the user would enter a bias; to raise the priority the user would be required to enter a password.

Other get Functions

Several other functions request information from the terminal and place it in the structure whose address is passed as an argument. These functions, getcopies( ), getclass( ), and getdescription( ), are essentially the same as the getpriority( ) function already described.

source file: get.c

```
1    #include "queue.h"
     .
     .
     .
32   getcopies( temp )
33   struct pqueue *temp;
```

(program continues)

```
34    {
35         temp->n_copies = 0;
36         while ( temp->n_copies < 1 || temp->n_copies > 10 )
37         {
38             printf( "Enter number of copies (1...10): " );
39             scanf( "%d", &temp->n_copies );
40             getchar(); /* excess newline */
41         }
42    }

       .
       .
       .

56    getclass( temp )
57    struct pqueue *temp;
58    {
59         char *strchr();
60
61         /* while no valid class identification */
62         while ( strcmp( temp->class, "") == 0 )
63         {
64             char *cpointer;
65
66             printf( "Enter class: " );
67             fgets( temp->class, 10, stdin );
68
69             /* get rid of newline that fgets() puts in there */
70             cpointer = strchr( temp->class, '\n');
71             *cpointer = '\0';
72
73         }
74    }
75
76    getdescription( temp )
77    struct queue *temp;
78    {
79         char *strchr();
80
81         /* while no valid description */
82         while ( strcmp( temp->description, "" ) == 0 )
83         {
84             char *cpointer;
85
86             printf( "Enter description: " );
87             fgets( temp->description, FILE_NAME_SIZE, stdin );
88
```

```
89                  /* get rid of newline that fgets() puts in there */
90                  cpointer = strchr( temp->description, '\n' );
91                  *cpointer = '\0';
92
93          }
94     }
```

.
.
.

The getsize( ) Function

This function calculates the size of the file and stores it in the structure whose
address is supplied as an argument. Although this information can usually be
obtained through built-in functions (e.g., in the UNIX system we can use the
stat() function), for portability reasons we have chosen to read the file and
count characters. The program is less efficient (especially for large files) but
more portable.

source file: get.c

```
  1    #include "queue.h"
```

.
.
.

```
 96    getsize( temp )
 97    struct pqueue *temp;
 98    {
 99         FILE *iptr;
100         long counter = 0;
101
102         /* open file to find its size */
103         /* could use OS facility to do this which would be
104             faster but not as portable */
105         if( (iptr = fopen( temp->filename, "r" )) != NULL )
106         {
107             while( fgetc( iptr ) != EOF )
108                 counter++;
109             temp->file_length = counter;
110             fclose( iptr );
111         }
112    }
```

In line 105, this function opens the file to be queued, stores the return value
of fopen() in the variable iptr, and checks the assigned value to ensure that
the open is successful. If successful, the function reads the file a character at a

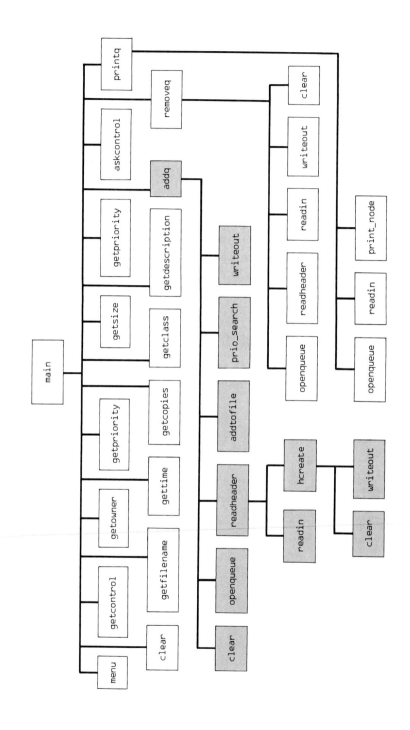

time, counting characters. The total number of characters is then stored in the structure member file_length.

The addq( ) Function

This function adds the temporary record just created to the print queue file and then logically inserts it as part of the linked list. In general, we add a record to the linked list as follows:

1. Find the correct place to insert the record. This procedure differs depending on how the list is going to be manipulated—as a stack, a queue, or, as in this example, a prioritized queue.

2. Take the previous record's "next" field in the list and store it in the new structure to be added to the prioritized queue. Then update this to disk.

3. Change the previous record's "next" field to point to the record being inserted. Then update this to disk.

In our example, the following code does this insertion:

source file: add.c

```
1    #include "queue.h"
2
3    FILE *ioptr;
4
5    addq( temp )
6    struct pqueue *temp;
7    {
8        node r_temp;      /* record number of inserted record */
9        node r_before;    /* record number of previous node   */
10       node addtofile();
11       node prio_search();
12       struct pqueue header, before;
13
14       clear( &before );
15       clear( &header );
16
17       openqueue();
18       readheader( &header );
19
20       r_temp = addtofile( temp );
21
22       r_before = prio_search( &header, temp, &before );
23
24       temp->r_next = before.r_next;
```

(program continues)

```
25          writeout( r_temp, temp );
26
27          before.r_next = r_temp;
28          writeout( r_before, &before );
29
30  }
    .
    .
    .
```

We use the record number (structure number) to form the records in the file into a linked list. The field holding the record number is of type node. You will recall that node is a synonym for int, as defined in the header file queue.h. Comments on function addq() follow:

Line	Comments
8–13	The variables in this function (as well as in the other functions in this source file) referring to record numbers are prefixed with the characters "r_". The structures holding the actual information are declared in line 12. Record-number variables are declared for the record to be inserted and the record that is already in the list and will precede our new record.
14–15	Since the structure variables header and before are declared as automatic, we cannot assume that the values of the members will be clear.
17	This function opens the file holding the print queue.
18	Each linked list has a header. The header is always in a known location and points to the record that logically begins the list. In this file, the first structure stored in the file is assumed to be the header record. If the readheader() function encounters an empty file it creates a header record.
20	The contents of the structure temp are written to the file. In this version of the program, the structure is always written to the end of the file. In later versions we will reuse those records in the file that have been logically deleted from the queue, either by a user request or because the file has been printed. The addtofile() function

returns the position at which the record is to be put in the file.

22   Now that the record has been physically positioned in the file, we need to find where it should be logically placed in the linked list. For this, we call the prio_search() function. This function requires three arguments:

&header   The header structure: This structure contains the information needed to start the search (the physical record number of the first logical record).

temp   The contents of the structure to be added: From this structure, we will extract the print request's priority and compare this to the other records in the list so that we can logically position the structure in the list.

&before   The address of a structure of type pqueue: When the record logically preceding the record to be inserted in the list is found, its contents are placed in this structure. The record number of this structure is the return value of the prio_search() function.

We now have the record number and the contents of the structure logically preceding the structure we are inserting into the list. Thus, we have determined the logical location of the new structure.

24–25   Set the new record's "next" field to the value of the previous record's "next" field and write the record to be inserted to disk.

27–28   Set the "previous" record to point to the inserted record as its logical "next" and write the updated "previous" record to disk.

At this point, the record is properly inserted in the queue. Now let's look at the openqueue(), readheader(), addtofile(), prio_search(), and writeout() routines in more detail.

The openqueue( ) Function

This function opens the print queue file if the file has not been previously opened; otherwise it rewinds the file.

source file: filemaint.c

```
1     #include "queue.h"
2
3     openqueue()
4     {
5         /* file has not already been opened */
6         if ( ioptr == 0 )
7         {
8             /* open queue file */
9             if ( (ioptr = fopen( PRINTER_QUEUE, "r+" )) == NULL )
10            {
11                fprintf( stderr, "Cannot open %s\n",
12                    PRINTER_QUEUE );
13                exit(1);
14            }
15            setbuf( ioptr, (char *)NULL );
16        }
17        else
18            fseek( ioptr, (long)0, 0 ); /*rewind file */
19    }
                    .
                    .
                    .
```

Line	Comments
6	Since the variable $ioptr$ is declared as external (line 3 of file main.c), we can assume it has a NULL initial value. If it has not yet been populated, the file is not yet open and we open it.
9–13	In line 9, we save the return value from fopen() in the variable $ioptr$ and check to see if the open is successful. If the open is not successful, we print an error to the standard error output and exit() the program with a nonzero (failure) status.

The name PRINTER_QUEUE represents the file to be opened; it is defined in the header file queue.h:

header file: queue.h

```
1    #include <stdio.h>
     .
     .
     .
4    char *getenv();
5    #define PRINTER_QUEUE getenv( "PRINTER_QUEUE" )
```

> The program assumes that an environment parameter containing the printer queue file has been set and labeled `PRINTER_QUEUE`.

15 > If the file open is successful, we turn off standard I/O buffering. If several users are accessing the file simultaneously, two users could attempt to update the same portion of the file at the same time. If buffering is not turned off it could lead to inconsistent views of the file, causing the file to be corrupted. As a rule, if it is possible that several users are attempting to update the same file simultaneously, shut off buffering through the `setbuf()` library function. This provides a more consistent view of files at the expense of (possibly) slower performance.

17–18 > If the file is already open, position the user at the beginning of the file. Alternatively, we could have used the `rewind()` library function.

The readheader( ) Function

This function is needed because the linked list is kept entirely on disk. The header structure is always the first record on the file. The header record does not need to be an entire structure; a simple variable of type `node` pointing to the first structure in the linked list would suffice. We have chosen to use a structure so that we can share common input and output routines with the functions that read and write records from and to the file. The code for the `readheader()` function is:

source file: filemaint.c

```
1    #include "queue.h"
     .
     .
     .
21   readheader( header )
22   struct pqueue *header;
23   {
24       /* read in header record from queue file */
```

(program continues)

```
25          if ( readin( 0, header ) == -1 )
26          {
27               /* no header on file */
28               hcreate( header );
29          }
30     }
31
32     hcreate( header )
33     struct pqueue *header;
34     {
35
36          printf( "Creating printer queue\n" );
37          clear( header );
38          writeout( 0, header );
39     }
```

Line	Comments
25	The readin() function is called with two arguments: 0, the record number, and header, the structure's memory address. If this function returns a value of -1, it is assumed that the header does not exist.
28	If the header does not exist, create one using the hcreate() function.
37–38	In the hcreate() function, the header structure is cleared and written to disk using the writeout() function. The writeout() function, as well as the readin() function, accepts two arguments: the record number and the memory address of the structure to be written (or read.) The record number is used to calculate the byte offset of the structure in the file.

The addtofile( ) Function

The next function called by addq() is the function that physically places the new record in the print queue file. This function always places the new record at the end of the file, whether or not any unused space is left from logically deleted records. In Case Study 4, we will see two methods for reclaiming space from deleted records—a free list and a bitmap. The addtofile() function is defined as follows:

source file: filemaint.c

```
1    #include "queue.h"
     .
     .
     .
41   addtofile( temp )
42   struct pqueue *temp;
43   {
44       /* always adds record to end of file */
45       long whereami, ftell();
46
47       fseek( ioptr, (long)0, 2 );   /* go to EOF */
48       whereami = ftell( ioptr );
49       fwrite( (char *)temp, sizeof(struct pqueue), 1, ioptr );
50
51       /* return record number in file */
52       return( byte_to_node(whereami) );
53   }
```

Line	Comments
41–42	The argument to the function is the address of the structure that is to be written to disk.
47	For the fseek() function, a final argument of 2 indicates a jump to the end of the printer queue file. The first argument is the external variable that holds the return value of the call to fopen().
48	Set the variable whereami to the current byte offset within the printer queue file. The offset will later be used to compute this function's return value.
49	Write the record contents to the file. The first argument to the fwrite() function is typecast to (char *). We will write one record of size:
	sizeof (struct pqueue)
	Using the sizeof operator is preferable to counting the number of bytes in the structure. This takes into consideration any unused holes, caused by alignment requirements, in the structure.
52	The addtofile() function returns the value generated by the byte_to_node() macro. This macro converts a supplied byte number to the equivalent record number.

Preprocessor Macros

In this function, we use the macro named byte_to_node(). Macros behave similarly to function calls but are actually substitutions performed by the preprocessor. In general, a macro is defined using the #define preprocessor directive in a slightly different form than we have seen it used:

```
#define macro_name(arg1, arg2) expression_involving_arg1_and_arg2
```

The opening parenthesis must immediately follow the last character in the macro name. The list of arguments to the macro may be used in the expression that follows it, along with any other fixed data.

It is customary for a macro not to rely on anything else but its argument list. For example, a macro should not assume that other variables exist; the expression should use only variables in the argument list. The macro named byte_to_node() is defined in the header file queue.h (most macros are defined in header files) as follows:

header file: queue.h

```
    .
    .
    .
 8  typedef int node;
    .
    .
    .
27  #define    byte_to_node(x) (x)/(sizeof(struct pqueue))
    .
    .
    .
```

In this example, the macro expects only one argument. For example, if the macro call is invoked as follows:

```
byte_to_node( 10000 )
```

the preprocessor substitutes the following:

```
(10000)/(sizeof(struct pqueue))
```

The preprocessor does not try to perform the computation; it only does the substitution. In addition to this macro, we also need the complementary macro node_to_byte() defined in the same file as follows:

header file: queue.h

```
      .
      .
      .
 8    typedef int node;
      .
      .
      .
26    #define    node_to_byte(x) (x)*(sizeof(struct pqueue))
      .
      .
      .
```

Some Rules for Macros

When defining macros, parentheses should surround the supplied arguments used in the resulting expression. The following example will demonstrate why. Assume we have the following macro:

```
#define abs(x)   x < 0 ? -x : x
```

and the following input:

```
a
```

The value of the substitution expression is:

```
a < 0 ? -a : a
```

But, if instead we pass −a to the macro, then the substitution yields:

```
-a < 0 ? --a : -a
```

If the value of the passed parameter is zero or positive (i.e., the conditional part is true), then the value of a is decremented and the resulting expression yields the decremented value of a instead of the negative value. A correct version of this macro is:

```
#define abs(x)   (x) < 0 ? -(x) : (x)
```

For similar reasons, when using a macro it is important never to pass any expression to it having a side effect. For example, if we pass our macro the following expression:

```
abs( --i )
```

the macro's expansion is:

$$(--i) < 0 ? -(--i) : (--i)$$

In the conditional part, the value of i is decremented and then checked to see if it is less than zero. If it is, then it is decremented *again* and the negative of the resulting value becomes the expression's value. If the condition yields a false value, the value of the variable i is decremented a second time.

For these reasons, make it very clear in the supporting documentation when macros are being used. Also, be careful never to pass any expression involving a side effect as a parameter; the parameter could be repeated several times in the macro call's expansion.

The prio_search( ) Function

Now that we have opened the queue file, read in the header, and physically placed the new record in the file, we need to find where it logically fits in the queue. To do this we compare the priority of the structure to be inserted against the priorities of the records already on the queue. The logic of this comparison is simple:

```
for ( each member of the queue )
{
        if ( priority of "member" > priority of inserted record )
        {
                return( record number of "member" )
        }
}
```

The function returns the record number of the record that logically precedes the record being inserted. If there are several jobs already on the queue with the same priority as the one being inserted, it is placed after all the others, thus maintaining a first-in, first-out ordering within a priority. The following code implements this:

source file: add.c

```
1   #include "queue.h"
2
3   FILE *ioptr;
    .
    .
    .
32  #define LIST_END 0
33  #define HEADER_RECORD 0
34
```

```
35     node prio_search( header, insert, previous )
36     struct pqueue *header, *insert, *previous;
37     {
38         struct pqueue current;
39         node r_previous, r_current;
40
41         /* set up initial conditions for search */
42         r_previous = HEADER_RECORD;
43         *previous = *header;
44
45         while ( (r_current = previous->r_next) != LIST_END )
46         {
47             if ( readin( r_current, &current ) == -1 )
48             {
49                 fprintf( stderr,
50                     "Corrupted linked list: searchq\n" );
51                 exit( 2 );
52             }
53             if ( current.priority > insert->priority )
54             {
55                 break;
56             }
57             r_previous = r_current;
58             *previous = current;
59         }
60         return( r_previous );
61     }
```

This function contains two markers: the record currently being inspected (current) and the one that logically precedes it (previous). The name of the record to be inserted is insert.

Line	Comments
35–36	The function requires three arguments:

- The first argument is used by the function to find the beginning of the list.
- The second argument is the address of the structure containing the record to be inserted into the queue. To determine the proper logical placement in the queue, we use the information in the structure's priority member.
- The third argument is the address of the structure that will eventually contain the

job information of the member logically preceding the new, inserted member. The calling function, addq(), will use this structure's r_next field to add the new element into the list logically.

42–43   These two statements set up the initial conditions for the loop. We have two markers in the list— the current and previous nodes. At the top of the loop, the r_next field of the previous node determines the current node. Setting the previous node to the header starts the loop at the list's first logical member.

45   Set the current record equal to the one that logically follows the "previous" node. The first time through the loop, the "previous" node is the header, otherwise it is the node we inspected the last time through the loop. If the value of the "previous" r_next field is zero, then we are at the logical end of the list. If this occurs the first time through the loop, then the queue is empty.

47–52   Read the current node into the structure current. If the read fails (returns a value of -1) this indicates that the "previous" record points to a record that does not exist. This is an abnormal condition resulting in the production of an error message and causing an exit from the program. The error message is printed to the standard error output.

53–56   If the record just read has a lower priority (1 is highest; 10 is lowest) than the record we are inserting, we have found the correct place to insert the record. We exit from the loop and return the previous record's record number (in line 60).

57–58   If the current record's priority is higher than or equal to the record we are inserting, continue looping until we encounter a lower priority or the logical end of the queue. These statements save the state of the record just inspected in the "previous" fields in preparation for the loop's next iteration.

60   This statement is executed under two conditions: the end of the queue is encountered (normal end of the while loop), or the point of insertion is found and the loop is prematurely terminated (line 55). In either case, the record number of the

previous record is returned. The appropriate information has already been saved in the `previous` structure either by line 43 (if the queue is empty) or by line 58. Both of these lines use the structure assignment facility.

I/O Support Functions

The following two functions provide I/O support for the add, remove, and print functions. Both functions require the record number of the record to read in (or write out) and a pointer to a structure as arguments. The code for the two functions is as follows:

source file: filemaint.c

```
1    #include "queue.h"
     .
     .
     .
55   writeout( r_source, source )
56   node r_source;
57   struct pqueue *source;
58   {
59       fseek( ioptr, (long)node_to_byte(r_source), 0 );
60       fwrite( (char *)source, sizeof(struct pqueue),
61           1, ioptr );
62   }
63
64   readin( r_dest, destination )
65   node r_dest;
66   struct pqueue *destination;
67   {
68       int val;
69
70       fseek( ioptr, (long)node_to_bypte(r_dest), 0 );
71       val = fread( (char *)destination,
72           sizeof(struct pqueue), 1, ioptr );
73       if ( val == 0 )
74       {
75           return( -1 );
76       }
77       return( r_dest );
78   }
```

The `writeout()` function returns no value while the `readin()` function returns −1 if the supplied record number does not correspond to an actual record on the disk. We use −1 as the value returned in case of error because 0 is a valid record number.

Line	Comments
59	Move the current offset in the file to the byte position calculated by the `node_to_byte()` macro. Remember, this macro multiplies the record number by the size of the structure to be written. This macro yields an integer value, but the `fseek()` function expects a long integer as its second argument, so the value must be typecast.
60–61	Write the contents of the structure to the file at the current position.
64–66	The `readin()` function requires the record number to be read and the address of a structure where the information in the record is placed.
70	Like the `writeout()` function, this function locates the current position in the file through the `fseek()` library function.
71–72	An attempt is made to read the structure. If this attempt fails, the return from `fread()` is zero (the number of records successfully read). Otherwise, the contents of the structure on disk will be placed in the structure pointed to by `destination`.
73–76	If the read request is unsuccessful, return a value of −1. If the calling function obtains a return value from this function of −1, then the contents of the structure that `destination` points to are not considered valid.
77	As a verification that the read is successful, return the record number supplied to this function.

REMOVING A PRINT REQUEST

Up to this point, all the routines were used for adding records to the printer queue. In this section, we discuss the procedures that permit a job already on the queue to be removed. To remove a print request it is necessary to identify it. Because multiple print requests may have the same file name we will not use filename as a means of identification. Instead we will use the control number that was assigned in the program's `add` section. The first function we discuss asks the user for the control number of the job to be removed. It is called `askcontrol()`:

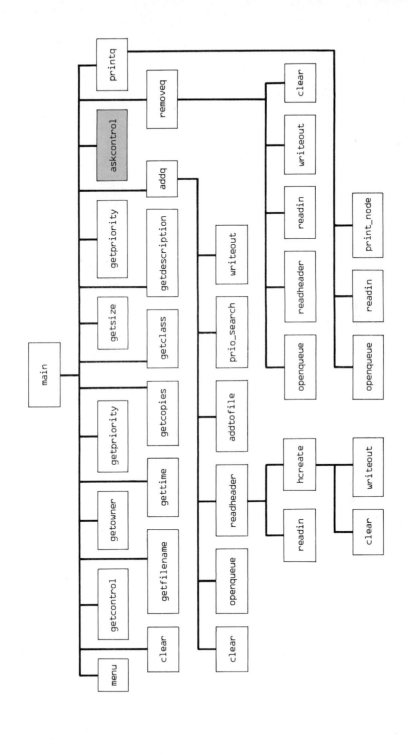

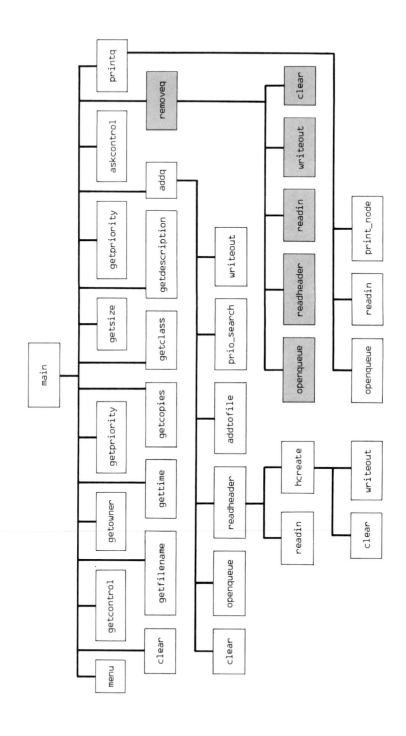

program: get.c

```
 1    #include "queue.h"
 .
 .
 .
44    askcontrol()
45    {
46        int answer = 0;
47
48        while( answer == 0 )
49        {
50            printf( "Enter control # of file to remove: " );
51            scanf( "%d", &answer );
52        }
53        return( answer );
54    }
```

The function returns the control number.

The removeq( ) Function

This function implements the job's logical removal from the queue. The function does not, however, physically remove the record from the print queue file. Standard facilities allowing us to shrink the size of a file do not exist, so the best we can do is to reclaim the physical space logically deleted from the queue. We will discuss procedures for this in Case Study 4. The removeq( ) function is defined as follows:

program: remove.c

```
 1    #include "queue.h"
 2    #define END_OF_LIST 0
 3
 4    removeq( control )
 5    node control;
 6    {
 7        struct pqueue previous, current;
 8        node r_previous, r_current;
 9
10        openqueue();
11        readheader( &previous );
12
13        r_previous = 0;
14
```

(program continues)

```
15          while( (r_current = previous. r_next) != END_OF_LIST )
16          {
17               if ( readin( r_current, &current ) == -1 )
18               {
19                    printf( "Corrupted print queue\n" );
20                    exit( 2 );
21               }
22
23               if( current.control_id == control )
24               {
25                    previous. r_next = current. r_next;
26                    writeout( r_previous, &previous );
27                    clear( &current );
28                    /* create hole in file */
29                    writeout( r_current, &current );
30                    return;
31               }
32               else
33               {
34                    r_previous = r_current;
35                    previous = current;   /* next node */
36               }
37
38          }
39          fprintf( stderr, "Print job %d not found\n", control );
40          exit( 3 );
41     }
```

Line	Comments
4–5	This function expects one argument—the control identification number of the print job to be deleted.
7	Like the prio_search() function, we search the queue using the current record and its predecessor.
10–13	Open the print queue file and set up the header as the first "previous" record.
15	Assign the record number of the record that logically follows the "previous" record to the current record number. If this assigned value is 0, then we are at the end of the list.
17–21	Read the contents of the next logical record in the list. If the read fails, we have a corrupted linked list. In this case, an error message is printed and the program terminates.

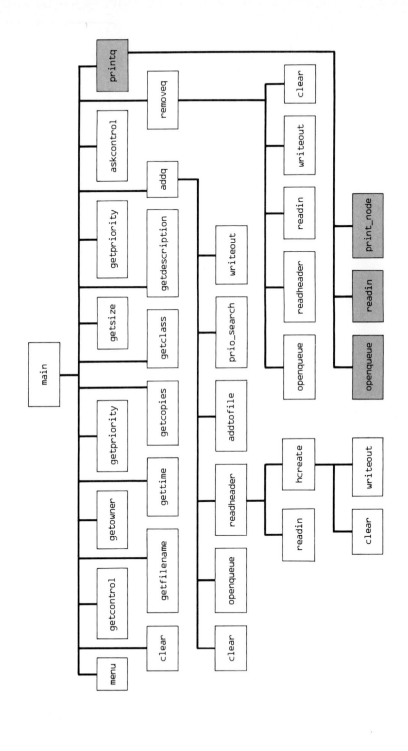

23	If the control identification of the current record matches the control identification of the job to be removed, we have found the correct record.
25	The record is logically removed by replacing its predecessor's r_next field with its r_next field. The current record is now logically not part of the linked list.
26	The substitution performed in statement 25 is written to disk using the writeout() function.
27–29	Clear out the deleted record and update the file. At this point, the record constitutes an unusable gap in the printer queue file. In Case Study 4 we will see how this problem can be resolved and the record space in the file recovered.
30	Return to the main() function; the remove has been accomplished.
32–36	If the current record does not generate a control identification match, store it as the previous record and continue with the loop.
39–40	If the end of the linked list is reached and the record has not been found, print an error message and exit the program.

PRINTING THE QUEUE

The following two functions are used to print the contents of the line printer queue. The first function steps through the print queue and then calls the second function to print each of the structure's elements.

The printq() Function

This function, as well as the function that prints the structure, is found in a file named print.c. The printq() function is defined as follows:

source file: print.c

```
1    #include "queue.h"
2    #define END_OF_LIST 0
3
4    printq( r_header )
5    node r_header;
6    {
7         node r_current;
8         struct pqueue current;
9
```

```
10          openqueue();
11
12          if ( readin( r_header, &current ) == BAD_READ )
13          {
14              printf( "Empty queue\n" );
15              return;
16          }
17
18          printf( "\n\n%-5s %-34s %4s %7s %-s\n",
19              "ID/", "FILENAME/", "PRI/",
20              "SIZE", "DESCRIPTION" );
21          printf( "%-5s %-34s %4s %7s %-s\n\n",
22              "OWNER", "TIME QUEUED", "COPY",
23              "", "CLASS" );
24
25          while ( (r_current = current.r_next) != END_OF_LIST )
26          {
27              if ( readin( r_current, &current ) == BAD_READ )
28              {
29                  printf( "Corrupted queue\n" );
30                  exit( 4 );
31              }
32              print_node( &current );
33          }
34      }
        .
        .
        .
```

Line	Comments
4–5	The function requires one argument—the record number of the header record in the file.
10–16	The header is read from the print queue file and becomes the current record. The header is not printed. If the file does not contain a header record then the message "Empty queue" is printed.
18–23	Print the field headings. You will notice that in the printf() control string, a dash (–) followed by a number appears between several of the format specifiers. The dash tells printf() that the field is to be left justified (right justified is the default if the field width is specified) and the number describes the field width.

25	Step through the queue a record at a time until the r_next field of the record indicates that the logical end of the list has been encountered.
27–31	Read the appropriate record into the structure current. If the read fails, then the linked list has been corrupted; print an error and exit the program.
32	For each record read from the file, print its contents using the print_node() function.

The print_node( ) Function

This function may be called from several places, but in this example it is only called from the printq() function. Its sole argument is the address of a structure whose contents it will print. The print_node() function is defined as follows:

program: print.c

```
 1   #include "queue.h"

     .
     .
     .
36   print_node( temp )
37   struct pqueue *temp;
38   {
39       char *ctime(), *strchr(), *cpointer, *newline;
40
41       /* prepare time field */
42       cpointer = ctime( &time->q_time );
43       newline = strchr( cpointer, '\n' );
44       *newline = '\0';
45
46       printf( "%-5d %-36s %2d %71d %s\n", temp->control_id,
47           temp->filename, temp->priority,
48           temp->file_length, temp->description );
49       printf( "%-5s %-36s %2d %7s %s\n\n", temp->owner,
50           cpointer, temp->n_copies, "", temp->class );
51   }
```

Line	Comments
42	The ctime() function's argument is the address of a long integer that holds the return value from the time() call. The time() function returns the number of seconds elapsed since a fixed point

in time. The c t i me ( ) function then converts the long integer into a 26-character string of the form:

Day Month Day_in_month Time Year

followed by a newline character.

43–44   Since the time will be printed in the middle of a line, we need to remove the newline character that c t ime ( ) placed in the string. We use the st r chr ( ) library function to find the newline and set it to null.

46–50   Using the same format as the header, we print the contents of the structure whose address is supplied. A few minor adjustments have been made to the field widths to ensure proper alignment.

THE CONTROLLER PROGRAM

So far, we have discussed those functions used to queue files to be printed. In this section we will discuss the program that takes requests from the queue and prints the files. The logic for this program is:

```
while ( forever )
{
        if ( something on queue )
        {
                read first record from queue;
                print file whose name is in
                        this queue structure;
        }
        else
        {
                sleep for a while and try again;
        }
}
```

This program is started when the system is booted and remains active until the system is brought down. On systems that cannot have background processes, the program would periodically be manually invoked, read records until there were no more on the queue, and then stop.

Assuming there is a structure on the queue (i.e., the "next" field of the header is nonzero), the program reads the contents of the structure and finds

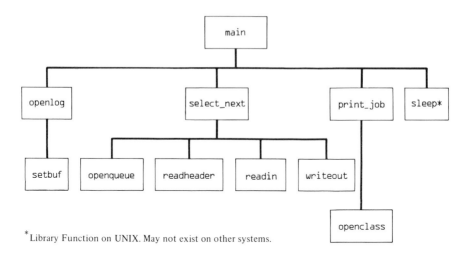

*Library Function on UNIX. May not exist on other systems.

the name of the file to be printed. The file printing procedure is contained in a separate function and will be discussed later in this case study. If there is no structure on the queue, then the program sleeps for a while and tries again later. If this is not a timesharing environment, the program exit()s at this point. The hierarchy of user-defined functions in this program is shown above.

The main( ) Function

The main() function for this program is defined as follows:

program: controller.c

```
 1    #include "queue.h"
 2
 3    #define FOREVER 1
 4    #define EMPTY −1
      .
      .
      .
10    main()
11    {
12         struct pqueue job;
13         unsigned sleep();
14
15         openlog();
16
17         while ( FOREVER )
18         {
19              if ( select_next( &job ) != EMPTY )
20                   print_job( &job );
```

```
21                else
22                    sleep( (unsigned)10 );
23        }
24  }
```

.
.
.

Line	Comments
15	As its name implies, the openlog() function opens a log file. Whenever a file is printed using our spooling system, the name and pertinent information about the file is recorded in the log.
17–23	This loop runs forever, looking for files to print. Whenever one appears on the queue, the print_job() routine is called to print the file; if no request is on the queue, the program calls the sleep() function which puts the program to sleep for a specified number of seconds. Most systems have a library function called sleep(), where the supplied argument is usually in seconds; sometimes the argument is interpreted as hundredths of seconds.

The select_next( ) Function

The select_next() routine picks the job with the highest priority from the queue. Since the linked list is organized as a prioritized queue, this will always be the first logical structure on the queue. The code for this function is shown on the following page:

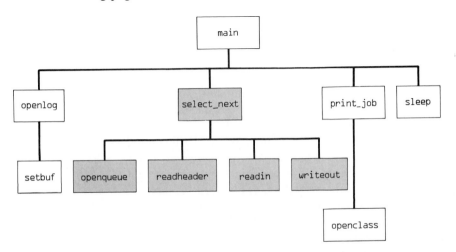

program: controller.c

```
1    #include "queue. h"
  .
  .
  .
4    #define EMPTY -1
  .
  .
  .
8    FILE *logptr;
  .
  .
  .
26   select_next( job )
27   struct pqueue *job;
28   {
29        static struct pqueue header;
30
31        openqueue();
32        readheader( &header );
33
34        if ( header. r_next != 0 &&
35             readin( header. r_next, job ) != -1 )
36        {
37             fprintf( logptr, "Printing file: %s\n", job->filename );
38             header. r_next = job->r_next;
39             writeout( 0, &header );
40             return( 1 );   /* record number selected */
41        }
42        else
43             return( EMPTY );
44   }
```

Line	Comments
31	This function opens the queue. The file position is set to the beginning of the file. If the file is already open, it rewinds it. This is the same openqueue ( ) function used in the queuing program.
34–35	Both of these conditions must be true for the compound statement between lines 36 and 41 to be executed. The header's "next" field must point to another record in the file and that record must exist in the file. If we have been careful in

the other program the second part should never fail.

37   A record has been successfully read from the file and placed in the structure job. Some of the information in this record is recorded in the log file using the pointer logptr.

38   The record is removed from the print queue by setting the header's "next" field to point to the record that follows the record being printed. If this is the last record on the file, then the value assigned is zero, emptying the queue.

39   The updated header is written out to the disk. Ideally, in a multiprocessing environment, some form of protection should be placed around lines 34 through 37 to ensure that a second process does not concurrently begin update. File/record locking or semaphores could do this.

40–43   Either return a value of 1 (the record number to be printed) or, if the queue is empty, return the defined value of EMPTY (−1).

The print_job( ) Function

When this program's main ( ) function finds a record that represents a file to be printed, it calls print_job(). File printing methodology is system dependent, and even within a system, there may be several different file printing commands, each useful in different circumstances. Therefore, we would like, as much as possible, to keep print command details out of the program. To do this we will set up a table of file-printing commands, where each command is associated with a class. (If you remember, all print requests had associated

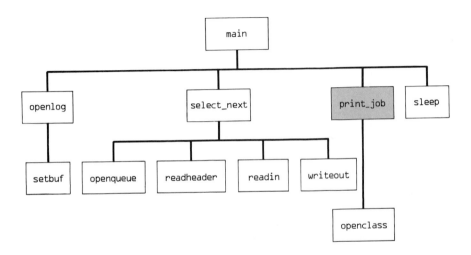

EXHIBIT CS2-2

The controller program command table

name of class	pre	post1	post2

print classes.) The print_job() function will scan this table until it finds the print class associated with the current print request and then it will construct the appropriate print command. We will use the system() library function (system() issues commands as if they were typed at the terminal) to issue the appropriate command to print the file whose name is stored. For example, in the UNIX system, the command to print a text file looks like:

```
cat filename >/dev/lp
```

The command name is "cat", the file name is "filename", and the phrase at the end of the line, ">/dev/lp", instructs the system to direct the output of this command to the printer. The first word and the last phrase will be the same for all files, but the file name changes. We keep track of this constant information by storing it in the command table. It, in turn, is stored in a file. The command table format is shown in Exhibit CS2-2. The first field labels the entry. All files identified as belonging to a given class will undergo processing as defined by the remainder of the line. The second field, pre, is the name of the command that reads and possibly formats the file. We allow for two postprocessing programs, but may only use one. Exhibit CS2-3 shows how the table entry for the UNIX cat command would appear. Another print command class (to print documents) is defined in Exhibit CS2-4 where filename is the name of the file being printed. If the class name is doc and the filename to be printed is frog, then the command generated is:

```
mm frog | col >/dev/lp
```

The print_job() function is defined on the facing page:

EXHIBIT CS2-3

Table entry for the UNIX cat command

name of class	pre	post1	post2
text	cat	>/dev/lp	

Table entry for the UNIX mm command

name of class	pre	post1	post2
doc	mm	| col	>/dev/lp

program: controller.c

```
1    #include "queue.h"
   .
   .
   .
5    #define SUCCESS 1
6    #define FAILURE -1
7
8    FILE *logptr;
   .
   .
46   FILE *classptr;
47   #define INPUT_SIZE 80
48   #define COMMAND_SIZE INPUT_SIZE+20
49
50   print_job( job )
51   struct pqueue *job;
52   {
53       char classline[INPUT_SIZE], command[COMMAND_SIZE];
54       char *prefix, *postproc, *postfix;
55       char *strchr(), *strtok(), *cptr;
56
57       openclass();
58       while( fgets( classline, INPUT_SIZE, classptr ) != NULL )
59       {
60           cptr = strtok( classline, "\t" );
61           if ( strcmp( job->class, cptr ) == NULL )
62           {
63               prefix = strtok( (char *)NULL, "\t" );
64               postproc = strtok( (char *)NULL, "\t" );
65               postfix = strtok( (char *)NULL, "\n\t" );
66
67               sprintf( command, "sh -c \"banner OWNER: %s %s %s\"",
68                   job->owner, job->description, postfix );
```

(program continues)

```
69              fprint( logptr, "command line: %s\n", command );
70              system( command );
71
72              sprintf( command, "sh -c \"%s %s %s %s\"", prefix,
73                  job->filename, postproc, postfix );
74              fprintf( logptr, "command line: %s\n", command );
75              system( command );
76
77              return( SUCCESS );   /* success */
78          }
79      }
80
81      fprintf( logptr, "CONTROLLER: class %s not found\n", job->class);
82      return( FAILURE );
83  }
```

Line	Comments
50–51	The argument supplied to this function is the address of a structure of type `pqueue`; the structure contains information about the file to be printed.
53	The `classline[]` array holds lines as they are read from the class file (the file that defines pre- and postprocessors for each different class type.) Eventually, the `print_job()` function formulates a command line to be sent to the system; the command line, including the filename, is stored in `command[]`.
54	These three pointers to characters point into the line read from the class file; they point to the beginning of the line (the printing/formatting command), the first postprocessor, and the second postprocessor, respectively.
57	If it is not already open, the class file is opened, otherwise the program sets the offset in the file to zero (rewinds the file.)
58	This line begins the loop and causes it to continue as long as there are lines remaining in the class file. Each line of information from the class file is read into the `classline[]` array.
60	The `strtok()` library function "tokenizes" the string. This function is passed two arguments: the character string's address and a string containing delimiters. When a delimiter is found in

the string, the strtok() replaces it with a NULL character, effectively ending the string. The return value of strtok() is the substring's starting address. Thus, cptr will point to the class name.

61   If the class name just read from the file matches the class for the file to be printed, then the file is printed (lines 63 through 79.) If there is no match, we will return the defined value of FAILURE to the calling process.

63   When the strtok() function is called a second time with a NULL first argument value, then it looks for the second field (next occurrence of the delimiter) in the same string as before. It is possible to use new delimiting characters but we continue to use only the tab character. The function's return value is the starting address of the second field in the string and the delimiter character is changed to a '\0' character. Thus, the prefix field will contain the address of the command line's second field (the printing/formatting command).

64–65   The same process is used to separate the classline[] array into substrings representing the postprocessor and the (optional) suffix. In the final invocation, two delimiting characters are supplied, a tab and a newline. When strtok() encounters either of these two, it will replace it with a string termination character.

67–68   Before the file is printed, a separate request is made to print a page header identifying each job. These lines are somewhat UNIX specific; they use the banner command to print the owner's name in large letters, and the sh −c command to invoke the UNIX shell to interpret and execute the rest of the command line. The sprintf() library function formulates the command line. It is similar to the fprintf() library function except for its first argument. The first argument of sprintf() is the address of a character array where the formatted output will be placed, rather than the file destination (the first argument of fprintf().) For example, if the file owner's name is hutch, and the description is "the password file", and the class file entry is the following:

text *tab* ca t *tabtab*> / d e v / l p

then the output line (placed in `command[]`) looks like:

`sh -c "banner OWNER: hutch the password file >/dev/lp"`

On a UNIX system, this command line prints the following in large letters:

`OWNER: hutch the password file`

69   The command line that prints the banner is recorded in the log file for auditing.

70   The `system( )` library function is called and supplied the command line formed in lines 67 and 68. The `system( )` function issues the command to the operating system which then executes it.

72–75   Similarly, we construct the command to print the file: a command is formed, the command line is recorded in the log file, and the command is executed using the `system( )` library function.

77   If the file prints successfully, return the defined value of `SUCCESS` to the calling function.

81–82   If we cannot find the current class type in the class table, then log the error and return the defined value of `FAILURE` to the calling process. This could be modified to assign a default class type if the supplied value is undefined in the class table.

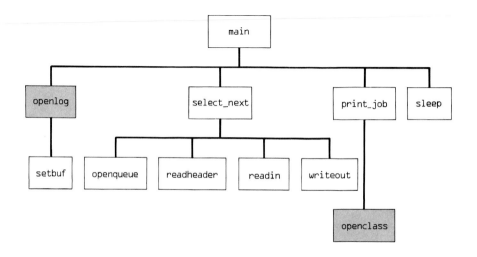

File Support Functions

This program uses several other functions, some of which we have already seen and are shared with the queueing program. Two additional functions, which open the log file and the class file, are listed here:

program: controller.c

```
1    #include "queue.h"
     .
     .
     .
8    FILE *logptr;
     .
     .
     .
46   FILE *classptr;
     .
     .
     .
85   openclass()
86   {
87       if ( classptr == 0 )
88       {
89           /* open queue file */
90           if ( (classptr = fopen( "/etc/classfile", "r" )) == NULL )
91           {
92               fprintf( stdferr, "Cannot open %s\n",
93                   "/etc/classfile" );
94                   exit( 1 );
95           }
96           setbuf( classptr, (char *)0 );
97       }
98       else
99       {
100          rewind( classptr );   /*rewind file */
101      }
102  }
103
104  openlog()
105  {
106      /* open log file */
107      if ( (logptr = fopen( "/tmp/logfile", "a" )) == NULL )
108      {
109          fprintf( stderr, "Cannot open %s\n",
110              "/tmp/logfile" );
```

(program continues)

```
111             exit( 2 );
112         }
113     setbuf( logptr, (char *)0 );
114  }
```

Line	Comments
87	Since c l a s s p t r is declared as an external variable, we are guaranteed its initial value is zero. Because we are setting it in this function, we can assume that if its value is nonzero, we must have run this function before. If this is the case, we reposition at the beginning of the file (line 100.)
96	In a multiprocessing environment, several users could be updating this file simultaneously. Therefore, we shut off standard I/O buffering to guarantee a more consistent view of the file. (The same technique is used in line 113 of the o p e n l o g ( ) function.)

SUMMARY

In this case study, we developed a large system for queuing requests to print files. Using a linked list, we implemented a prioritized queue. This is slightly different from the queue we implemented in Chapter 17. In this example, the elements of the list are arranged in order by priority, with higher priority records at the beginning of the list and lower priority records at the end. Strictly speaking, only records of the same priority are arranged and accessed in first-in, first-out order.

The implementation is somewhat UNIX specific, although with minor modification it could be made to run on any system. It is usually good practice to consider portability issues when developing software. It is difficult, however, to write a system of any significant size without introducing system dependencies. One technique that facilitates portability is to isolate all machine-dependent functions in a single source file. When the software is to be ported (moved to another machine type) the functions to be modified can be easily located.

CASE STUDY 3

USING HASHING TO MAINTAIN A DICTIONARY OF KEYWORDS AND DEFINITIONS

OVERVIEW

This case study describes hashing as a technique for maintaining and accessing a list of objects. We will build a system that stores and retrieves definitions of keywords in a dictionary.

HASHING

Hashing is a useful technique for managing the insertion, deletion, and access of elements in a data base. It is an efficient data maintenance methodology implemented by building a table of pointers (called the *hash table*) that points into the database. A mathematical function (called the *hashing function*) translates each element to be stored in the database into a number. This number is then used as an index into the hash table, which contains, at this table address, a pointer to the element's location in the database. Thus, access to any element is direct; when presented with an element, we apply the hashing function, create the number associated with this element, and proceed directly to this table address. At this table address we will find a pointer to the element in the database. In the application we will develop in this case study, the elements are words in a dictionary. We will create a function that translates these words into numbers between 0 and 63. This number will be an index into a hash table. The location of the word in the dictionary database will be the value stored in the hash table.

What happens if multiple entries map into the same value? This is called a *collision* and it causes a problem because two (or more) element addresses cannot occupy the same table location at the same time. A good hashing function will minimize collisions, but they will always occur and we need to devise a method for resolving them.

To resolve collisions, we will apply the technique of linked lists that we developed in Chapter 17. Whenever an element maps into a table address that is already occupied, we create a linked list, or *chain*, in the database. As additional elements map into the occupied slot in the hash table, we simply extend the chain that starts there. The address of the first record in the chain is stored at the proper location (as defined by the hashing function) in the hash table. When searching for a word we proceed to its table address. If the word pointed to by the address in the table does not match the target word, we proceed down

EXHIBIT CS3-1

The hash table and the dictionary file. Although the connections between and within the files are represented by pointers, they are actually file offsets. Entries 1 and 3 hash to the same value.

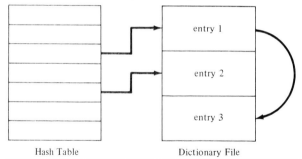

Hash Table   Dictionary File

the chain until we find the word, or the end of the list, whichever comes first. We are guaranteed that if the word exists in the database it will be on the selected list.

Exhibit CS3-1 represents a conceptual view of the table structure.

The Dictionary Application

The application we will implement using hashing is fairly straightforward: we will build a system that permits us to insert, delete, modify, and access key-words stored in a dictionary. The information stored with each word includes the definition of the word, the name of the person who entered the word, the name of the person who last modified the word or its definition, and up to five "see also" references.

To store all this information we create three data structures:

- a *hash table* containing sixty-four entries, each of which points to the location of a word in the dictionary file
- the *dictionary file*, which is a collection of structures containing words and associated information (but not the word definition)
- the *definitions file* containing variable-length word definitions. Each record in the dictionary file points to a location in the definitions file corresponding to the starting location of the definition.

These three data structures are linked, as shown in Exhibit CS3-2.

To add a word to the dictionary we first pass the word through the hashing function, which translates the word into an offset into the hash table. If this location in the hash table is empty, we add the word and its associated information (without the definition) at the end of the dictionary file and place the location of the dictionary file record into the hash table. However, if this location in the hash table is occupied, then another word has already hashed into this table location and we have a "collision." In this case, we replace the current pointer in the table with a pointer to the new structure. We add the new

EXHIBIT CS3-2

The hash table and the dictionary file with the definitions file added. Pointers to latter file are also file offsets.

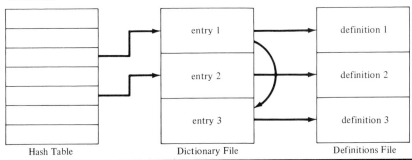

| Hash Table | Dictionary File | Definitions File |

word and associated information to the end of the dictionary file. Then we place the address of the record that had been in the hash table into the next field of the new record. Thus, we have effectively extended the linked list by "bumping" all entries down the chain and we have placed the new dictionary record at the beginning of the correct hash list.

As we add each new record to the end of the dictionary file we also place this word's definition at the end of the definitions file. We place the offset of the beginning of the definition in the new record in the dictionary file as well as the length of the definition.

The dict Program

This program has four functions, two of which we will describe in detail in this chapter, the other two will be left as a student exercise. The four functions are:

add( )	This allows us to add a definition to the file. We will use a text editor to enter the definition so that we can easily edit our entries. We will permit up to five "see also" references for each keyword definition.
change( )	We will use this function to change the definition of an existing entry using the same text editor as in the add function.
delete( )	This function allows us to remove an entry from the dictionary file.
lookup( )	This function prints a definition from the file. If there are any "see also" references, the definitions of these are also printed.

A diagram of the complete function hierarchy is shown on the next page.

The main( ) Function

This function controls the program execution at the highest level. The logic for the main( ) function is:

```
main( )
{
    open necessary files
    do
    {
        prompt for command
        accept command input
        parse into command and arguments
        if( command is valid )
            execute appropriate function

    } while( "end" was not entered as command )
}
```

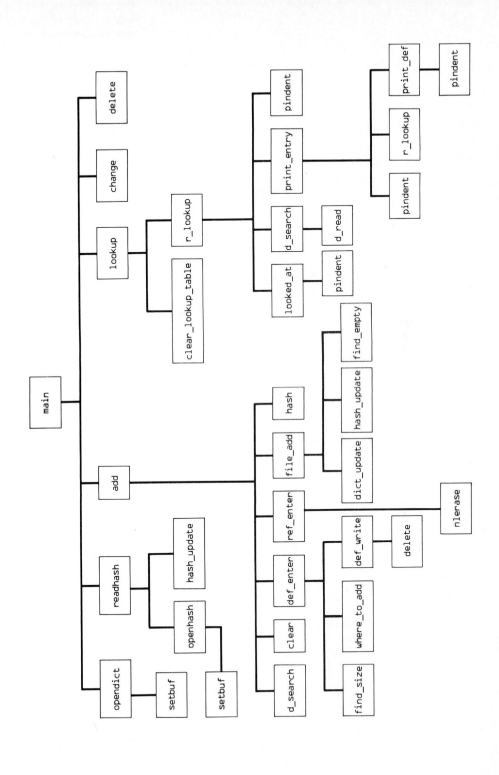

The C language implementation of this pseudocode is:

source file: main.c

```
1     #include <stdio.h>
2     #include "general.h"
3     #include "command.h"
4     #include "word_def.h"
5
6     struct word_def temp;
7
8     main()
9     {
10        char command[ COMMAND_LENGTH ];
11        char *arg, *cmd, *strtok();
12        int sub;
13
14        opendict();
15        readhash();
16
17        do
18        {
19            printf( "\nEnter command: " );
20            fgets( command, COMMAND_LENGTH, stdin );
21            cmd = strtok( command, "\t\n" );
22            arg = strtok( (char *)0, "\n" );
23
      .       /*  process command  */
      .
      .
33        } while ( strcmp( command, "end" ) != 0 );
34    }
```

Line	Comments
2–4	Three local header files are included. They contain general information, information describing a command line, and information describing the definition of a word. Details will be supplied later in this case study.
10	A character array named command[], that will eventually hold a command typed in from the terminal, is allocated. This array's length is the defined constant COMMAND_LENGTH. It is defined as 80 in the header file command.h.
14	This function opens the file that contains most of

the information about entries in the dictionary, including the word itself, who defined the word (entered the definition), who last changed the definition, where the definition begins in the definitions file, as well as other information.

15   This file contains a table that is used to access entries in the dictionary. The hash table will be described in more detail later in this case study.

17–33   This do loop prompts the user for a command. It then parses the input line into the command and its arguments, after which the command is executed.

19–20   A prompt is issued and the user is asked to enter a command line containing the name of the command and the appropriate arguments.

21   The character pointer cmd is set to the address of the beginning of the command line after the strtok() function "tokenizes" the string. It does so by searching for the first occurrence of either a tab, space, or newline character. The strtok() function replaces the first delimiting character in the string with a null '\0' character.

22   The strtok() library function is used with a null first argument to continue parsing the same string. The return value, the beginning of the second field, is stored in the variable arg. The string termination character replaces the newline at the end of the string. Notice that the delimiting characters in this call are different from the first call; we want the rest of the input line to be stored in the second string.

33   If the command entered is end then the program falls out of the loop and the program ends. If not, it prompts the user for the next command.

POINTERS TO FUNCTIONS

Lines 24 through 32 of the main() function execute the function that corresponds to the command the user types. In this section we describe the technique used to branch to the appropriate function; in the next two sections we will show you the C language code that implements this technique.

To branch to the appropriate function we compare the command typed in against a list of valid command names and then execute the appropriate function by using a pointer to the function. Functions, like variables, have addresses that can be stored in pointer variables. A pointer to a function is defined as follows:

```
return_type (*pointer_name)();
```

We note that return_type is the type of the function's return value and pointer_name is the name of the pointer variable.

A pointer to a function can be assigned a function's starting address. A function name, like the name of an array, if used all by itself in an expression, has the value of the function's starting address. For example, the following code fragment declares a pointer to an integer-returning function and assigns the function address to the pointer variable:

```
main()
{
    int function();
    int (*fpointer)();

    fpointer = function;
}

int function()
{
    /* body of function */
}
```

(We need to declare the function named function() in main() if we want to reference its value, even if it returns an integer value.)

To execute the function from the pointer variable, we use the following statement:

```
( *fpointer )( arguments );
```

The parentheses are needed to force the pointer dereferencing to occur before the execution of the function.

In our program, we declare an array of structures, each containing a command name (as it would be typed from the terminal) and the corresponding function's address. This array's format is found in a header file named command.h and is defined as follows:

header file: command.h

```
1    #define COMMAND_LENGTH   80
2
3    struct cmmd
4    {
5        char cmd_name[10];
6        int (*cmd_addr)();  /* pointer to function */
7    };
8
9    extern struct cmmd cmdarray[];
10   extern int number_commands;
```

In each of these structures we store the name of the command in the array named cmd_name[] and the address of the function that carries out the command in the pointer variable cmd_addr. All other source files that reference the array include this file.

The cmdarray[] array is declared in the source file command.c. The array declaration is as follows:

source file: command.c

```
1    #include <stdio.h>
2    #include "general.h"
3    #include "command.h"
4    #include "hash.h"
5    #include "word_def.h"
6
7    int add(), change(), delete(), lookup();
8
9    struct cmmd cmdarray[] =
10   {
11       { "add", add };
12       { "change", change }
13       { "delete", delete },
14       { "lookup", lookup }
15   };
16
17   int number_commands = 4;
```

In lines 9 through 15, we declare and initialize an array of four cmmd structures. The first field of each structure contains the command as the user enters it at the terminal and the second field contains the address of the function carrying out the command. The array size is kept in the external variable number_commands.

You have probably noticed that this source file does not contain any functions, only declarations of external variables. The compiler permits this and allows us to neatly package our software.

Adding New Functionality to Software

Storing the commands and corresponding function names in a separate source file permits us to update the software easily. To add functionality we only have to update the command.c source file; the modules containing the code that actually performs the processing do not have to be modified or recompiled when new functions are added.

Let's add a new function that prints a definition and the name of the person who last changed it. The command typed in at the terminal is:

owner

followed by the name of the term (or keyword). To accommodate this new command we simply update the file command.c with the new command definition:

source file: command.c

```
 1    #include <stdio.h>
 2    #include "general.h"
 3    #include "command.h"
 4    #include "hash.h"
 5    #include "word_def.h"
 6
 7    int add(), change(), delete(), lookup(), owner();
 8
 9    struct cmmd cmdarray[] =
10    {
11            { "add", add },
12            { "change", change },
13            { "delete", delete },
14            { "lookup", lookup },
15            { "owner", owner }
16    };
17
18    int number_commands = 5;
```

In line 7 we declare the new function's return type, in line 15 we associate the new function's address with the user command, and in line 18 the value of the variable containing the table size is increased by one.

To implement the new feature we write the function, compile it, recompile command.c, and then link these two object modules with those for main() and the other functions.

Executing User Commands

Now we can fill in the main() function's missing pieces:

source file: main.c

```
1    #include <stdio.h>
2    #include "general.h"
3    #include "command.h"
4    #include "word_def.h"
5
6    struct word_def temp;
7
8    main()
9    {
10       char command[ COMMAND_LENGTH ];
11       char *arg, *cmd, *strtok();
12       int sub;
13
14       opendict();
15       readhash();
16
17       do
18       {
19           printf( "\nEnter command: " );
20           fgets( command, COMMAND_LENGTH, stdin );
21           cmd = strtok( command, "\t\n" );
22           arg = strtok( (char *)0, "\n" );
23
24           for( sub = 0; sub < number_commands; sub++ )
25           {
26               if ( strcmp( cmd,
27                       cmdarray[sub].cmd_name ) == 0 )
28               {
29                   ( *cmdarray[sub].cmd_addr )( arg );
30                   break;
31               }
32           }
33       } while ( strcmp( command, "end" ) != 0 );
34   }
```

Line	Comments
24	We inspect up to number_commands entries in the array of structures.
26–31	If the user command matches a command in the table, we execute the function (line 29) associated with the command, and supply a pointer to the argument (list). The value of the expression:

```
cmdarray[sub].cmd_addr
```

is a pointer to a function that returns an integer value; we execute the function by dereferencing the pointer. After the function is executed, we break out of the inner for loop and prompt the user for another command.

DICTIONARY STRUCTURE

As we discussed earlier, three files are used to maintain the dictionary. The first file, previously identified as the dictionary file, contains a collection of structures each of which is used to store the keyword and its associated information (not including the definition). The format of the structures in this file are:

header file: word_def.h

```
 1    #define WORD_SIZE 20
 2    #define NAME_SIZE 10
 3
 4    struct word_def
 5    {
 6        char word[ WORD_SIZE ];
 7        char creator[ NAME_SIZE ];
 8        char last_ch[ NAME_SIZE ];
 9        long definition;              /* start of definition in file */
10        long def_length;
11        char see_also[5][ WORD_SIZE ];   /* 5 external references */
12        long next;                       /* linked list linkage    */
13    };
14
15    extern struct word_def temp;
```

Line	Comments
6	This 20-character array contains the keyword to be defined.
7–8	These two arrays contain the name of the person who first defined the word and the name of the person who last made a change to the word.
9–10	These two fields are used to access the file where the word definition is stored. The first field, definition, contains the definition's starting

location (the byte offset) in the file; the second contains the definition length.

11   This is a two-dimensional array of characters that contains up to five "see also" references.

12   The `next` variable points to the location in the dictionary file of another definition structure (if one exists); this is used to form the hash list. Remember, the hash list, which is in the form of a linked list, is used to handle "collisions"—multiple entries that hash into the same value in the hash table.

The dictionary and definitions files are opened through a call to the function `opendict()`, defined as follows:

source file: fileio.c

```
       .
       .
       .
10     opendict()
11     {
12         /* file has not already been opened */
13         if ( ioptr == 0 )
14         {
15             /* open queue file */
16             if ( (ioptr = fopen( DICTIONARY, "r+" )) == NULL )
17             {
18                 fprintf( stderr, "Cannot open %s\n",
19                     DICTIONARY );
20                 exit(1);
21             }
22             setbuf( ioptr, (char *)NULL );
23         }
24         else
25             fseek( ioptr, (long)0, 0 );  /*rewind file */
26
27
28         if ( defptr == 0 )
29         {
30             /* open queue file */
31             if ( (defptr = fopen( DEFINITIONS, "r+" )) == NULL )
32             {
33                 fprintf( stderr, "Cannot open %s\n",
34                     DEFINITIONS );
```

(program continues)

```
35                  exit(1);
36              }
37              setbuf( defptr, (char *)NULL );
38          }
39      else
40          fseek( defptr, (long)0, 0 ); /*rewind file */
41  }
```

If the files have not been opened before, they are opened for update
(`"r+"`). After opening the files, the `setbuf()` function turns off the standard
I/O buffering so that multiple concurrent updates do not interfere with one
another. If the files are already open, the current offset in the file is set back to
the beginning.

A third file contains the hash table, which is an array of sixty-four pointers
to entries in the dictionary file. This table is used whenever a word is added or
referenced. Each of these entries begins a linked list. To locate the dictionary
structure for a word, we pass the word through a *hashing function*, that generates a number between zero and sixty-three, one less than the hash table size.
This locates the appropriate linked list for this word.

> *Note: Although these array entries point into the file they are not
> pointer variables; they are* long *offsets from the beginning of the file.
> Pointer variables can only point to objects in memory.*

The definition of the hash table is as follows:

source file: fileio.c

```
        .
        .
        .
7   long hash_tbl[ HASH_TABLE_SIZE ];
        .
        .
        .
```

where HASH_TABLE_SIZE is defined as 64 in the local header file hash.h.
This table's size must be an even power of two.

To translate a word into a number between 0 and 63 we use the following
hashing function, found in the file hash.c:

source file: hash.c

```
1   #include <stdio.h>
2   #include "general.h"
3   #include "command.h"
4   #include "hash.h"
```

```
 5    #include "word_def.h"

         .
         .
         .

24    hash( keyword )
25    char *keyword;
26    {
27         long hash_value = 0;
28
29         /* hashing function adds the ASCII values of
30             all characters in the string and truncates high
31             order bits. Hash table must be an even power of
32             two elements in length */
33
34         while ( *keyword != '\0' )
35         {
36             hash_value += *keyword;
37             keyword++;
38         }
39
40         return ( (int)(hash_value & (HASH_TABLE_SIZE - 1)) );
41    }
```

In this hashing function, we treat each of the characters in the string as an integer and sum the characters' ASCII values. In line 40, we remove the high-order bits resulting in a number between 0 and 63, which the calling function then uses as an offset into the hash table.

The third file in the dictionary system contains the word definitions. This file will be described in more detail later in this case study.

The readhash( ) Function

At the beginning of the main( ) function, the readhash( ) function is called to read the hash table from disk into an external array in memory. At other times during program execution, this table is written back to disk. The following three functions open the hash table file, read the file into memory, and update the file to disk.

source file: fileio.c

```
1    #include <stdio.h>
2    #include "general.h"
3    #include "hash.h"
4    #include "word_def.h"
5
6    FILE *ioptr, *defptr, *hashptr;
7    long hash_tbl[ HASH_TABLE_SIZE ];
```

(program continues)

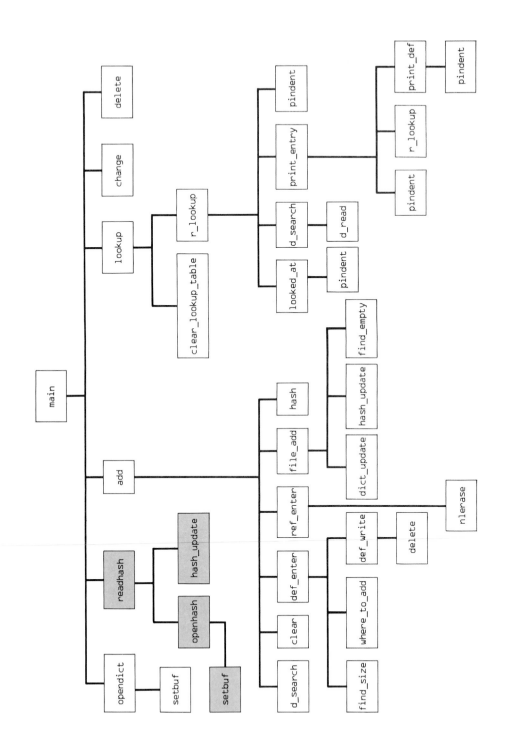

```
  8    extern struct word_def temp;

       .
       .
       .
 45    readhash()
 46    {
 47        openhash();
 48        if ( fread( hash_tbl, sizeof(long), HASH_TABLE_SIZE,
 49            hashptr ) < sizeof(long) * HASH_TABLE_SIZE )
 50        {
 51            /* first time; hash table is empty */
 52            hash_update();
 53        }
 54    }
 55
 56    openhash()
 57    {
 58        /* file has not already been opened */
 59        if ( hashptr == 0 )
 60        {
 61            /* open queue file */
 62            if ( (hashptr = fopen( HASH_FILE, "r+" )) == NULL )
 63            {
 64                fprintf( stderr, "Cannot open %s\n",
 65                    HASH_FILE );
 66                exit(1);
 67            }
 68            setbuf( hashptr, (char *)NULL );
 69        }
 70        else
 71            fseek( hashptr, (long)0, 0 ); /*rewind file */
 72    }

       .
       .
       .
109    hash_update( )
110    {
111        rewind( hashptr );
112        if ( fwrite( hash_tbl, sizeof(long),
113            HASH_TABLE_SIZE, hashptr ) == 0 )
114        {
115            fprintf( stderr, "WRITE ERROR ON HASH TABLE\n" );
116            exit( 3 );
117        }
118    }
```

Line	Comments
47	If the hash table file is not already open, it is opened. If it is already open, we rewind the file (set the current offset to the beginning of the file).
48–49	The hash table is read from the file into the external array named hash_tbl[].
50–53	If the read fails (there is no hash table on disk), a blank table is written to disk. This is a normal condition encountered the first time the program is run with a newly created hash table file.
57–72	If the file is already open, we are positioned at the beginning of the file through a call to the fseek() library function. If the file is not open, we open it, save the return value in the field hashptr, and check for a successful open. If the open is not successful, we print an error and end the program.
68	Since the file can be opened by many users simultaneously, we shut off standard I/O buffering, providing a consistent view of the data in the file to all users.
111	Return to the beginning of the file.
112–117	Write out the hash table contents in memory to the disk. If there are any problems, print an error message and exit.

Adding a Definition

To add a definition to the dictionary, we interact with the add() function as follows:

```
Enter command: add pointer

Enter definition:
A variable type that holds the
address of another variable or
function. Can be accessed through
the dereferencing operator "*".

Enter references (5 max)
declaration
<empty line>
```

The following pseudocode represents the logic to add a definition to the dictionary:

```
add( keyword )
{
     if ( definition already on file )
         return ( error )

     get definition using editor
     add definition to definitions file

     get references (5 max)
     fill in rest of dictionary structure
     add structure to dictionary file

     logically place entry on appropriate hash list
     update hash table to disk
}
```

This logic is implemented in the add ( ) function, whose name is listed in the array of command structures:

source file: add.c

```
 1    #include <stdio.h>
 2    #include "general.h"
 3    #include "command.h"
 4    #include "hash.h"
 5    #include "word_def.h"
 6
 7    add( keyword )
 8    char *keyword;
 9    {
10        char *strcpy();
11
12        if ( d_search( keyword ) == 1 )
13        {
14            fprintf( stderr,
15                "add: DEFINITION IS ALREADY THERE\n" );
16            return;
17        }
18
19        clear();
20        strcpy( temp.word, keyword );
21
22        printf( "Enter definition:\n" );
23        def_enter();
24        printf( "Enter references (5 max)\n" );
```
(program continues)

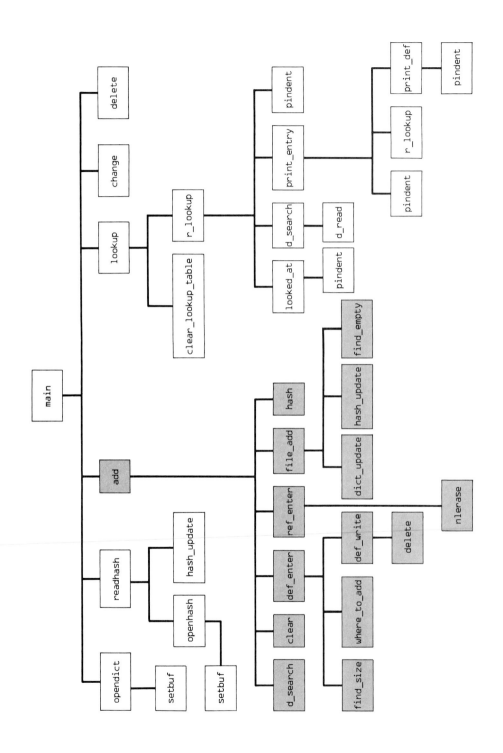

```
25        ref_enter();
26
27        file_add ( hash( keyword ) );
28    }
```

Line	Comments
7–8	The function is given an argument containing the address of a string of characters containing the keyword.
12–17	If the keyword has already been defined in the dictionary, we print an error message and return. The d_search() function looks for the keyword in the dictionary. If the keyword is found, the dictionary structure contents are placed in the temporary dictionary structure named temp and a value of 1 is returned. If the keyword is not found, then a value of 0 is returned.
19	The clear() function clears the temporary external structure named temp.
20	The keyword is copied into the temporary structure.
22–23	A prompt is issued to the user to enter the definition. The definition is then entered through the def_enter() function. This function provides an external text editor as a user interface for entering the definition.
24–25	The five "see also" references are requested and entered through the ref_enter() function.
27	The new dictionary structure is added to the dictionary file and to the hash list. The file_add() function assumes that all the necessary information is stored in the temporary structure named temp. The hash() function supplies file_add() with the hash list index to which this entry is added.

The clear( ) Function

In line 19 of the add() function, the clear() function is used to clear the temporary structure. The clear is performed this way:

source file: add.c

```
1    #include <stdio.h>
2    #include "general.h"
```

(program continues)

```
3   #include "command.h"
4   #include "hash.h"
5   #include "word_def.h"
    .
    .
    .
65  clear()
66  {
67      int sub;
68
69      strcpy( temp.word,  "" );
70      for ( sub = 0; sub < 5; sub++ )
71      {
72          strcpy( temp.see_also[sub],  "" );
73      }
74      temp.definition = 0L;
75      temp.next = 0;
76  }
```

To clear a character array, we use the strcpy() library function and copy the null string into the array. Assigning the value ' \0 ' to the array's first element is an alternate method.

The def_enter( ) Function

This function executes the text editor whose name is stored in the environment variable EDITOR. The def_enter() function is defined as follows:

source file: defmaint.c

```
1   #include <stdio.h>
2   #include "general.h"
3   #include "command.h"
4   #include "hash.h"
5   #include "word_def.h"
6
7   extern FILE *defptr;
8
9   def_enter()
10  {
11      char command[ COMMAND_LENGTH ], tempfile[20];
12      char *strcpy(), *mktemp();
13      long size, find_size(), where_to_add();
14
15      strcpy( tempfile, TEMP_FILE_NAME );
16      mktemp( tempfile );
```

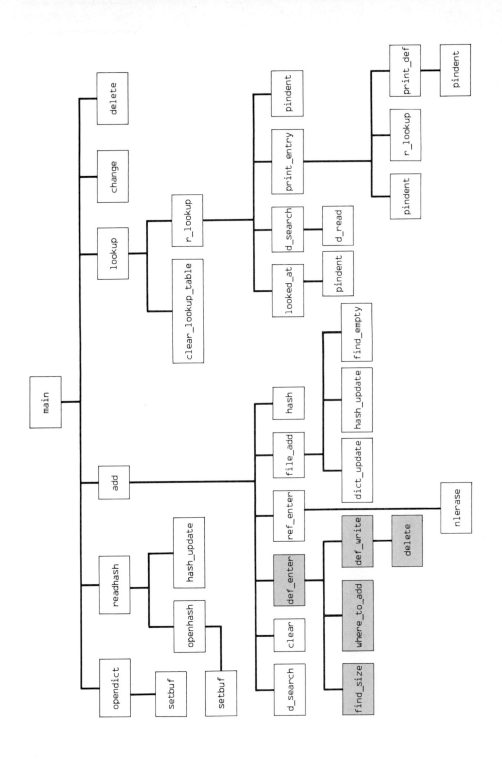

```
17
18        sprintf( command, "%s %s\n", EDITOR, tempfile );
19        system( command );
20
21        size = find_size( tempfile );
22        temp.def_length = size;
23        temp.definition = where_to_add( size );
24        def_write( tempfile, size );
25    }
```

.
.
.

Line   **Comments**

15–16   The text editor we will invoke creates a tempo-
            rary file containing the keyword definition.
            We will then add the contents of the temporary
            file to the definitions file. The value of
            TEMP_FILE_NAME is defined in the local header
            file general.h as follows:

            `#define TEMP_FILE_NAME "/tmp/dictXXXXXX"`

            which is the format the library function
            mktemp() expects. From this template,
            mktemp() creates a unique file name. Although
            this procedure is UNIX-specific, other operating
            systems should have similar functions available.

18   A command line is formulated to execute the edi-
            tor on the temporary file created in lines 15 and
            16. The value of the defined constant EDITOR is
            found in the general.h file:

            header file: general.h

            ```
            char *getenv();
            #define  EDITOR   getenv("EDITOR")\
               !=NULL?getenv("EDITOR"):"/bin/ed"
            ```

            The value of the resulting expression depends on
            whether the environment variable EDITOR ex-
            ists. If it does, then the expression's value is the
            return value from the getenv() library function
            (that character string's starting address). If not, it
            is the value of the expression:

"/bin/ed"

which designates the default editor.

19   The command line formulated in line 18 is executed through the system() library function.

21   The find_size() function is executed to determine the size of the temporary file created
during the editing session. The file size, and
hence the definition size, is stored in the variable
size.

22   The file size is stored in the temporary structure.

23   The function where_to_add() locates space in
the definitions file. In this version of the program
the function adds the definition to the end of the
file. In Case Study 4 the function will be en-
hanced to look for unused file space large enough
to store the new definition.

24   The def_write() function writes the definitions to the definitions file at the location stored
in the definition member of the temporary
structure. The number of bytes to be written to
the file is stored in the variable named size.

The find_size( ) Function

This function opens the temporary file containing the definition, counts the
number of characters in the file, and then closes the file. The return value from
this function is the file size. The find_size() function is defined as follows:

source file: defmaint.c

```
   .
   .
   .
27  long find_size( filename )
28  char *filename;
29  {
30      FILE *iptr;
31      long size = 0;
32
33      /* find size */
34      if ( (iptr = fopen( filename, "r" )) == (FILE *)NULL )
35      {
36          printf( "DEFINITION NOT CREATED\n" );
37          exit( 4 );
38      }
```

(program continues)

```
39          while( fgetc( iptr ) != EOF )
40          {
41              size++;
42          }
43          fclose( iptr );
44          return( size );
45      }
        .
        .
        .
```

If the supplied file name does not correspond to an existing file, this is a fatal error causing the program to terminate.

The where_to_add( ) Function

This function returns the position at which the new definition will be added:

source file: defmaint.c

```
1       #include <stdio.h>
2       #include "general.h"
3       #include "command.h"
4       #include "hash.h"
5       #include "word_def.h"
6
7       extern FILE *defptr;
        .
        .
        .
47      long where_to_add( size )
48      long size;
49      {
50          long ftell();
51
52          fseek( defptr, 0L, 2 ); /* EOF */
53          return( ftell( defptr ) );
54      }
```

As written, this function always returns the position of the end of the file. In a system in which definitions can be changed or removed, this scheme is inefficient because it does not reuse space. In Case Study 4, we will see how we can recover this space through another data structure—the map.

The def_write( ) Function

This function reads the definition from the temporary file and adds it to the definitions file at the appropriate place. It requires two arguments: the name of the temporary file and its length. The def_write() function is defined as follows:

source file: defmaint.c

```
 1    #include <stdio.h>
 2    #include "general.h"
 3    #include "command.h"
 4    #include "hash.h"
 5    #include "word_def.h"
 6
 7    extern FILE *defptr;
 .
 .
 .
56    def_write( filename, length )
57    char *filename;
58    long length;
59    {
60        FILE *iptr;
61        int c;
62
63        if ( (iptr = fopen( filename, "r" )) == (FILE *)NULL )
64        {
65            printf( "DEFINITION NOT CREATED\n" );
66            exit( 4 );
67        }
68        if ( fseek( defptr, temp.definition, 0 ) != 0 )
69        {
70            printf( "fseek() ERROR\n" );
71            exit( 6 );
72        }
73        while ( (c = fgetc( iptr )) != EOF )
74        {
75            fputc( c, defptr );
76        }
77        fclose( iptr );
78        delete( filename );
79    }
```

Line	Comments
63–67	Open the file whose name is supplied as an argument. The return value is stored in the variable iptr, which is then used to refer to the file. Unless the file has been deleted, this open should not fail.
68–72	The second argument to the fseek( ) function indicates where in the file the definition is to be placed. The current offset in the file is set to this value; if the fseek( ) fails, the program exits.
73–76	Characters are copied from the temporary file to the definitions file, one at a time.
77–78	The temporary file is closed and then removed via the local function delete( ). Deleting files is system dependent, so the deletion command is placed in a separate function. This function's definition is found in the machdep. c file:

source file: machdep.c

```
1   delete( filename )
2   char *filename;
3   {
4      unlink( filename );
5   }
```

The definitions file remains open for future reference.

The ref_enter( ) Function

This function allows the user to add up to five "see also" references. These references are stored directly in the dictionary structure with the keyword, the creator's identification, and so on. The ref_enter( ) function is defined as follows:

source file: add.c

```
1   #include <stdio.h>
2   #include "general.h"
3   #include "command.h"
4   #include "hash.h"
5   #include "word_def.h"
    .
    .
    .
```

```
30    ref_enter()
31    {
32        int sub;
33
34        for ( sub = 0; sub < 5; sub++ )
35        {
36            fgets( temp.see_also[sub], WORD_SIZE, stdin );
37            nlerase( temp.see_also[sub] );
38            if( strlen( temp.see_also[sub] ) == 0 )
39            {
40                break;
41            }
42        }
43    }
```

Up to five references may be entered; entering an empty line (with only the newline character) causes the loop to terminate prematurely through the break in line 40. We use the fgets() library function, rather than gets(), to read the information because it respects the array size limits (gets() reads characters into its destination without checking the array size and can overwrite other variables). The fgets() function stores the entered newline character in the array. To remove it we call the nlerase() function:

source file: add.c

```
 1    #include <stdio.h>
      .
      .
      .
78    nlerase( string )
79    char *string;
80    {
81        char *strchr(), *cpointer;
82
83        if ( (cpointer = strchr( string, '\n' )) != NULL )
84            *cpointer = '\0';
85    }
```

The file_add() Function

This function adds the new dictionary structure to the dictionary file. It searches the file for room to add the structure, logically adds the structure as part of the appropriate linked list, and then physically writes the dictionary structure to the file. The function is defined as follows:

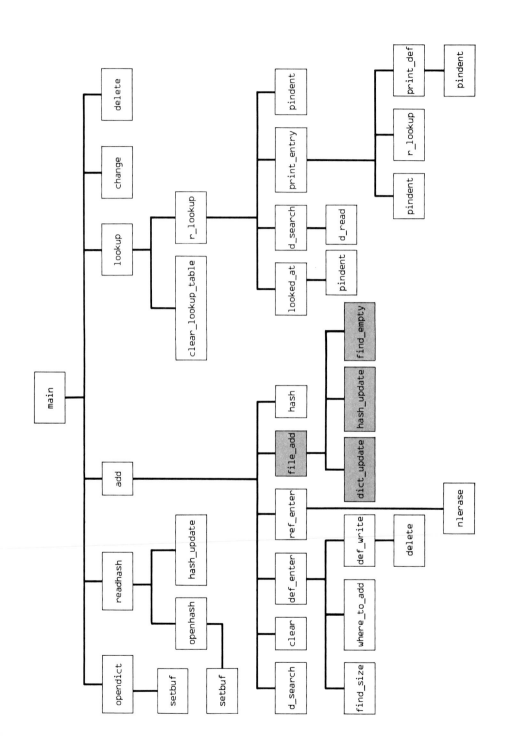

source file: add.c

```
1    #include <stdio.h>
2    #include "general.h"
3    #include "command.h"
4    #include "hash.h"
5    #include "word_def.h"
     .
     .
     .
45   file_add( hash_value )
46   int hash_value;
47   {
48        long record, position, find_empty();
49        char *getenv();
50
51        temp.next = hash_tbl[hash_value];
52
53        record = find_empty();
54        hash_tbl[hash_value] = record;
55
56        strcpy( temp.creator, getenv( "LOGNAME" ) );
57        strcpy( temp.last_ch, getenv( "LOGNAME" ) );
58
59        position = record * (long)sizeof(struct word_def);
60        dict_update( position );
61        hash_update();
62
63   }
```

Line	Comments
51–54	The structure is logically added to the beginning of the appropriate hash list. The hash value is supplied to this function as an argument; it is used as an index into the hash table, which begins the linked list of dictionary structures for all keywords that map to the same hash table slot.
56–57	These members contain the names of the users who created and made changes to an entry. These lines are UNIX specific and may have to be adjusted for other operating systems.
59	The starting position in the dictionary file for the new structure is equal to the record number returned by the find_empty() function, multiplied by the size of one of the dictionary struc-

tures. The find_empty() function will be defined in Case Study 4.

60   The function dict_update() writes the dictionary structure to the appropriate place in the file.

61   The hash table is updated to the disk.

The dict_ update( ) Function

This function writes the temp structure to the supplied location in the dictionary file. The function is defined as follows:

source file: fileio.c

```
1    #include <stdio.h>
2    #include "general.h"
3    #include "hash.h"
4    #include "word_def.h"
5
6    FILE *ioptr, *defptr, *hashptr;
7    long hash_tbl[ HASH_TABLE_SIZE ];
8    extern struct word_def temp;
     .
     .
     .
93   dict_update( position )
94   long position;
95   {
96       if ( fseek( ioptr, position, 0 ) != 0 )
97       {
98           printf( "SEEK ERROR\n" );
99           exit( 1 );
100      }
101      if ( fwrite( &temp, sizeof(struct word_def),
102              1, ioptr ) == 0 )
103      {
104          printf( "WRITE ERROR\n" );
105          exit( 2 );
106      }
107  }
```

The fwrite() library function writes the structure to the dictionary file. The fseek() function finds the proper location.

LOOKING UP A DEFINITION

The dictionary of definitions forms a data type. It is a list of keywords, each of which can reference other keywords. If we start at any definition, the "see also'' references and their references form a treelike structure of related definitions. If some of the references, in turn, point back to the original keyword or other referenced keywords, the data structure may form a *network*.

The lookup() function prints the keyword definition, the definitions of all its references, the definitions of all of their references, and so on. This function never prints a definition twice; doing so is likely to lead to an infinite loop (actually infinite recursion in this program.) The lookup() function prints the definitions in the following manner:

```
Enter command: lookup malloc
KEYWORD: malloc

A general purpose memory allocation
library function. Expects as its
argument the amount of memory (in
bytes) to allocate. Returns the
address at which it allocated the
memory.

SEE ALSO: calloc
    KEYWORD: calloc

    A memory allocation library function
    which also clears the memory it
    allocates. This function expects two
    arguments: the two are multiplied to
    find the amount of memory to allocate.

    SEE ALSO: free
        KEYWORD: free

        The library function which deallocates
        memory allocated through either malloc()
        or calloc(). Expects as its argument
        the return value of a previous call to
        calloc() or malloc() and returns a true
        value if successful.

        SEE ALSO: calloc
        *** DEFINITION OF calloc ALREADY PRINTED ***
        SEE ALSO: malloc
        *** DEFINITION OF malloc ALREADY PRINTED ***
    SEE ALSO: malloc
    *** DEFINITION OF malloc ALREADY PRINTED ***

SEE ALSO: free
*** DEFINITION OF free ALREADY PRINTED ***
```

The function uses an outline form to print the definitions thus emphasizing the terms' relationships. If a definition has already been printed, it is noted in the output. The program keeps track of which words have already been referenced through the table called so_far[]. This is a table of pointers to character strings, where each member points to dynamically allocated memory holding the keyword. This table's size is fixed at 100 entries. Thus, the program is only capable of tracing through 100 linked references. (This limit can be removed by replacing the fixed table with a linked list of structures, each of which is dynamically allocated as needed.) The n_so_far variable is used to keep track of the number of valid entries in the table.

The lookup() function is defined by the following pseudocode:

```
lookup( keyword )
{
        find definition
        print definition
        for ( each valid reference )
        {
                lookup ( reference )
        }
}
```

This is implemented through the following C language function:

source file: lookup.c

```
1      #include <stdio.h>
2      #include "general.h"
3      #include "command.h"
4      #include "hash.h"
5      #include "word_def.h"
       .
       .
       .
9      lookup( keyword )
10     char *keyword;
11     {
12         clear_lookup_table();
13         r_lookup( keyword );
14     }
```

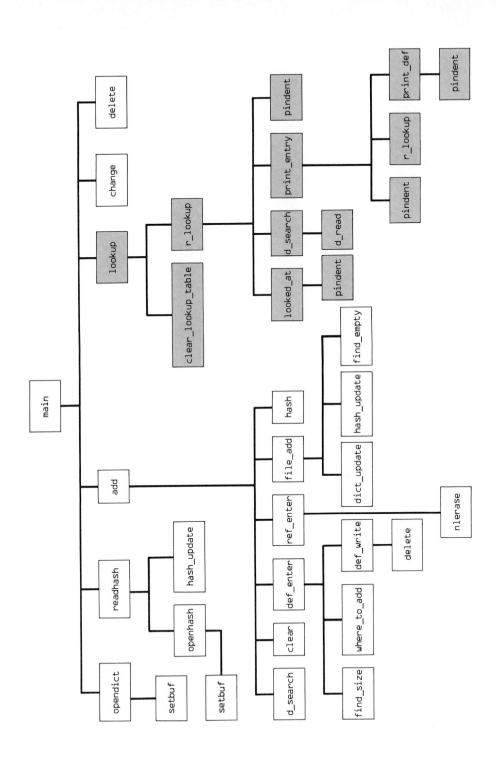

The clear_lookup_table() function clears the so_far[] table and the character strings to which it points. The r_lookup() function is defined as follows:

source file: lookup.c

```
     .
     .
     .
16   r_lookup( keyword)
17   char *keyword;
18   {
19        struct word_def contents;
20
21        if ( looked_at( keyword ) == TRUE )
22        {
23             return;
24        }
25
26        if ( d_search( keyword ) )
27        {
28             contents = temp;
29             print_entry( keyword, contents );
30        }
31        else
32        {
33             pindent();
34             printf( "*** %s not in dictionary ***\n", keyword );
35        }
36   }
```

Line	Comments
21–24	Since this routine prints a term in the dictionary as well as its references, it must make sure the references have not already been printed. The looked_at() function does this. If a reference has been printed before, looked_at() returns a FALSE value as defined in the general.h header file.
26–30	The d_search() function searches the dictionary file for the structure containing the supplied keyword and populates the global structure temp with the dictionary information. It returns a TRUE value if the search is successful.

28 If the term is found we save a copy in the variable `contents` because we will make other (recursive) calls to `r_lookup()`; this will destroy the contents of the variable `temp`.

29 The `print_entry()` function prints the definition of the keyword and of all the references. It also indents the printout properly.

31–35 If the keyword is not defined, then the `d_search()` function fails and the error message:

    ★★★ *keyword* not in dictionary ★★★

is printed. The `pindent()` function prints the appropriate number of spaces so that the next `printf()` prints its output in the correct place.

The looked_at( ) Function

This function finds out whether a definition has already been printed. For example:

```
Enter command: lookup recursion
KEYWORD: recursion

A function defined in terms of itself.

SEE ALSO: recursion
*** DEFINITION OF recursion ALREADY PRINTED ***
```

The `looked_at()` function is defined this way:

source file: lookup.c

```
1    #include <stdio.h>
2    #include "general.h"
3    #include "command.h"
4    #include "hash.h"
5    #include "word_def.h"
     .
     .
     .
63   static char *so_far[100];
64   static int n_so_far;
```

(program continues)

```
75   looked_at( keyword )
76   char *keyword;
77   {
78        char *malloc(), *cpointer;
79        int sub;
80
81        for ( sub = 0; sub < n_so_far; sub++ )
82        {
83             if ( strcmp( *(so_far + sub), keyword ) == 0 )
84             {
85                  pindent();
86                  printf( "*** DEFINITION OF %s ALREADY PRINTED ***\n",
87                       keyword );
88                  return( TRUE );
89             }
90        }
91        cpointer = malloc( (unsigned)(strlen( keyword ) + 1) );
92        strcpy( cpointer, keyword );
93        so_far[n_so_far] = cpointer;
94        n_so_far++;
95        return( FALSE );
96   }
```

Line	Comments
75–76	The argument supplied to this function points to the keyword.
81–90	Compare the keyword to be printed to each valid entry in the so_far[] table. If a match occurs, the word has already been printed. We print a message to that effect and return the defined value of TRUE back to the calling function.
91–92	The word has not yet been printed; we add it to the list. In line 91, we allocate enough memory to hold the character string (one extra byte to hold the string termination character '\0'). In line 92, we copy the keyword into the allocated memory.
93–94	Update the so_far[] table so that the last entry points to the new word (stored in line 92) and increase the number of valid entries in the table. The n_so_far field, when used as an index, always points to the next available slot in the table.

> When used as a counter, it is the number of valid
> entries in the table.
>
> 95   Return the defined value of FALSE. The entry
> was *not* already printed.

The clear_lookup_table() function called from the lookup() function in line 12, clears the so_far[] table. It deallocates the memory allocated by the malloc() library function and is defined as follows:

source file: lookup.c

```
        .
        .
        .
63   static char *so_far[100];
64   static int n_so_far;
65
66   clear_lookup_table()
67   {
68       int sub;
69
70       for( sub = 0; sub < n_so_far; sub++ )
71           free( so_far[sub] );
72       n_so_far = 0;
73   }
        .
        .
        .
```

Since entries in this table point to character strings whose memory was dynamically allocated, we clear the memory to which these entries point. In line 71, the library function free() is called to deallocate the memory allocated in line 91 of the looked_at() function. After all memory is released, the index (counter) is reset. There are now no valid entries in the table and the next empty slot is indexed by 0.

The d_search( ) Function

This function searches for a keyword in the dictionary. The keyword is hashed and used as an index into the hash table. The linked list starting at this hash table slot is searched sequentially. The d_search() function is defined as follows:

source file: hash.c

```
1   #include <stdio.h>
2   #include "general.h"
```

```
3     #include "command.h"
4     #include "hash.h"
5     #include "word_def.h"
6
7     d_search( keyword )
8     char *keyword;
9     {
10        int record;
11
12        for ( record = hash_tbl[ hash( keyword ) ];
13              record != 0 && d_read( record );
14              record = temp.next )
15        {
16            if ( strcmp( temp.word, keyword ) == 0 )
17            {
18                return( TRUE );
19            }
20        }
21        return( FALSE );
22    }
```

.
.
.

Line	Comments
12	The for loop initialization sets the record variable equal to the record number of the first record (structure) in the hash list. The return value from the function hash() is used as an index into the hash table.
13	The conditional part of the loop checks for the end of the linked list and the existence of another list member. The d_read() function reads in the structure associated with the current record number, returns a true value if it finds the record, and stores the structure in the temp variable.
14	The record variable is set equal to the record number of the linked list's next member.
16–19	If the keyword stored in the structure is the same as the one supplied as an argument, return the defined value of TRUE.
21	If the keyword does not match any of the members on the corresponding hash list, then the term is not defined in the dictionary; the defined value of FALSE is returned.

The d_read() Function

The previous function calls d_read() to read the structure from the dictionary file. The function is defined as follows:

source file: fileio.c

```
1     #include <stdio.h>
2     #include "general.h"
3     #include "hash.h"
4     #include "word_def.h"
5
6     FILE *ioptr, *defptr, *hashptr;
7     long hash_tbl[ HASH_TABLE_SIZE ];
8     extern struct word_def temp;
      .
      .
      .
74    d_read( record )
75    int record;
76    {
77        if ( fseek ( ioptr,
78            (long)(record * sizeof(struct word_def)),
79            0 ) != 0 )
80        {
81            printf( "SEEK ERROR\n" );
82            return( FAILURE );
83        }
84        if ( fread( &temp, sizeof(struct word_def),
85                1, ioptr ) == 0 )
86        {
87            printf( "RECORD NOT FOUND: d_read\n" );
88            return( FAILURE );
89        }
90        return( SUCCESS );
91    }
```

In lines 77 through 79, we use the fseek() function to find the correct position in the dictionary file as a function of the current record number and the size of a structure. In lines 84 through 89, we read in the dictionary structure; if a problem is encountered during the read, we print an error message and return the defined value of FAILURE, otherwise we return the defined value of SUCCESS.

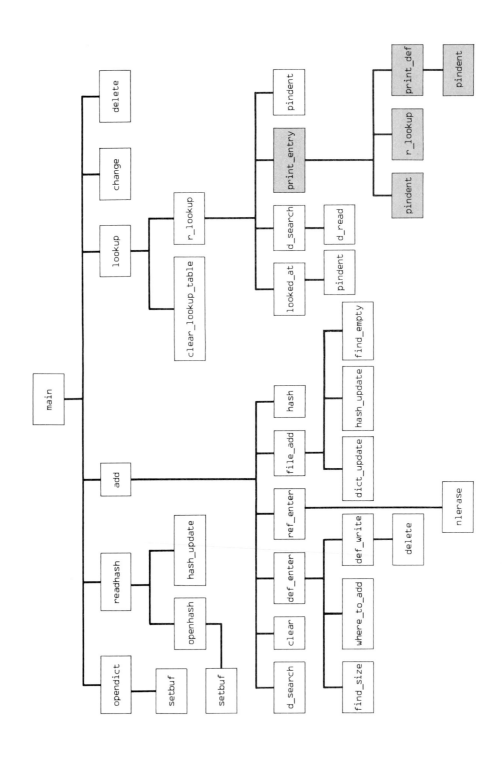

The print_entry( ) Function

In the r_lookup() function, when a keyword has been successfully matched and the dictionary record read into the temp structure, the print_entry() function is called to print the keyword name, the definition, and each valid "see also" reference. The print_entry() function is defined as follows:

source file: lookup.c

```
      .
      .
      .
 7    int   indent = 0;
      .
      .
      .
38    print_entry( keyword, contents )
39    char *keyword;
40    struct word_def contents;
41    {
42         int sub;
43
44         indent++;
45
46         pindent();
47         printf( "KEYWORD: %s\n", keyword );
48         print_def();
49
50         for ( sub = 0; sub < 5; sub++ )
51         {
52             if ( strlen( contents.see_also[sub] ) > 0 )
53             {
54                 pindent();
55                 printf( "SEE ALSO: %s\n",
56                     contents.see_also[sub] );
57                 r_lookup( contents.see_also[sub] );
58             }
59         }
60         indent--;
61    }
```

Line	Comments
7	The pindent() function uses the indent variable to print spaces, creating the output in outline form.

38–39   This function expects two arguments: a pointer
         to the keyword and a structure containing the
         dictionary information for the keyword. On ear-
         lier C compilers, instead of passing the entire
         structure, it would have been necessary to pass a
         pointer to the structure.

47–48   The "KEYWORD" label is printed followed by the
         definition from the definitions file.

50–59   The definition is printed for each of the five
         possible references by recursively calling the
         r_lookup() function.

The print_def( ) Function

The print_def() function is called in line 48 of the print_entry() function. As its name implies, it prints the keyword definition.

The function begins printing from the offset in the definitions file described
in the dictionary structure's definition member. It prints def_length
characters from that point, properly indented. The print_def() function is
defined this way:

source file: defmaint.c

```
1    #include <stdio.h>
2    #include "general.h"
3    #include "command.h"
4    #include "hash.h"
5    #include "word_def.h"
6
7    extern FILE *defptr;
     .
     .
     .
80   print_def()
81   {
82       extern int indent;
83       int c;
84       long to_print, ftell();
85
86       printf( "\n" );
87       pindent();
88       if ( fseek( defptr, temp.definition, 0 ) != NULL )
89       {
90           printf( "DEFINITION NOT THERE\n" );
91           return;
92       }
```

```
 93            for ( to_print = 0; to_print < temp.def_length; to_print++ )
 94            {
 95                c = fgetc( defptr );
 96                fputc( c, stdout );
 97                if ( c == '\n' )
 98                    pindent();
 99            }
100            printf( "\n" );
101    }
```

Line	Comments
7	The defptr pointer holds the return value from the opening of the definitions file in the opendict() function.
88–92	We "seek" to the location in the definitions file where this term's definition begins. If the seek fails, we print an error message and return.
93–99	We print the number of characters as defined in temp.def_length. Whenever a newline character is printed, we call the pindent() function to indent the next line of the definition.

Several functions in this program call the pindent() function to print an indentation based on the indent variable. The pindent() function is defined as follows:

source file: lookup.c

```
        .
        .
        .
 98    pindent()
 99    {
100        printf( "%*s", (indent − 1) * 8, "" );
101    }
```

This function uses the * option to the printf() library function. This allows us to specify the width of the string field dynamically. The character string to be printed is empty, but the field width is based on the value of indent.

This completes the add() and lookup() command definitions. Implementing the change() and delete() functions are left as an exercise for the student.

SUMMARY

In this case study, we introduced the powerful technique called hashing. Using hashing we can gain efficient access into any list because the hashing function maps directly into the appropriate location. If collisions occur, we may have to navigate a linked list until we encounter the correct record. Good hashing functions will minimize collisions.

We also introduced the concept of pointers to functions and showed how function calls can be stored and executed from a table. This technique makes it easier to expand a system's functionality by providing a simple method for adding new commands.

MANAGING RESOURCES WITH FREE LISTS, BITMAPS, AND MAPS

OVERVIEW

In the previous case studies, we introduced several C language data structure applications. These data structures were stored in disk files, but did not reuse deallocated resources (e.g., records or space in a file.) New records were always added to the end of the file without consideration for available space in the middle of the file. In this case study, we will see three techniques—free lists, bitmaps, and maps—for recovering this space.

FREE LISTS

One method for keeping track of unallocated structures in a linked or hash list is to use another linked list, called a *free list*. When a record (structure) is deallocated, it is put on this list. For example, in Case Study 2's line printer spooler program, when a queue structure was deallocated, it was discarded and an empty "hole" was created in the middle of the file. When another queue structure was created, it was added to the end of the list. This example could be improved using the following logic:

in remove routines:

```
dealloc_structure( record )
{
        record.next = free_list_header.next;
        free_list_header = record;
        update( header );
        update( record );
}
```

in add routine:

```
allocate_structure()
{
        return_value = free_list_header.next;

        free_list_header.next =
            "next" member of that structure;

        return( return_value );
}
```

We need to make one small change to the queue file's layout: a second header structure needs to be added (presumably after the first header). The second header is the starting point of the "inactive" or free list. Exhibit CS4-1 illustrates this.

All references in the program to the header remain the same; it is still physically the first record in the file. The routine that creates the header is modified so that it will create two records—the original header and the new header, which is the beginning of the free list.

EXHIBIT CS4-1

Adding a free list header to the line printer spooler. Entries 2 and 4 have been deallocated and are available for use.

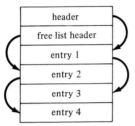

Deallocation

Whenever a record is logically removed from the queue, it is added to the free list by the following function:

source file: free.c

```
1    #include <assert.h>
2    #include "queue.h"
3
4    void dealloc( r_current, current )
5    node r_current;
6    struct pqueue *current;
7    {
8        static struct pqueue free_list;
9
10       assert( readin( FREE_LIST, &free_list ) != BAD_READ );
11
12       current->r_next = free_list.r_next;
13       free_list.r_next = r_current;
14
15       writeout( FREE_LIST, &free_list );
16       writeout( r_current, current );
17   }
```

Line	Comments
4–6	The arguments supplied to this function are the record number in the file and the address of the structure being deallocated.
10	The free list header is read into the static struc-

ture free_list. The assertion fails if the free
list header is not present. The assert() macro
is defined in the standard header file assert.h.

12–13   The record is added to the free list by swapping
pointers. The deallocated record now points to
the header's "next" field and the header points
to it.

15–16   Since both records have been modified, they are
written to disk.

This function needs to be referenced in the queueing and controller programs. In Case Study 2, we created the removeq() function; it removed a job from the print queue by logically removing its record from the linked list, thus creating an unusable gap in the list. We can now modify the removeq() function so that the deallocated space can be reclaimed:

source file: remove.c

```
 1   #include "queue.h"
     .
     .
     .
 4   removeq( control )
 5   node control;
 6   {
     .
     .
17       while ( (r_current = previous.r_next) != END_OF_LIST )
18       {
     .
     .
     .
25           if( current.control_id == control )
26           {
27               previous.r_next = current.r_next;
28               writeout( r_previous, &previous );
29               dealloc( r_current, &current );
30               return;
31           }
     .
     .
     .
41   }
```

Now `removeq()` calls the `dealloc()` function to add the record to the free list so that the space can be reused.

Allocation

Previously, we always added new records to the end of the file. Now, before adding a record to the end of the file, we check for structures that have been deallocated. The `alloc()` routine finds an unused record and is defined as follows:

source file: free.c

```
 1   #include <assert.h>
 2   #include "queue.h"
     .
     .
     .
19   node alloc()
20   {
21       static struct pqueue free_list, temp;
22       node ret_val;
23
24       assert(readin( FREE_LIST, &free_list ) != BAD_READ );
25       if ( free_list.r_next != 0 )
26       {
27           assert( readin( free_list.r_next, &temp ) != BAD_READ );
28           ret_val = free_list.r_next;
29           free_list.r_next = temp.r_next;
30           writeout( FREE_LIST, &free_list );
31           return( ret_val );
32       }
33       return( EMPTY_FREE_LIST );
34   }
```

Line	Comments
19	This function requires no arguments; it will always allocate one structure and return its record number.
24	It is assumed that the free list header is present. It is read into the `free_list` variable. If this read fails (no free list header present), then the program fails through the assertion.
25	If the "next" member of the free list header is not empty, then there are gaps in the middle of the file that we will use before extending the size of the file.

27	We read in the record that appears as the ''next'' member on the free list.
28	We save the record number of the first record on the free list in ret_val.
29	The first record in the free list (after the header) is removed from the linked list.
30	The free list header is updated to the disk.
31	If a record is removed from the free list, its record number is returned.
33	If the free list was empty, return the value EMPTY_FREE_LIST as defined in the file queue.h (−1).

Changes are also required to the add_to_file() function:

source file: filemaint.c

```
 1   #include "queue.h"
     .
     .
     .
45   addtofile( temp )
46   struct pqueue *temp;
47   {
48        long whereami, ftell();
49        node alloc(), freenode;
50
51        if ( (freenode = alloc()) != EMPTY_FREE_LIST )
52            {
53                whereami = node_to_byte( freenode );
54                fseek( ioptr, whereami, START_OF_FILE );
55            }
56        else
57            {
58                fseek( ioptr, (long)0, END_OF_FILE );
59                whereami = ftell( ioptr );
60            }
61
62        fwrite( (char *)temp, sizeof(struct pqueue), 1, ioptr );
63
64        return( byte_to_node(whereami) );
65   }
     .
     .
     .
```

Rather than automatically searching for the end of file using fseek(), we first check to see if alloc() has returned the record number of any unused space in the file. If alloc() returns a value not equal to EMPTY_FREE_LIST, then the value it returns is the record number of the structure just removed from the free list. We use this number to calculate the record's offset in this file and then write the new record to this location.

If the alloc() function returns the defined value of EMPTY_FREE_LIST, we add the new record to the end of the file, as before.

BITMAPS

Bitmaps are useful for managing a collection of resources of any type. To determine if a resource is in use, we need to store only one bit of information per resource. Assume the picture in Exhibit CS4-2 represents the dictionary file from Case Study 3. The file is a collection of structures, each of a fixed size. Some of these structures hold words currently defined in the dictionary and others hold words that have been deleted from the dictionary. Since these are structures, we could link the structures to form a free list. As an alternative, we will maintain another file, called a bitmap. The bitmap file has one bit associated with each structure, grouped together in *banks* of 32 bits (Exhibit CS4-3).

EXHIBIT CS4-2

Dictionary file from Case Study 3. Assume words 2, 4, and 6 have been deleted.

| word 1 |
| .. word 2 .. |
| word 3 |
| .. word 4 .. |
| word 5 |
| .. word 6 .. |

EXHIBIT CS4-3

Dictionary file with bitmap showing deleted words and unused records.

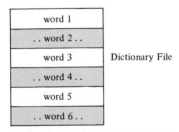

Bitmap | 10101000   00000000   00000000   00000000

Allocation Using a Bitmap

To allocate from a bitmap we search the data structure for a zero bit, one bank, or group of 32 bits, at a time. The logic is:

```
find_empty()
{
        for ( each "bank" in the bitmap file )
        {
                for ( each bit in "bank" )
                {
                        if ( bit not set )
                        {
                                turn on bit
                                return( bit offset in bitmap )
                        }
                }
        }
        /* bitmap solidly packed */

        allocate( new bank )
        turn on first bit
        return( bit offset in bitmap )
}
```

In Case Study 3, we referenced, but did not define, the `find_empty()` function, which is an implementation of the previous logic:

source file: bit.c

```
1    #include <stdio.h>
2    #include <assert.h>
3    #include "bitmap.h"
4
5    long find_empty()
6    {
7        long bank, bank_no, read_bank(), alloc_bank();
8        int offset, find_set_next_zero();
9
10       openbit();
11
```

```
12          while ( (bank_no = read_bank( &bank )) != END_OF_BITMAP )
13          {
14              /* if room left in "bank" */
15              if ( (offset = find_set_next_zero( &bank )) !=
16                  BANK_FULL )
17              {
18                  return( bit_pos( bank_no, offset ) );
19              }
20          }
21
22          bank_no = alloc_bank( &bank );
23          offset = find_set_next_zero( &bank );
24          assert( offset == 0L );
25
26          return( bit_pos( bank_no, offset ) );
27      }
            .
            .
            .
```

This method can be considered advantageous over maintaining a free list. In a free list, the allocation and deallocation routines must be application specific because they change values stored in the application-dependent structure. The bitmap routines are completely self-contained and application independent.

Line	Comments
5	The function is called without any arguments. It returns a long integer corresponding to the bit offset within the file at which the first zero is encountered.
10	The openbit() function opens the bitmap file for update. This function will be seen in detail shortly.
12–20	Read a group of 32 bits from the bitmap file. If there is a zero in the bank, set it to one and return its offset in the file. If the bank has all bits turned on, proceed to the next bank in the file. If the end of file is encountered, increase the size of the bitmap by one.
15	The find_set_next_zero() function searches the bank for zeroes. If one is found, it is set to one and its bit position is returned. This function's return value will either be between zero and 31 or the defined value of BANK_FULL (−1) if no zeroes are found in the bank.

18   Return the offset of the zero bit within the bit-
          map. The bit_pos() macro is defined in the
          local header file as follows:

header file: bitmap.h

          .
          .
          .

4   #define BITS_IN_LONG   32

          .
          .

8   #define bit_pos(bank,offset) (long)(bank * \
     BITS_IN_LONG + offset)

          This macro converts a given bank number and
          the offset within the bank to a bit offset within
          the file.
22   If all banks in the bitmap have their bits set to
          one, the size of the bitmap is automatically ex-
          tended by one bank. The alloc_bank() func-
          tion writes 32 zero bits to the end of the bitmap
          and clears the long integer whose address it was
          given as an argument.
23–24   We use the find_set_next_zero() function
          to find the first zero in the new bank and set it to
          one. We then assert that this is true through the
          assert() macro, as defined in the standard
          header file assert.h.
26   The bit_pos() macro converts the supplied in-
          formation into a bit offset within the bitmap file.

The find_set_next_zero() function is implemented as follows:

source file: bit.c

```
1    #include <stdio.h>
2    #include <assert.h>
3    #include "bitmap.h"
     .
     .
     .
```

```
29    find_set_next_zero( bank )
30    long *bank;
31    {
32        int offset = 0;
33
34        for ( offset = 0; offset < BITS_IN_LONG; offset++ )
35        {
36            if ( (*bank & ( 1L << offset )) == 0L )
37            {
38                *bank |= (1L << offset);
39                update( bank );
40                return( offset );
41            }
42        }
43        return( BANK_FULL );
44    }
```

For each bit position in the long integer, shift a 32-bit representation of the number 1 to the left and test if the bit at that position is off. If the bit is zero, set it to one (line 38), update the bitmap file, and return the offset. If the condition in line 36 is false for each bit, return the defined value of BANK_FULL. Exhibit CS4-4 shows this.

EXHIBIT CS4-4

Note that (*bank & (1L << offset)) is never = 0L until offset = 23

```
Bitmap    11111111  01111111  11111111  11111111

1L        00000000  00000000  00000000  00000001
```

Releasing the Resource

The return value from the find_empty() function is a number associated with a resource. When the resource is no longer in use, we find the appropriate bit in the bitmap and set it back to zero. This is done as follows:

source file: bit.c

```
1    #include <stdio.h>
2    #include <assert.h>
3    #include "bitmap.h"
```

(program continues)

```
46    long restore_bit( resource )
47    long resource;
48    {
49         long bank, bank_no, bit, find_bank();
50
51         openbit();
52
53         bank_no = resource / BITS_IN_LONG;
54         bit = resource % BITS_IN_LONG;
55
56         bank_no = find_bank( bank_no, &bank );
57         assert( bank & ( 1L << bit ) );
58         bank &= ~( 1L << bit );
59         update( &bank );
60
61         return( resource );
62    }
```

Line	Comments
46–47	The resource number is the only argument supplied to this function. The restore_bit() function finds the bit in the bitmap corresponding to the resource, sets the bit to zero, and returns the supplied argument as a verification.
53	To find the correct group of 32 bits, we perform integer division.
54	The offset within the bank is calculated using the modulous (remainder) operator.

EXHIBIT CS4-5

Deallocating resource number 24 in bank
Before resource is deallocated:

```
11111110  11111111  00011111  00000000    bank
```

Releasing the resource at bit 24:

```
00000000  00000000  00000000  00000001    1L

00000000  10000000  00000000  00000000    1L << bit

11111111  01111111  11111111  11111111    ~( 1L << bit )

11111110  11111111  00011111  00000000    bank

11111110  01111111  00011111  00000000    bank & = ~( 1L << bit )
```

56	The bank number, as calculated in line 53, is used to locate the appropriate place in the file to have the bank read. The bank is stored at the address supplied to the find_bank() function.
57	We make sure this resource was indeed previously allocated.
58	The bit is turned off by "anding" a mask into the bank. The mask is created using the offset to shift a 32-bit representation of 1 to the left, and then taking its complement. In Exhibit CS4-5, we can see that all bits are as before except for the target bit which has been set to zero.
59–61	Update the bitmap file and return the resource number released.

Support Functions

The following functions are needed to support the bitmap functions. These functions open the bitmap file, read the next record from the file, update the file and locate a given bank in the file.

The openbit() function opens the bitmap file; it is similar to other file opening functions we have already seen:

source file: bitfile.io.c

```
1    #include <stdio.h>
2    #include <assert.h>
3    #include "general.h"
4    #include "bitmap.h"
5
6    FILE *bitptr;
7    long file_pos;
8
9    openbit()
10   {
11       if ( bitptr == 0 )
12       {
13           bitptr = fopen( BITMAP, "r+" );
14           if ( bitptr == (FILE *)NULL )
15           {
16               fprintf( stderr, "Cannot open %s\n",
17                   BITMAP );
18               exit( 5 );
19           }
20           setbuf( bitptr, (char *)NULL );
21       }
```

(program continues)

```
22          else
23          {
24              rewind( bitptr );
25              file_pos = 0;
26          }
27      }
        .
        .
        .
```

The next function takes the pathname for the bitmap from the defined value
BITMAP:

source file: bitmap.h

```
1   extern char *getenv();
2   #define BITMAP              getenv( "BITMAP" )
    .
    .
    .
```

Since the getenv() library function returns a value other than an integer,
it must be declared. As a result of the #define statement, whenever the
phrase BITMAP is referenced in a source file, the phrase is replaced with a call
to getenv().

The read_bank() function reads the next bank from the bitmap:

source file: bitfile.io.c

```
 1   #include <stdio.h>
 2   #include <assert.h>
 3   #include "general.h"
 4   #include "bitmap.h"
 5
 6   FILE *bitptr;
 7   long file_pos;
     .
     .
     .
42   long read_bank( bank )
43   long *bank;
44   {
45       int fread();
46
```

```
47         if ( fread( (char *)bank, sizeof(long), 1, bitptr ) == 0 )
48         {
49             return ( END_OF_BITMAP );
50         }
51         return( file_pos++ );
52     }
        .
        .
        .
```

Several functions use the file_pos variable to keep track of the current bank number in the bitmap file. If the call to fread() fails, then we are at the end of the bitmap. When the calling function returns the defined value of END_OF_BITMAP it extends the bitmap size by calling alloc_bank(). It is defined as follows:

source file: bitfile.io.c

```
1     #include <stdio.h>
2     #include <assert.h>
3     #include "general.h"
4     #include "bitmap.h"
5
6     FILE *bitptr;
7     long file_pos;
        .
        .
        .
54    long alloc_bank( bank )
55    long *bank;
56    {
57        *bank = 0L;    /* clear bank */
58
59        fwrite( (char *)bank, sizeof(long), 1, bitptr );
60        return( file_pos++ );
61    }
        .
        .
        .
```

This function, called from the find_empty() function, clears a long integer and writes it to the end of the file.

The next function, update(), is called whenever a change has been made to the bitmap. It assumes that the last bank read is the one to be updated. Therefore, it "backs up" one record in the file before writing:

source file: bitfile.io.c

```
 1    #include <stdio.h>
 2    #include <assert.h>
 3    #include "general.h"
 4    #include "bitmap.h"
 5
 6    FILE *bitptr;
 7    long file_pos;
      .
      .
      .
29    update( bank )
30    long *bank;
31    {
32         long current, ftell();
33         current = ftell( bitptr );
34
35         if ( current > 0 )
36         {
37              fseek( bitptr, (long)(current - sizeof(long)), 0 );
38         }
39         fwrite( (char *)bank, sizeof(long), 1, bitptr );
40    }
      .
      .
      .
```

The find_bank() function reads a specified bank from the bitmap. It is called when a resource is to be deallocated and its bit in the bitmap restored (set to zero). This function is defined as follows:

source file: bitfile.io.c

```
 1    #include <stdio.h>
 2    #include <assert.h>
 3    #include "general.h"
 4    #include "bitmap.h"
 5
 6    FILE *bitptr;
 7    long file_pos;
      .
      .
      .
```

```
63    long find_bank( bank_no, bank )
64    long bank_no, *bank;
65    {
66         long ret_val, position, read_bank();
67
68         position = bank_no * sizeof(long);
69         assert( fseek( bitptr, position, 0 ) == 0 );
70
71         file_pos = bank_no;
72         ret_val = read_bank( bank );
73         return( ret_val );
74    }
```

MAPS

In addition to the dictionary file in Case Study 3, there was also a separate sequential definitions file, in which new definitions were added to the end of the file. Although we did not fully develop the routines for removing and changing definitions, it should be obvious that these actions will create gaps in the file that can be reused. More generally, we are concerned with the problem of *contiguous allocation* in a large pool of resources (in this case, bytes in a file) and the need to allocate and deallocate contiguous "chunks" from the resource pool.

One popular method for managing contiguous (de)allocation is through a *map*. A map is simply a list of holes in the resource. In the dictionary application, it would be a list of gaps in the file created by the deletion of definitions. Exhibit CS4-6 illustrates how a map may be used to point to gaps in the definitions file.

The map is kept in order by location. This permits us to combine several small, contiguous areas into a larger area. As in the bitmap example, if we determine that a sufficiently large gap does not exist for a new definition, we add the definition to the end of the file.

Map Definition

In this example, we will develop a nonapplication specific map to keep track of a pool of resources. The map is defined this way:

header file: map.h

```
1    char *getenv();
2    #define MAP_FILE getenv("MAP")!=NULL ? getenv("MAP") : "map"
3
```

(program continues)

```
 4    struct generic_map
 5    {
 6         long size;
 7         long start;
 8    };
 9
10    extern int v_mapsize; /* virtual map size */
11    extern int p_mapsize; /* physical map size */
12
13    extern struct generic_map available[];
```

Line	Comments
1–2	Since many users may access the map simultaneously, we keep an up-to-date copy in a file whose name is stored in the environment variable MAP. If the environment variable is not set, the program defaults to accessing a file named map in the current working directory.
4–8	The map file's structure is defined. For each gap (or hole) in the resource pool, we keep the starting location and the gap size. Like the bitmap routines, these routines are generic; it is the calling function's responsibility to interpret these

EXHIBIT CS4-6

Map pointing to gaps in the definitions file

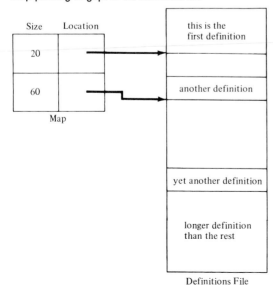

values. In the dictionary example, the starting location corresponds to a position in the definitions file and the length is the length of the definition.

10　　This variable holds the map table's "virtual" length—the number of valid entries. When used as an offset into the map table, it always points to the next unused slot in the table.

11　　This variable holds the table's physical size—the total number of possible entries. Its value is initialized once and remains constant.

13　　This is the external reference to the map table itself.

The map table is declared in its own source file. This source file is the only place where a constant value describes the table size. All the other modules can access the table size through the external variable p_mapsize. This permits us to change the map size without changing or recompiling any of the other modules. The file in which the map table is declared is:

source file: map.c

```
1    #include "map.h"
2    #include "general.h"
3
4    #define MAP_SIZE 300
5
6    struct generic_map available[ MAP_SIZE ];
7
8    int v_mapsize = 0;          /* empty */
9    int p_mapsize = MAP_SIZE;
```

Had we defined the map size in the map.h header file we would have had to recompile all the modules whenever this value changed. Line 6 declares the map structure to be three hundred entries long; we can keep track of three hundred gaps (or holes) in the resource pool (the definitions file).

Allocation

To allocate a contiguous segment using a map we use the following logic:

```
allocate( amount )
{
        for ( each entry in the map )
        {
                if ( size of gap > amount )
                {
```

(pseudocode continues)

```
                              reduce size of gap
                              increase starting location of gap
                              return( previous location of gap )
                    }
                    else if ( size of gap == amount )
                    {
                              /* shrink number of valid map
                                 entries */
                              move up all entries below this
                                        one in the map
                              return( previous location of gap )
                    }
          }
          return ( NO_ROOM )
}
```

If the calling function cannot locate a gap large enough to grant the request, it adds the information to the end of the file. The calling function interfaces with this function as follows:

```
main( )
{
          /* part of program omitted */

          if ( (starting_location = map_alloc( size ))
                    == NO_ROOM )
          {
                    find end of file
                    starting_location = end of file
          }
          write information at starting_location
}
```

The allocation function is implemented as follows:

source file: alloc.c

```
1    #include <stdio.h>
2    #include "map.h"
3    #include "general.h"
4
5    long map_alloc( request )
6    long request;
7    {
8         int sub;
```

```
9          long ret_val;
10
11         for ( sub = 0;  sub < v_mapsize;  sub++ )
12         {
13             /* first fit */
14             if ( available[sub].size > request )
15             {
16                 available[sub].size -= request;
17                 ret_val = available[sub].start;
18                 available[sub].start += request;
19                 return( ret_val );
20             }
21             /* exact fit */
22             else if ( available[sub].size == request )
23             {
24                 ret_val = available[sub].start;
25                 moveup( sub ); /* condense */
26                 return( ret_val );
27             }
28         }
29         return( NO_ROOM );
30     }
```

Line	Comments
5–6	The size of the request is passed as an argument to the function. In the dictionary example, this request is the size of the definition we would like to add to the file. The function finds a sufficiently large contiguous block using the map file and returns the starting location of the allocated space.
11	We look at each entry in the map until we find a sufficiently large block. Whenever the table's virtual size is increased, the variable v_mapsize is incremented; when gaps are combined and the table size is reduced, the variable v_mapsize is decremented.
13–20	In this program we use a *first fit* algorithm to allocate space, in contrast with a *best fit*. We stop searching the map table when we find a sufficiently large block. In this part of the if statement, we consider only blocks that are larger than we need.
16	Decrease the size of the gap by the amount we are allocating from it.

17	Save the gap's starting location to return to the calling function.
18	Move the start of the gap back by the amount allocated.
19	Return the allocation's starting location to the calling process.
21–27	If we have an exact fit (the size of the gap is the same as the amount of the request), then we completely eliminate the gap. We remove the entry from the map table by moving all the other entries below it in the map up one entry. The moveup() function will be described next.
29	If we have tested and rejected all the entries in the map table, we return a value indicating that a sufficiently large gap did not exist to accommodate the new information. The application may choose to add to the end of the file (extendable pool) or may treat this as an error condition (fixed size pool).

To condense the file after a properly sized gap has been found, the mapalloc() function calls the moveup() function. This function is defined as follows:

source file: dealloc.c

```
1    #include <stdio.h>
2    #include "map.h"
3    #include "general.h"
     .
     .
     .
79   moveup ( sub )
80   int sub;
81   {
82        int tsub;
83
84        for( tsub = sub; tsub < (v_mapsize - 1); tsub++ )
85        {
86             available[tsub] = available[tsub + 1];
87        }
88        v_mapsize--;
89   }
```

The function iterates only until the subscript reaches $v\_mapsize - 1$ (the number of valid entries in the table). This function uses the assignment of structures feature. On older C compilers this function would have to be revised to call another function to make the assignment.

Deallocation

Whenever space is released, we provide two pieces of information to the deallocation function: the amount of space released and its starting location. When the deallocation function enters the new gap into the map, it tries to combine this block with the preceding gap in the file and, if possible, with the gap following the deallocated block. The following function implements this:

source file: dealloc.c

```
1    #include <stdio.h>
2    #include "map.h"
3    #include "general.h"
4
5    long map_dealloc( amount, location )
6    long amount, location;
7    {
8         int sub;
9
10        for ( sub = 0; sub < v_mapsize; sub++ )
11        {
12             if ( available[sub].start > location )
13             {
      .
      .
      .
                  /* add to the map */
48             }
49        }
      .
      .
      .
65   }
```

The function looks at each valid entry in the map until the address recorded in the map entry is greater than the starting location of the block we are deallocating. Exhibit CS4-7 shows the insertion of an entry into the map.

We also attempt to construct a larger gap from the one being deallocated and one(s) already in the map by determining if they border one another. This is known as *coalescing adjacent blocks*. The function continues:

EXHIBIT CS4-7

Inserting a new gap into the map

Map before inserting new gap:

Amount	Location
25	50
75	125
25	450
100	575
20	900
40	940

Map after inserting gap at location 475, amount 75

Amount	Location
25	50
75	125
20	450
75	475
100	575
20	900
40	940

source file: dealloc.c

```
      .
      .
      .
 5    long map_dealloc( amount, location )
 6    long amount, location;
 7    {
 8        int sub;
 9
10        for ( sub = 0; sub < v_mapsize; sub++ )
11        {
12            if ( available[sub].start > location )
13            {
14                /* combine with below */
15                if ( location + amount ==
16                    available[sub].start )
```

```
17                    {
18                          available[sub].start = location;
19                          available[sub].size += amount;
20
21                          /* combine with above also */
22                          if ( sub > 0 && location ==
23                                available[sub-1].start +
24                                available[sub-1].size )
25                          {
26                                available[sub-1].size +=
27                                        available[sub].size;
28                                moveup( sub );
29                          }
30                          return( SUCCESS );
31                    }
        .
        .
        .
48                {
49            }
        .
        .
        .
```

First, we see if the ending boundary of the new gap borders the beginning location of the gap which follows it. If so, we combine the new entry with the following gap (lines 18 and 19). Exhibit CS4-8 illustrates this. Next, we see if the starting boundary of the newly merged block borders the end of the previous block. If so, we combine the preceding gap with the newly merged block, creating a still larger block. The moveup() function then removes the extra entry from the map.

If the new entry does not border the gap whose map entry follows it, we see if the preceding gap borders the block being deallocated:

source file: dealloc.c

```
        .
        .
        .
5    long map_dealloc( amount, location )
6    long amount, location;
7    {
8          int sub;
9
```

(program continues)

Coalescing adjacent blocks in a map

Map before inserting new gap:

Amount	Location
30	60
10	100
25	125

Inserting gap at location 110, amount 15

Amount	Location
30	60
10	100
15	110
25	125

Map after coalescing adjacent blocks:

Amount	Location
30	60
50	100

```
10          for ( sub = 0; sub < v_mapsize; sub++ )
11          {
12              if ( available[sub].start > location)
13              {
14                  /* combine with below */
15                  if ( location + amount ==
16                      available[sub].start )
17                      {

    .
    .
    .

                    /* possibly combine with
                       above also */
31                  }
32                  /* combine with above only */
33                  else if ( sub > 0 && location ==
34                      available[sub-1].start +
35                      available[sub-1].size )
36                  {
37                      available[sub-1].size += amount;
38                      return( SUCCESS );
39                  }
```

.
.
.

```
48                }
49              }
```

.
.
.

```
65    }
```

If the deallocated block borders the previous block, the two are combined.

If the new block cannot be combined with either the preceding or following gap, room is allocated in the map for this block. The movedown() function is called to create the new table entry:

source file: dealloc.c

.
.
.

```
 5    long map_dealloc( amount, location )
 6    long amount, location;
 7    {
 8        int sub;
 9
10        for ( sub = 0; sub < v_mapsize; sub++ )
11        {
12            if ( available[sub].start > location )
13            {
14                /* combine with below */
15                if ( location + amount ==
16                    available[sub].start )
17                {
```

.
.
.

```
21                    /* combine with above also */
22                    if ( sub > 0 && location ==
23                        available[sub-1].start +
24                        available[sub-1].size )
25                    {
```

.
.
.

```
30                    }
31                }
```

(*program continues*)

```
32                     /* combine with above only */
33                     else if ( sub > 0 && location ==
34                         available[sub-1].start +
35                         available[sub-1].size )
36                     {

   .
   .
   .

39                     }
40                     /* make new hole */
41                     else
42                     {
43                         movedown( sub );
44                         available[sub].start = location;
45                         available[sub].size = amount;
46                         return( SUCCESS );
47                     }
48                 }
49             }

   .
   .
   .

65   }
```

In line 43, the movedown( ) function moves the entries in the map down one at a time from the point of insertion. Then the starting location and amount of the new entry is inserted. The movedown( ) function is defined this way:

source file: dealloc.c

```
1     #include <stdio.h>
2     #include "map.h"
3     #include "general.h"

   .
   .
   .

67    movedown( sub )
68    int sub;
69    {
70         int tsub;
71
```

```
72              for( tsub = v_mapsize;  tsub > sub;  tsub-- )
73              {
74                   available[tsub] = available[tsub - 1];
75              }
76          v_mapsize++;
77      }
```

This version of the function has one serious flaw: it fails to see if v_mapsize is equal to p_mapsize (i.e., the table is full). To check for this condition, we change the function as follows:

source file: dealloc.c.

```
1    #include <stdio.h>
2    #include "map.h"
3    #include "general.h"
     .
     .
     .
67   movedown( sub )
68   int sub;
69   {
70        int tsub;
71

          if ( v_mapsize >= p_mapsize )
          {
               return( FAILURE );
          }
72        for( tsub = v_mapsize;  tsub > sub;  tsub -- )
73        {
74               available[tsub] = available[tsub - 1];
75        }
76        v_mapsize++;
          return( SUCCESS );
77   }
```

When small gaps totally fill the table, we encounter a condition called *fragmentation*. This can be addressed in several ways:

- Print a system message to the user warning that the map is fragmented. This is probably the least desirable solution because the user may not understand the message and is not likely to have permission to increase the size of the map.
- Clean up the map. For example, if the block being deallocated is two hundred units long and a smaller gap exists in the map, delete the smaller entry and store the larger gap.

EXHIBIT CS4-9

Adding a gap to the end of the map and extending the virtual map size

Map before inserting new gap:

Amount	Location
25	70
10	110
30	170

Map after inserting gap at location 220, amount 55:

Amount	Location
25	70
10	110
30	170
55	220

- Redesign the map file as a series of linked structures instead of as an array. As many of these structures can be maintained as necessary. In addition, insertions and deletions in the linked list would be more efficient. Since records (map entries) can be removed from the linked list, we would need to keep track of them through a free list or bitmap. A bitmap may be preferable because we already have generic routines to manage a bitmap.

Choosing the proper method really depends on the particular application. If the file governed by the map is fairly stable, as with a dictionary, the array map is adequate. If several hundred users make changes to the file many times a minute, the linked list approach is preferable.

We now need to add one final feature to the `map_dealloc()` function. If the deallocated block's starting location is greater than the location of all of the gaps currently in the map, we add the new gap to the end of the map. Exhibit CS4-9 illustrates this.

In this case, we have to extend the map's virtual size and add the deallocated gap to the end. The following code implements this in the `map_dealloc()` function:

source file: dealloc.c

```
 5     long map_dealloc( amount, location )
 6     long amount, location;
 7     {
 8          int sub;
 9
10          for ( sub = 0;  sub < v_mapsize;  sub++ )
11          {
         .
         .
         .
49          }
50          /* map is solid—extend if possible */
51          if ( v_mapsize == p_mapsize )
52          {
53               /* map table full */
54               fprintf( stderr, "FRAGMENTED MAP\n" );
55               return( FAILURE );
56          }
57          else
58          {
59               /* extend map table */
60               available[v_mapsize].size = amount;
61               available[v_mapsize].start = location;
62               v_mapsize++;
63               return( SUCCESS );
64          }
65     }
       .
       .
       .
```

First, we (in lines 51 through 56) see if the map's virtual size is equal to the physical size. In this case, the table is full and we cannot increase the map size; we return the defined value of FAILURE. If there is still room in the table, we add the new entry to the end of the map and increase the virtual size of the map.

SUMMARY

In this chapter, we have seen three methods for managing resources: the free list, the bitmap, and the map. The free list is only applicable when we are managing a linked list. Using a free list is efficient; little time is consumed in either adding an entry to the list or removing one from it. However, if several structures are to be allocated at the same time, a record needs to be read from the disk for each allocation, in contrast to the bitmap, where one long integer can be used to allocate up to 32 resources.

Bitmaps keep track of resources generically. These routines do not require any knowledge of the resource they are managing, only the resource number. The main advantage to this method is that it is easily made into a generalized solution, unlike free lists. It is also useful when the allocation of several resources in one request is required (our routines would have to be slightly modified). However, in certain situations, bitmaps may not be as fast as the free list.

The map is used for contiguous allocation. Like the bitmap, it is a generic solution; the map allocation and deallocation routines know nothing about the application calling them. The only information needed for deallocation is the starting location and the amount. The application using these routines places interpretations (e.g., scale) on these values. For allocation, the only information needed is the amount of the request. Relative efficiencies depend on how the map is to be stored—as an array with or without clean up, or as a linked list.

APPENDIXES

APPENDIX A

ASCII CHART

ASCII CHART

The following chart describes the ASCII sequence of characters and the numbers (shown here in octal) assigned to them:

000	nul	001	soh	002	stx	003	etx	004	eot	005	enq	006	ack	007	bel
010	bs	011	ht	012	nl	013	vt	014	np	015	cr	016	so	017	si
020	dle	021	dc1	022	dc2	023	dc3	024	dc4	025	nak	026	syn	027	etb
030	can	031	em	032	sub	033	esc	034	fs	035	gs	036	rs	037	us
040	sp	041	!	042	"	043	#	044	$	045	%	046	&	047	'
050	(	051	)	052	*	053	+	054	,	055	–	056	.	057	/
060	0	061	1	062	2	063	3	064	4	065	5	066	6	067	7
070	8	071	9	072	:	073	;	074	<	075	=	076	>	077	?
100	@	101	A	102	B	103	C	104	D	105	E	106	F	107	G
110	H	111	I	112	J	113	K	114	L	115	M	116	N	117	O
120	P	121	Q	122	R	123	S	124	T	125	U	126	V	127	W
130	X	131	Y	132	Z	133	[	134	\	135	]	136	^	137	_
140	`	141	a	142	b	143	c	144	d	145	e	146	f	147	g
150	h	151	i	152	j	153	k	154	l	155	m	156	n	157	o
160	p	161	q	162	r	163	s	164	t	165	u	166	v	167	w
170	x	171	y	172	z	173	{	174			175	}	176	~	177	del

APPENDIX B

ANSI C PROPOSALS

OVERVIEW

The ANSI committee, X3J11, has been meeting on setting standards for the C language. This appendix describes some of the significant changes suggested by the committee. Some of these changes are intended to increase the flexibility of the language while others are attempts to standardize features previously left to the discretion of the compiler implementor. Previously, the only "standard" available was the book The C Programming Language by B. Kernighan and D. Ritchie, which was not specific on some language details, thus causing a divergence among compilers. The ANSI proposal intends to remove these ambiguities. Although a few of the proposed changes could cause problems for some previously written programs, they should not affect most existing programs.

CONSTANTS

For character strings and character variables, two "escape" sequences have been added:

\a	When printed, this character will ring the bell on the terminal. This replaces the ever popular \07 escape sequence. The a in this sequence refers to *alert*.
\v	When printed, this will cause the output device (printer) to skip to its next vertical tab.

Although an escape sequence for the "escape" character (\033) was discussed, no "escape" escape sequence was added because it may not have an equivalent in other character sets, such as EBCDIC.

Floating-point constants now can have suffixes like integers do. The default type for floating-point constants is double, but if necessary they can be represented as float (with the suffix F) or as long double (with the suffix L).

Integer constants may also have the suffix U or u appended to their value to represent them as unsigned entities.

CHARACTER STRINGS

Two changes have been made concerning character strings. These are:

1. Strings are now constants. This means that the contents of character strings are not changeable, as was illustrated in Chapter 4, program temp_file. c. This program would have to be changed to store the modifiable string in a character array and pass the address of the array.

This change allows compiler writers to put the strings in an area of memory sharable among users executing the same program.

2. Strings can now be concatenated. If two strings appear next to one another with only white space in between, they are considered one character string. Therefore, the following expressions are equivalent:

```
"string one string two"
```

and

```
"string one " "string two"
```

or

```
"string one"
"string two"
```

VARIABLE NAMES

Automatic, register, and static variable name length can be at least 31 characters long. Compilers may recognize more than 31, but to conform to the ANSI
standard, they must support at least 31. External variable name length must be
at least six characters long, case insensitive. Although an extension to greater
than six characters would be desirable, the decision to limit it to six makes
ANSI C compatible with existing assemblers and linkage editors. If a structure
is defined as external, its name must be less than six characters long but the
member names can be up to 31 characters.

NEW DATA TYPES

The following data types, not mentioned in *The C Programming Language* are
added:

void	Although available on most compilers, this data type is added officially. It is usually used to type the return value of a function that returns nothing.
void *	This is used to declare a "typeless" pointer. Variables of this type may be assigned values but they cannot be dereferenced without being cast to another type.
signed char	This new type was introduced to enhance program portability. Some older compilers treat all character variables as signed while others store character variables unsigned. This enables the programmer to request a signed integer explicitly even if the default type for the machine is unsigned.
unsigned char	This requests an unsigned character variable for machines that treat characters as signed entities.
unsigned short	These variables can store integers between 0 and 64K.
unsigned long	These variables can store integers between 0 and 4G (billion).
long double	This was introduced to support machines that can have more precision than the average double-precision floating-point number. As of the ANSI standard, double variables must have at

least the precision of float variables and long double variables must have at least the precision of double variables.

Variables can now be modified by the type modifier const. When used with variable initialization, this modifier will cause the value of the variable to be constant. This permits these variables to be placed in read-only sharable storage. A second type modifier, volatile, when applied to a variable declaration, will force the variable to be stored in read/write memory. Sometimes the optimizer puts certain variables in unused registers to speed the execution of the routine. In certain circumstances, such as variables shared between processes (operating system dependent) and for signal handling (also operating system dependent), it is necessary to make the variables volatile so they are stored in memory rather than in registers.

OPERATORS

The unary plus (+) operator permits the programmer to explicitly direct the compiler in its order of subexpression evaluation. For example, the expression:

```
( a + b ) + c
```

can be reordered by the compiler for convenience or efficiency. If the unary plus operator is applied to a parenthesized expression, it forces that expression to be evaluated first. This may be necessary if the operand types are a mixture of floating-point and/or integer types. In these cases, the programmer has the option to control arithmetic operations of the same precedence level.

The conditional expression:

```
expression1 ? expression2 : expression3
```

has been extended to allow the expression value to be a structure or a union. This can be used in conjunction with structure or union assignment.

The sizeof operator now has a defined type. In most pre-ANSI compilers, expressions using the sizeof operator had the type int, but this was not standard. ANSI compilers will have the type of a sizeof expression defined by a symbolic constant size_t defined in the header file stddef.h.

CONTROL CONSTRUCTS

The switch construct has been changed to allow for any integral type in the case part. In previous compilers, only integer values were allowed in the case part.

FUNCTION PROTOTYPES

Perhaps the largest change to the C language is in the area of passing arguments to functions. Before ANSI C, the compiler didn't check the types of arguments. Although the UNIX lint program checks this, type checking was not built in to the C compiler. The ANSI proposal suggests the use of function prototypes, defined as follows:

- When a function's return value is defined in a calling function, the argument types may be specified as follows:

```
main()
{
        int abc;
        char *func( int, char * );
        float xyz;
        /* remainder of program omitted */
}
```

This informs the compiler that the function named func() returns a pointer to a character and expects two arguments, an integer and a pointer to a character. If types other than these are given as arguments to the function, an error is produced at compile time.

- If a function has a variable number of arguments where only a few are defined, the remainder are represented by ellipsis (. . .) as follows:

```
main()
{
        int printf( char *, ... );
        /* more program omitted */
}
```

- If a function requires no arguments, it is defined as follows:

```
main()
{
        int rand( void );
        /* more program omitted */
}
```

This informs the compiler that the function does not expect an argument and a compile-time error should be generated if an argument is supplied. If a function is defined with nothing between the parentheses, function arguments will not be checked.

- If desired, the programmer may specify a name along with the argument type. This does not limit the function to using these names when calling the function; any expression can still be passed. It is used for documentation purposes only. For example:

```
main()
{
        int fputc( char c, FILE *stream );
}
```

Defining functions this way makes the program more closely resemble the notation used in the manual pages describing the functions.

- The argument specification in the function itself would remain the same. The names the function assigns to the arguments are listed in the parentheses following the function name and their types are defined following the closing parenthesis and before the function's initial brace.

- In pre-ANSI compilers, certain variable types are automatically widened. For example, all characters are converted to integers and floating-point numbers are converted to doubles. With function prototyping, these conversions do not take place when small data types are passed to functions.

PREPROCESSOR STATEMENTS

In the proposed ANSI standard, preprocessor statements can be indented. Some earlier compilers insisted that all preprocessor directives begin in column one.

SUMMARY

These proposed changes are only a subset of all the suggestions being made, although they are the most important. The rest of the changes are really of more concern to compiler writers than to application programmers.

APPENDIX C

USING THE C LANGUAGE WITH THE UNIX OPERATING SYSTEM

OVERVIEW

This appendix acquaints the programmer with some of the many facilities available in the UNIX operating system that aid in C program development.

COMPILING C PROGRAMS

In the UNIX system, C programs are compiled in several stages, all of which are controlled through the cc command. This command is given the name of one or more source files and creates an executable file from these source files. The basic command usage is:

cc program.c

where cc is the command name and program.c is the source file name. By default, this command line produces an executable file with the name a.out. To change this name, the programmer can specify the −o option to the cc command followed by the name of the executable file, as follows:

cc −o executable program.c

Stages of Compilation

The cc command actually runs several programs in sequence:

preprocessor
This phase processes all lines that begin with the "sharp" (#) symbol. The preprocessor deletes all comment lines (unless the -C option is supplied on the cc command line), performs token and macro substitutions, and locates include files. If on the include directive, the file name is placed within angle brackets:

#include <stdio.h>

then the preprocessor looks for the file in the /usr/include directory. If the file name is enclosed in quotes:

#include "pqueue.h"

the preprocessor looks for this file first in the same directory as the source file and then in the /usr/include directory.

It is possible to halt the cc command after the preprocessor phase and view the substititions the preprocessor made. One of two command line options will do this:

−E
This causes the preprocessor output to be directed to the terminal. If this option is selected, it

is often best to "pipe" this command's output to the command line:

```
hp -m
```

or any other program that reduces multiple contiguous blank lines to a single blank line. The preprocessor usually sends many blank lines to its output.

-P   This stores the preprocessor output in a file whose name is modeled after the name of the original source file. The ". c" suffix is replaced with a ". i ".

It is also possible to send information to the preprocessor through the cc command line. The following options permit this:

-I   This informs the preprocessor where to look for included files. If the included file name is enclosed in double quotes, the preprocessor looks in the directory name that follows this option letter as well as in the current directory.

-D   This option allows symbolic names to be defined through the cc command line. For example:

```
cc -D "VERBOSE=0"
```

is equivalent to the following preprocessor directive in the file itself:

```
#define VERBOSE 0
```

By putting the directive on the command line, the programmer does not have to change any code or header files if the value of the symbolic name changes.

compiler   The compiler translates the preprocessor output into assembly language. There are several cc command line options that can be passed to the compiler. They are:

-O   This option causes the compiler output to be optimized.

-S   Stop the cc command after compilation. The assembly language output is stored in a file suffixed by the characters ". s " with the same base name as the source file. This option is helpful if the programmer wishes to study how the compiler translates certain language constructs.

-P   This produces code that, when compiled and run, will gather statistics on the running program and store it in a file called mon.out. This data can be analyzed through a program called prof. An example of this program's output is shown below:

name	%time	cumsecs	#call	ms/call
_write	64.2	1.35		
__exit	21.5	1.80		
_close	10.7	2.02		
__flsbuf	5.6	2.14		
__print	1.8	2.18		
_look_st	0.8	2.20	7	2.29
_read	0.8	2.21		
.				
.				
.				
_getcomm	0.0	2.26	15	0.00
.				
.				
.				
_main	0.0	2.26	1	0.00
.				
.				
.				
_monitor	0.0	2.26		
_pop_sta	0.0	2.26	7	0.00
_printf	0.0	2.26		
_profil	0.0	2.26		
_push_st	0.0	2.26	4	0.00
.				
.				
.				
_strchr	0.0	2.26		
_strcpy	0.0	2.26		
_strlen	0.0	2.26		
.				
.				
.				

assembler

The output contains the amount of time, in microseconds, taken to execute each of the functions called during the program invocation as well as other important information. For more details see the manual page for the `prof` command. Often when developing large programs, the programmer separates the functions into several source files and compiles them independently. When all the modules have been compiled, they are then linked producing an executable output. If the −c option is given to the `cc` command, it will cause the command to stop after assembling the assembly language output of the compiler and will leave the output in a file with the suffix ".o". A typical development and compilation process looks like:

```
$ cc -o main.c
$ cc -o fileio.c
$ ls                      <lists filenames>
fileio.c
fileio.o
main.c
main.o
$ cc -c stack.c
                          <link all parts of program>
$ cc main.o fileio.o  stack.o
                          <run program and find mistake>
$ a.out
                          <program has mistake in stack function>
                          <use "ed" editor to correct>
$ ed stack.c
                          <recompile stack.c>
$ cc -c stack.c
                          <relink all modules>
$ cc main.o fileio.o  stack.o
```

link editor

The linking stage of the process is very short in comparison with the compilation and assembly. Therefore, it is most efficient not to recompile and reassemble the program's unchanged parts. The link editor resolves external references and links user-defined modules together with the library routines they call. The link editor may be passed several arguments through the cc command line:

-f
> Some systems have floating-point hardware support. For these systems, the compiler will produce code that uses this hardware. For systems without this support, it is necessary for the programmer to specify the -f option to the cc command line. This links the object program created with floating-point software routines. The following command line compiles and creates an executable file from the floater.c program (it uses floating-point arithmetic):

```
cc -f -o floater floater.c
```

> If a machine does not have floating-point hardware support and the -f option is omitted from the compiling command line, the program will fail at runtime and produce a core dump and the error message:

```
illegal instruction-core dumped
```

-l library
> If functions from an external library are referenced, this option informs the link editor where to locate these library files. For example, if a function from the math library is referenced in the prog.c program, it is compiled and linked as follows:

```
cc prog.c -lm
```

Some machines require that the library reference appear last on the `cc` command line; others allow it to appear anywhere. These libraries are stored in either of the following two directories:

```
/lib
/usr/lib
```

The file name will be the library letter specified (`m` in this example) prefixed with the characters `lib` and suffixed with the characters `.a`. In this example, the link editor looks for files with the name

```
libm.a
```

in either of the directories.

Pathnames

Like many other operating systems, pathnames in the UNIX system identify files. They are made up of a series of directory names delimited by slashes (/). The following is an example of a UNIX-style pathname:

```
/usr/hutch/book/lstack.c
```

UNIX C LANGUAGE PROGRAMMING UTILITIES

Several programming tools are available that help write understandable, portable, and, most important, working code. These include:

cb This program indents the source program and places the "beautified" version on the standard output. The program is indented using standard indentation conventions. It is useful in finding misplaced parentheses or braces. The following program:

source file: sloppy.c

```
 1    main()
 2    {
 3    int x,y,z;
 4
 5    x=14;
 6    if(x==10)
 7    {
 8    z=15;
 9    y=12;
10    }
11    }
```

would be transformed by the cb program to look like:

```
$ cb sloppy.c
main()
{
        int x,y,z;
        x=14;
        if(x==10)
        {
                z=15;
                y=12;
        }
}
```

The "beautified" version of the program is displayed on the standard output and could be saved in a file through output redirection.

lint

This program alerts the programmer to potential problems, such as a function with incorrectly typed arguments or variables whose values have been referenced before they have been set. It is executed as follows:

```
$ lint lstack.c
lstack.c
===============
warning: illegal pointer combination
    (132)              (180)
```

```
warning: possible pointer alignment problem
    (132)
```

```
===============
function argument ( number ) used inconsistently
    free( arg 1 )          llib-lc(178) :: lstack.c(116)
function returns value which is always ignored
    strcpy          fgets               fprintf
    fputs           printf
```

make
The make program simplifies large system development by allowing the programmer to define rules concerning program module compilation. A detailed description of the make program should be part of any standard UNIX system documentation.

adb and sdb
These two programs allow the developer to debug and trace a running program interactively. The system documentation should be consulted concerning the operation of these debuggers.

ctrace
Included with newer systems is a utility called ctrace. This program translates C source code into verbose C code that, when compiled, will print a trace of the executing program on the terminal. The following program:

source file: loan.c

```
1    main()
2    {
3        /* this program calculates and prints the
4           future amount of an invested amount; formula
5           used is:
6
7           future value =
8             present( 1 + interest rate)number periods
9        */
10
11       double rate, periods, savings_amount, f_amount;
12       double future();
13
14       printf( "Enter interest rate: " );
15       scanf( "%lf", &rate );
16
17       printf( "Enter savings amount: " );
```

(program continues)

```
18          scanf( "%lf", &savings_amount );
19
20          printf( "Enter number of years: " );
21          scanf( "%lf", &periods );
22
23          f_amount = future( rate, savings_amount, periods);
24          printf( "Future value = %.2f\n", f_amount );
25      }
26
27   double future( rate, amount, periods )
28   double rate, amount, periods;
29      {
30          double pow();
31          double f_amount;
32
33          /* percentage conversion */
34          rate = rate / 100.0;
35          /* interest is compounded monthly */
36          rate = rate / 12.0;
37          /* rate was converted to monthly base */
38          periods = periods * 12.0;
39          f_amount = amount * pow( (1.0 + rate), periods);
40          return( f_amount );
41      }
```

will produce the following output if it has been previously run through the ctrace program:

```
 1 main()
14      printf( "Enter interest rate: " ); Enter interest rate:   10
15      scanf( "%lf", &rate );
17      printf( "Enter savings amount: " ); Enter savings amount:   100
18      scanf( "%lf", &savings_amount );
20      printf( "Enter number of years: " ); Enter number of years:   2
21      scanf( "%lf", &periods );
23      f_amount = future( rate, savings_amount, periods );
        /* periods == 2.000000e+00 */
        /* savings_amount == 1.000000e+2 */
        /* rate == 1.000000e+01 */
27 future( rate, amount, periods )
34      rate = rate / 100.0;
        /* rate == 1.000000e+01 */
        /* rate == 1.000000e-01 */
36      rate = rate / 12.0;
```

```
         /* rate == 1.000000e-01 */
         /* rate == 8.333333e-03 */
38       periods = periods * 12.0;
         /* periods == 2.000000e+00 */
         /* periods == 2.400000e+01 */
39       f_amount = amount * pow( (1.0 + rate), periods);
         /* amount == 1.000000e+02 */
         /* periods == 2.400000e+01 */
         /* rate == 8.333333e-03 */
         /* f_amount == 1.220391e+02 */
40       return( f_amount );
         /* ( f_amount ) == 1.220391e+02 */
         /* f_amount == 1.220391e+02 */
24       printf( "Future value = %.2f\n" f_amount );
         /* f_amount == 1.220391e+02 */ Future value = 122.04

   /* return */
```

Other tools may be available on your UNIX system. Refer to the *UNIX System V Programmer's Reference Manual* or equivalent for more details.

APPENDIX

USING THE C LANGUAGE WITH THE MS-DOS OPERATING SYSTEM

OVERVIEW

In this appendix we provide some information that will be helpful in creating C language programs under MS-DOS. When reading this appendix please be aware of two important points:

• Although the C language has now been assimilated into many different operating system environments, its UNIX ancestry is still clearly visible. You will find that the MS-DOS compiler developers have relied heavily on UNIX-like procedures for developing and executing C programs. Therefore, it would be worthwhile to read Appendix C, Using the C Language with the UNIX Operating System, because much of that information is relevant to running C programs under MS-DOS.

• There are many C compilers under MS-DOS, marketed by a wide variety of vendors. Although most of the procedures for developing and executing C language programs are similar, if not identical, across compilers you should check the documentation that came with your system for specific details. The procedures we document are largely common among compilers, but your system could have its own idiosyncrasies.

COMPILING PROGRAMS

The steps in compiling a program under MS-DOS are virtually identical to UNIX. In general, a command (usually called c or cc) will compile, assemble, and link your programs or permit you to stop at any point in the process by using the appropriate command options. It is usually expected that the C language source file will have a filename with the extension (suffix) ".c". The compiler is invoked with the command line:

```
cc [options] filename.c
```

The compiler produces an object module usually with the filename followed by a ".o" or ".obj" extension. So for example, the command:

```
cc myfile.c
```

produces an object file with the name myfile.o.

The compiler will automatically invoke the assembler and then delete the assembly language source file after creating the object file. Most compilers have an option that will permit you to save the assembly language source file. You can also specify your own name for the object file by using the –O option. For example, the command:

```
cc -O vers1.new myprog.c
```

creates an object file with the name `vers1.new`, instead of the default name `myprog.o`.

Other UNIX-like compiler options, such as −D for defining symbolic constants at compile time, are also usually available. Your compiler documentation should have a complete list of compiler options.

Searching for #include Files

You can direct the compiler (preprocessor) to search for `#include` files using one of several methods. By default, it will search the current directory, which is usually the directory containing the source file. If you want the compiler to search other directories you have two options:

- Use the −I compiler option as described in Appendix C.
- Set an MS-DOS environment variable called `INCLUDE` equal to the directories you want searched. For example:

```
set INCLUDE=c:\just\incl1;c:\just\incl2
```

instructs the compiler to search in the two directories `\just\incl1` and `\just\incl2` on the `c` drive.

Memory Models

Most MS-DOS compilers have memory models that define the size of the memory allocated to the program and to data. Typically, you will have a choice of:

small program, small data
small program, large data
large program, small data
large program, large data

where:

- *small program*—limits the executable code size to 64K bytes
- *large program*—permits unlimited (bounded by available memory) size programs
- *small data*—limits the size of data, plus the stack, plus the heap to 64K
- *large data*—limits data to 64K, the stack to 64K, but the heap is bounded only by available memory

Memory model choice is dictated by the application size, but it is usually advantageous to use the smallest memory model possible. If the executable code size exceeds 64K it is still possible to use the small program model through overlays.

The Link Editor

The link editor's function is to take all the user-defined object files, link them with any external library functions, and produce an executable module. Some MS-DOS C compilers provide their own link editor, others instruct you to use the MS-DOS link editor link.

Typically, you will be required to link in a library containing all the non-floating-point library functions. If you are using floating-point arithmetic in the program, you will also be required to link in the floating-point math library. If the computer has a hardware floating-point processor (like an Intel 8087), floating-point calculations will be done in hardware, otherwise they will be done through software routines.

Unlike UNIX, where the executable program is named by default a.out, the executable program under MS-DOS is typically given the name of the original source file with the extension .exe. For example, the source file:

```
prog1.c
```

when compiled, produces the object file:

```
prog1.o
```

and when linked, produces the executable file:

```
prog1.exe
```

MS-DOS-Specific External Library Functions

Most MS-DOS C compilers have special library functions that interface with the personal computer environment and permit the programmer to have greater control over input and output procedures. Typically, there will be routines for changing foreground and background color, placing the computer in graphics mode, boxing text, drawing simple graphic objects, terminal emulation, accessing the extended character set, and so on. There are also third-party libraries containing hundreds of these functions, in addition to routines for other common procedures such as data communications.

UNIX Tools

As we mentioned earlier, the C language under MS-DOS still has close ties to the C language under UNIX. Over the years, a variety of tools useful to programmers have been developed under UNIX. Many of these tools have been ported to MS-DOS and are either bundled with the MS-DOS compiler or are available for separate purchase. Among the UNIX tools you will find on MS-DOS are:

- vi—the UNIX full screen text editor
- make—a utility for managing the development of large systems with many files
- grep—a pattern-matching program that searches for specified character patterns in one or more files
- sdb (source level debugger)—a useful tool for debugging C programs
- diff—a program for comparing the contents of two files
- ls—a file-listing utility

INDEX

INDEX